BY THE EDITORS OF CONSUMER GUIDE®

MUSTANG ENCYCLOPEDIA

BEEKMAN HOUSE
New York

CONTENTS

We transformed a '65 fastback from beater to beauty.
You can work similar magic on any Mustang
with these easy-to-follow, fully illustrated
instructions on body repairs, interior trimming,
engine cosmetics, and parts removal and replacement.

Louis Weber, President
Publications International, Ltd.
3841 West Oakton Street
Skokie, Illinois 60076

Permission is never granted for commercial purposes.

Manufactured in the United States of America
10 9 8 7 6 5 4 3 2 1

Library of Congress Catalog Card Number: 82-61174

ISBN: 0-517-359863

This edition published by:
Beekman House
Distributed by Crown Publishers, Inc.
One Park Avenue
New York, New York 10016

Credits

Principal Author
Richard M. Langworth (Mustang
  history)

Contributing Authors
Rick Kopec (Shelby history)
Barbara Langworth (Source Guide)
Greg Wells (Accessories Guide)

Photo Credits
Ford Motor Company Photomedia
  Department
David Gooley
Tony Hossain, *Old Cars Weekly*
Richard M. Langworth
Shelby American Automobile Club

Restoration Credits
Eckhardt Auto Glass & Trim, Ltd.
Morton Grove, Illinois

Mustang Country
Paramont, California

Mustang of Chicago
Bensenville, Illinois

River Trail Auto Body, Inc.
Wheeling, Illinois

Ye Olde Tunesmith, Ltd.
Skokie, Illinois

Jacket Design
Frank E. Peiler

INTRODUCTION

One of the things that sets Mustangs apart from most other cars is that they are so easily recognized, even by people who aren't car enthusiasts. The early Mustangs are among the most identifiable cars on the road with their trend-setting long hood/short deck styling, the simulated air scoops on the body sides, and the famous running horse emblems on the grille and fenders. Most everyone knows it's not just another small, sporty car or just a Ford—it's a Mustang. They might not know what year it is, but there's no doubt about the breed. As the Mustang grew larger in the late 60s and early 70s, it was still easy to spot one among hordes of other cars of similar size and intentions. And as gas prices became higher in the mid-70s, the Mustang was redesigned to meet the demands of a different time when economy was more important than acceleration. The Mustang II was smaller than the original ponycar while retaining many of the original ingredients. It looked far different, yet the familiar running horse was still galloping across the grille and subtle side sculpturing inspired memories of the first Mustang. When it was restyled again for 1979, the trademark running horse disappeared from the grille, but the new breed of Mustang still had the long hood/short deck design of the original. The appealing new body was shaped to cheat the wind as well as please the eye and the interior made much more efficient use of space than previous models. Just as the first Mustang was right for its time, the current edition is right for the 80s. Its low, wedge-shaped profile and wide wraparound taillights are distinguishing features, continuing the tradition of distinctive styling.

There aren't many other cars that have survived as long as the Mustang and retained so much of its original personality. Car lines come and go, and many of those that linger on are produced in much different form than the first models. Yet, the 1983 Mustang line will feature a convertible and a more muscular V-8 engine. The base engine is an economical 4-cylinder. The options list is longer than your arm, so you can still build the kind of car you want, from mild to wild, just like you've always been able to do with the Mustang. It's still a sporty personal car that's fun to drive, and it's still affordable. Mustangs have been criticized over the years both for what they were and what they weren't, but it's hard to deny that they've been affordable. The first Mustang sold for a base price of $2368, which meant that if you could afford a new car, you could afford a Mustang. The base price of a 1983 Mustang is much more than the 1964½ model, but still very competitive in today's market. It's a car that most drivers can tailor to their tastes and it's a car that most new car buyers can afford. That's no small accomplishment, combining broad appeal with an attractive price.

Precious few cars have had the winning combination of the Mustang: low price, broad appeal, and a special flair that is hard to define. Whether it was the new styling, or the name (described by one Ford executive as "American as hell"), the promise of adventure behind the wheel, or all of those ingredients and more, the original Mustang had a special flair. It didn't need a high-performance V-8 under the hood to set hearts beating faster either. The sporty looks, bucket seats, and nimble size were standard equipment on 6-cylinder versions as well. It looked just as good in its economy modes as it did in racier trim.

The story of the first generation of Mustangs, and the succeeding generations, are told in the first section of *Mustang Encyclopedia*, where Ford Motor Company insiders explain decisions that led to the creation of the first ponycar. The Mustang was created in the mind of Lee Iacocca, one of the greatest car salesmen of all time, who grasped the mood of the marketplace long before others to give Ford a big head start in the lucrative sporty personal car field. **The Mustang Story 1964–83** traces the evolution of the original ponycar over nearly 20 years of production and provides detailed references of body dimensions, engine specifications, and production figures by model year. A separate chapter on the exciting Shelby-Mustangs highlights the ultra high performance branch of the Mustang family that became a terror on road racing circuits.

Those early Mustangs that set sales records in the mid-60s are now collectors' cars, and growing interest in rebuilding these classics into showroom condition (or close to it) has resulted in a plethora of shops and companies that specialize in Mustang parts

and restoration services. We too were bitten by the restoration bug and wanted to get in on the act. What better way is there to explain how to restore your Mustang than to use a Mustang of our own as an example? We did not completely strip our 1965 fastback and rebuild it from the frame up, but we think the step-by-step restoration section is a valuable guide for the do-it-yourselfer who wants his Mustang to look as good as ours. The car that you will see restored on the pages of this book is the same one all the way through. We didn't start on one Mustang and then switch to another to illustrate different steps. It's the real thing, from start to finish.

To help readers choose a Mustang for restoration, and identify optional equipment that was available for each model year, *Mustang Encyclopedia* has a **Parts and Accessories Guide** that lists what was offered and the suggested retail price. Our guide also provides helpful commentary on which options are the most desirable to the Mustang collector. This guide will be an authoritative reference for those who need help in determining the authenticity of a restored Mustang. Many restored cars have parts that weren't offered by the manufacturer, though the owners will claim the parts are original or authentic reproductions. Let the buyer beware, but also let him be informed.

The last section of *Mustang Encyclopedia* is designed to encourage more Mustang enthusiasts to embark on restoration projects or revive late model Mustangs with fresh parts and accessories. **The Mustang Source Guide** lists parts suppliers, shops that provide special services, and clubs that are mainly devoted to the Mustang. These companies and organizations can help you with hard-to-find parts, advice, publications, and services. The source guide will make your restoration easier by reducing some of the leg work involved.

Few other cars have inspired a following as great as the Mustang's, a tribute to the original concept and how it has been carried out for nearly 20 years. The number of clubs, specialty shops, and publications for the Mustang lover testify to the widespread interest. That makes it much easier to find parts—new, used, and reproductions—than with other cars that never enjoyed the popularity of the Mustang. Those who have restored Mustangs or are in the middle of a project now can surely appreciate the benefits of having most parts and accessories readily available. A restoration project is always a lot of work; conducting a nationwide search for parts to complete the project can make it a frustrating experience.

The great popularity of older Mustangs means that many of them, especially the good ones, are being snatched up for restorations. Early Mustangs that are in restorable condition and don't have rusted bodies and frames or haven't been butchered with add-on parts never intended for Mustangs are still available, though they're harder to find and getting more expensive. We urge anyone interested in buying an older car for restoration to take their time in finding a suitable vehicle, looking carefully for rust, damage to structural pieces that were bent or broken in accidents, and missing parts that will have to be replaced. Also consider how much work the engine and transmission will need and whether the suspension is safe and sound. Before you jump in with both feet, find out whether you'll be able to keep your head above water in your restoration. You can find some nasty surprises once you start taking a car apart, greatly increasing the cost of your project and the energy you will have to expend on it. Take your time with your restoration; make it as enjoyable as possible.

If you never restore a Mustang, or have never even owned one, we think you'll enjoy *Mustang Encyclopedia,* a comprehensive volume for all types of car buffs. Probably no other American car has created as much excitement as the original ponycar did in the mid-60s. That glorious beginning for the Mustang made it an instant legend. Other cars have made big splashes when introduced, though few have rivaled the sales success of the Mustang or its longevity in an industry that is forced to change frequently to meet the whims of buyers and pressures of the times. The Mustang has survived through some of the most tumultous years in the history of the automobile, yet it still holds a strong share of the sporty personal car market and commands a strong following among enthusiasts. The Mustang hasn't survived because of the legend built in the 60s. It has survived because it has built on the legend that was started back then.

DESIGNING A LEGEND

The original ponycar did not begin in 1962 with the experimental Mustang I or in 1955 with the two-seat Thunderbird, though both have a place in the Mustang story. The tale really begins with developments in the auto industry as early as 1946, when America was emerging from World War II into an age of unbridled optimism.

When car production resumed, it didn't really make sense for most auto manufacturers to offer all-new models. Prewar body dies were still available and practically unused in some cases, which made it uneconomical to scrap them. Besides, there wasn't much time to design and retool completely fresh designs, so the industry returned with simply warmed-over '42s for the 1946 model year. Of course, at that time a company could sell literally anything on wheels, so there was little incentive to introduce something truly new right away. (Only Studebaker among the prewar makes was entirely redesigned, and that was for 1947.) But the seller's market waned as time went on and a war-starved public's appetite for new cars was satiated. Soon, buyers began hungering for new engineering and new styling. Indeed, the manufacturers had baited buyers throughout the war with promises of "cars of tomorrow" that would appear after hostilities ended. Still, it wasn't until 1949 that the Big Three—Ford, Chrysler, and General Motors—offered entirely new models.

While getting back into production, some manufacturers began to consider how their prewar designs, which by now were quite familiar, could be made to appear new, at least on the surface. One idea was to create a few low-production specials to maintain interest until all-new models were ready. Chrysler, Ford, and Nash each fielded a special for 1946. All had conventional production bodies embellished with wooden exterior trim comprising a framework of white ash, maple, or yellow birch and inserts of real mahogany wood or woodgrain decals.

Nash's Suburban and Chrysler's Town & Country were sedans built on wheelbases about 10 feet long and powered by middle-sized L-head sixes. Chrysler also offered a Town & Country convertible built on an even longer chassis and equipped with a big straight eight. Chrysler sold over 12,000 Town & Countrys during 1946-48, while Nash sold 1000 of its Suburbans. These models served their purpose of maintaining floor traffic in dealer showrooms until the all-new Chryslers and Nashes were introduced for 1949. Although Nash dropped the Suburban that year, Chrysler continued the T&C convertible and added a hardtop version for the 1950 model year. After that, Town & Country simply became a name used for Chrysler station wagons.

The first limited-editions created by the makers of the future Mustang were the Ford and Mercury Sportsman convertibles. These were inspired by a customized Model A built during the war years by then-styling director Bob

Detroit carmakers were stuck with early 1940s styling when they resumed passenger car production after World War II. They achieved new looks by offering special wood-bodied models. Ford's woodie was the Sportsman convertible (opposite page). Chrysler sold sedan and ragtop versions of its Town & Country (below). Nash's special was the Suburban (right).

Limited production models such as the 1950 Ford Custom Crestliner (above) helped generate showroom traffic with appealing paint schemes and special trim. The hardtop styling of the 1951 Ford Custom Victoria (right) was inspired by the pillarless "hardtop convertible" look pioneered by General Motors in 1949. The 1949 Buick Roadmaster Riviera (opposite page) was one of the first hardtops that featured the sporty appearance of a convertible.

Gregorie. Henry Ford II, just released from the Navy to help salvage the ailing Ford Motor Company, was searching for something different to offer the public. After seeing Gregorie's wood-trimmed custom, he ordered a similar treatment for production, and the Sportsman was born. The planking was no problem, because Ford owned a stand of timber in Northern Michigan, and this had been a source of wood for wagon bodies since 1929.

The Mercury Sportsman was offered only for 1946, and a mere 205 were sold. Built on a longer wheelbase, it was heavier than Ford's version and shared the same 100-horsepower flathead V-8, so it did not perform as well. It was also priced more than $200 higher, which may explain why it did not significantly contribute to Mercury sales traffic.

The Ford Sportsman, however, was a minor success, with close to 3500 built for 1946–48. Although such figures were not very significant from a sales standpoint, the car added a much-needed touch of glamour to the rest of Ford's staid, carryover postwar line. The Sportsman was phased out in early 1948 in preparation for the all-new 1949 models, which didn't need a special for added zest.

For 1950, however, Ford was back with limited editions, the Ford Custom Crestliner and the companion Mercury Monterey. Each was essentially a customized rendition of the standard two-door sedan. The Crestliner featured a two-tone color scheme, with a contrasting color sweep on the bodysides and a padded, color-keyed vinyl top. The Monterey offered a choice of padded tops in canvas or leather plus a deluxe interior. The idea behind both cars was to offer the appearance of a true convertible with its feeling of sportiness in lieu of a pillarless "hardtop convertible." That body style had debuted at GM for 1949, and was already selling at a rapid clip.

Responding more directly to this sales threat, Ford then introduced its Victoria hardtop for 1951, but retained the Crestliner. Mercury and Lincoln, however, didn't get their own versions, so Mercury continued with the Monterey, and Lincoln added similar customs, called Lido and Capri, to its line. None of these were particularly successful. For the redesigned 1952 Mercury and Lincoln, true pillarless styles replaced the padded-top specials, and the Monterey and Capri designations remained as series names.

Aside from the Nash Suburban, there were no note-

worthy postwar limited editions from the independent makers until 1949. In that year, upstart Kaiser-Frazer, the new auto company that began production after the war in Willow Run, Michigan, entered the field with its Kaiser Virginian. This was the product of a prior management decision to make a convertible sedan out of K-F's pillared, fixed-roof four-door. But the ragtop's engineering was of the patchwork variety, as shown by the engineer's choice of a ponderous reinforced frame to prevent body flex. As a spinoff from the convertible, the Virginian was the first four-door "hardtop sedan," although it had small, metal-framed glass pillars that did not roll out of sight. Like the Ford Crestliner, this so-called hardtop offered an optional roof covering to simulate a convertible top, and most were fitted with this. But at $3000, the Virginian was prohibitively expensive for its day, and only 1000 were sold through 1950.

The "personal" Kaiser for 1951 was the Dragon, offered initially as a trim package for the upper-series Kaiser Deluxe and distinguished from other models only by its interior. Seats, door panels, and dashboard were covered with embossed "dragon" vinyl, the name being chosen to avoid confusion with the skin of alligators whose survival was, even then, of concern to ecologists. This was the first car from a major Detroit automaker to use vinyl as an upholstery material, starting a trend that would quickly spread throughout the industry. Later that season, K-F offered a "Mark II" Dragon with a vinyl top as well as a vinyl interior. The pattern was now called "dinosaur," so there would be no mistaking it for the hide of any endangered species. A later version with bamboo-like vinyl trim was known appropriately as the Jade Dragon. Although these cars were slow sellers, they at least kept customers coming in.

Kaiser skipped a limited edition for 1952, but revived the series with the "Hardtop Dragon" the following year. Taking a cue from Ford, K-F promoted this four-door sedan as a hardtop by virtue of its padded "bambu" vinyl top. Richly upholstered, the 1953 Dragon was embellished with gold-plated medallions and hood ornament, and carried a gold owner's nameplate for the dash. Priced at about $3800, it sold about as poorly as the Virginian. Fewer than 1300 were built, and many were unsold at the end of the model year.

But 1953 was a good year for other limited-edition "per-

General Motors took bold steps in the 1953 model year to expand its personal car lines with introduction of the Cadillac Eldorado (above), Olds Fiesta (opposite page, top), and the Corvette. Corvette models shown are a 1954 roadster (right) and a 1955 roadster (opposite page). Sales of the Fiesta and the richly appointed Buick Skylark, also introduced in 1953, were disappointing.

sonal" cars. Packard, for example, offered a svelte new convertible called the Caribbean. This took many of its styling themes from the interesting Pan American two-seater, which had been developed with the Henney Body Company in 1952 for publicity purposes under the hard-driving leadership of Packard's new president James J. Nance. Listing at $5200 and equipped with a potent 180-bhp straight eight, the Caribbean stood apart from standard Packard convertibles with its ultra-clean lines and a custom hood with full-width air scoop. Elegantly trimmed, it was the star attraction at Packard showrooms. The Caribbean continued for 1954 with an even larger 212-bhp engine. Production was low—750 of the '53s and only 400 of the '54s—but it was an important prestige offering, and convinced customers that Packard was serious about regaining its preeminence in the luxury market.

The Caribbean was restyled for 1955 and, like the rest of the line, benefited from Packard's new ohv V-8 with 275 bhp. For 1956, power rose to 310. Convertible prices remained at around $6000, and a companion hardtop priced at $5500 was added that year. But falling sales of the higher-volume models and tight finances resulting from Packard's purchase of Studebaker in 1954 condemned the Caribbean to extinction after '56.

Certainly the strongest exponent of the personal-car theme in the early '50s was General Motors. In 1953, four of its five divisions introduced limited-production specials: the Cadillac Eldorado, Buick Skylark, Oldsmobile Fiesta, and Chevrolet Corvette. Their main purpose was to test public reaction to certain styling and engineering ideas that might be used on future mass-production models.

The $5700 Oldsmobile Fiesta had a custom leather interior, a 170-bhp version of the Rocket V-8, and was one of the first production cars to have a wraparound windshield. Standard equipment also included Hydra-Matic transmission and power brakes, steering, windows, and seats. But the Fiesta was dropped after only one year and a mere 458 units. Management had apparently decided it didn't need a limited edition to appeal to the typical Olds buyer, who was thought to be somewhat less interested in personal expression than a Buick or Cadillac prospect.

The Skylark was a more ambitious project. It was a sectioned, chopped, and channeled Buick convertible, four inches shorter and more cleanly styled than the standard issue. It sported Kelsey-Hayes wire wheels and the finest quality upholstery. Buick built only 1690 Skylarks for 1953, priced at $5000 a copy. The model returned for '54 with the price cut to $4500 and without many of its exclu-

sive styling touches. Only 836 were sold, and the Skylark vanished at the end of the season.

Cadillac's Eldorado was the most successful GM personal car of the '50s, and as such would strongly influence product planners at Ford. Initially priced at what seemed like an astronomical $7750, it was targeted as an upper-crust specialty item, and only 432 were sold its first year. Like the Skylark, it used a cut-down convertible body and wraparound windshield. A metal cover that concealed the top when stowed gave a smooth look to the rear deck. For 1954, Cadillac decided to capitalize on the Eldorado's prestige by making the car more salable. Price was cut by $2000, and the body was now the same as the standard Cadillac convertible's. The '54 lacked the custom styling of the '53, but its lower price sparked sales. The division sold 2000 for 1954, 4000 of the '55s, and 6000 for 1956. Eldorados were easily distinguished from other Cadillacs by a distinctive rear end sporting sharply pointed fins and, from 1955 on, a slightly more powerful version of Cadillac's brawny V-8. For 1957–58, Cadillac fielded an even more upmarket specialty model, the $13,000 Eldorado Brougham, a close-coupled hardtop sedan. Eldorado sales picked up in the early '60s and rose to significant levels by 1967, when a new Eldorado was introduced. Designed around the front-wheel-drive system of the Olds Toronado, this new-generation Eldorado became one of the most successful high-priced personal cars in history. Not surprisingly, it is still with us today.

But the public's taste wasn't limited just to big, flashy convertibles and hardtops. By the mid-1950s, the sports car had also captured America's fancy. Returning GIs had brought home MGs and Jaguars from England, and the popularity of these cars immediately after the war led to other European sports models aimed squarely at American buyers—the Triumph TR2, Austin-Healey 100, Alfa Romeo Guilietta, Mercedes-Benz 190SL. Although sports cars accounted for only .027 percent of the U.S. market in 1953, the public in general seemed fascinated by European features like bucket seats, floor-mounted gearshifts, and lithe two-seat bodies. Detroit's marketing mavens began to wonder whether a sports car in the lineup might help sales even more than a customized special.

Two independent manufacturers had launched sports cars by 1953, the Nash-Healey in 1951 and the Kaiser-Darrin, which arrived in 1953 as a '54 model. Another sporting entry was the very low-volume Hudson Italia of 1954–55, a four-seat grand tourer based on the firm's compact Jet chassis. But the independents were simply too strapped for money to compete with the European sports cars. They had to be more concerned with higher-volume family models on which their profits and survival depended.

Chevrolet's Corvette, on the other hand, sprang from the highest-selling single make and the most successful corporation in the world. Powered by a low-suds six-cylinder engine mated to an uninspired automatic transmission and having an unorthodox fiberglass body complete with old-fashioned side curtains, the 1953 Corvette was really more of a tourer than a sports car. MG and Triumph fans were appalled by its trendy styling and unsporting automatic. Those who admired Eldorados didn't like its plastic side curtains and limited luggage and passenger space. At one point, around 1954–55, GM actually considered dropping the Corvette altogether. Fortunately for future Corvette fans, Chevy was able to develop the car further. Corvette thus got its first V-8, the classic 265-cid Chevy small-block, for 1955, followed the next year by smooth new styling from the pen of Harley Earl, then fuel injection for 1957. It was thus transformed into a true sports car, and enjoyed increasing sales success into the '60s and '70s.

At Ford Motor Company's Dearborn headquarters, where GM's every move was carefully watched, the Corvette's arrival sparked a good deal of debate. Ford itself had been transformed from the disorganized company of 1945 into a dynamic competitor thanks to Chairman Henry Ford II and President Ernest Breech. It was traditional for Ford to respond to any GM product innovation with one of its own. Should it now field a challenger to the low-volume plastic sports car?

According to former product planner Tom Case, "There wasn't any question about it. Mr. Ford wanted a civilized sports car, if we were going to build a two-seater at all. The Corvette was too spartan, too much like an MG. You just couldn't imagine Mr. Ford struggling to raise one of those plastic side curtains." The company's response appeared in due course at the end of 1954: Thunderbird.

This new steel-bodied two-seater was pushed into production by Henry Ford's lieutenant, Lewis B. Crusoe, general manager of Ford Division. Crusoe was a marketing man first, a car buff second, and the Thunderbird reflected this in being primarily a brilliant marketing maneuver designed to outflank Chevrolet. In its early design phases

Crusoe decreed the new car would be powered by a V-8; a six wouldn't even be offered. The engine chosen turned out to be a 292-cubic-inch unit with close to 200 bhp. Crusoe also mandated automatic transmission and a bolt-on hardtop as options. A deluxe interior complete with conventional roll-up windows was also planned from the start. Styling, which was largely the work of Robert Maguire and Damon Woods, was spectacular. Priced at $2944, the T-Bird was competitive with the new V-8 Corvette, and given buyer preference for luxury features, the outcome was predictable. For the 1955 model year Chevrolet sold 674 Corvettes; Ford sold 16,155 Thunderbirds.

For 1956, Thunderbird got a mild facelift. The 1957 edition was more extensively reworked, gaining a combination bumper/grille, modest tailfins, and a revised interior. Available horsepower ran as high as 300. Sales for 1956 were 15,631, rising to 21,380 for '57. But even as the first Thunderbird rolled off the line, an all-new four-seat successor was being prepared for the 1958 model year. The marketing decisions that influenced this evolution are crucial to the Mustang story for, as Tom Case likes to say, "The Mustang was really the original Thunderbird revived—with two extra seats." The change came after Crusoe moved up in the company hierarchy. Taking his place as Ford Division general manager was Robert S. McNamara (later U.S. secretary of defense, then president of the World Bank). A no-nonsense financial man, McNamara decided that Ford Motor Company would no longer build cars just for the sake of image. From now on, every Ford product would be designed mainly to make money. If it was also interesting, so much the better.

The effects of this policy reached far beyond Ford Division, and McNamara was soon exerting considerable influence on top corporate management. For example, at his behest a Mercury production expert was brought in to make recommendations on how the exclusive Continental Mark II could be built and sold more profitably. The Mark II had been Ford's ultimate car in 1956–57, but the company lost about $1000 on every one it sold despite a lofty $10,000 price. Under McNamara's direction, the replacement Mark III was designed to share components with the higher-volume 1958 Lincoln. The result was a far less distinctive car, but one that was much cheaper to build. For the first time, Continental made a profit.

Ford's answer to the Corvette was the Thunderbird, a more refined two-seater than Chevy's sports car. The 1956 T-Bird (opposite page, inset) is distinguished from '55 models by Continental-type spare tire. The classic Continental Mark II (above) was Ford's ultimate personal car for 1956–57.

The 1955 Crown Victoria (above) was a personal car venture that had disappointing sales. The '57 T-Bird (right), last of the two-seaters, sold better than rival Corvette, but not enough to satisfy Ford management. Ford's brass wanted something more like the 1957 Studebaker Golden Hawk (opposite page, bottom), which combined performance and luxury in a car that could seat four people. The result was the 1958 Thunderbird (opposite page, top), a swank and powerful personal-luxury car that sold in high volume.

At Ford Division, making money was even more important, aside from its perennial rivalry with Chevrolet. Accordingly, McNamara ditched the flashy but slow-selling 1955–56 Crown Victoria, which featured an optional—and costly—transparent plastic roof. The novel Skyliner, a convertible with a retractable steel roof instead of a folding cloth top, was already in the design stage when McNamara arrived, and he was too late to stop it for 1957. But when the Skyliner failed to sell in significant numbers for three successive seasons, he axed it for 1960.

As for the future of the Thunderbird, McNamara had three options. He could continue the car in its two-seat form as a prestige item, selling it at a loss or perhaps a small profit. He could also drop it entirely. Or he could remake the T-Bird into something that would sell in greater numbers than the two-seater had. Given his orientation, the choice was obvious, and a four-seat Thunderbird was given a green light for 1958. McNamara also adamantly

refused to continue the two-seater as a companion model. He felt it would divert attention from the new, larger car, which would need to have maximum impact to stimulate initial sales.

Even before the decision was made to drop it, the two-seat Thunderbird had been a car of vastly different character compared to the Corvette. It was not a race-and-ride sports car, which the Corvette definitely was after 1955; rather, it was a boulevard sports car. Though it looked sporty, it handled with little more agility than a standard Ford Fairlane. Thunderbirds were rarely seen in competition, where they were not very successful anyway. But because it combined the allure of a sports car with the special styling and luxury of the early postwar limited editions, Thunderbird had outsold Corvette handily. Even so, the two-seater's annual sales rate of 15,000–20,000 units was too low for McNamara. The four-seat T-Bird would have to triple or quadruple those figures to earn a

permanent place in the line.

McNamara's judgment proved correct: the 1958 Thunderbird was a sweeping sales success. It had a newly designed unit body with a low, ground-hugging stance, and was offered as a convertible or a fixed hardtop. To make up for its added weight compared to the two-seater, the new T-Bird had a more powerful 300-bhp, 352-cid V-8 standard. Production was around 40,000 units for '58, the vast majority being hardtops. The 1960 production total exceeded 90,000. After 1963, the T-Bird was more luxury car than grand tourer, but it never lost the cachet of "personal luxury" established by the '58 "Squarebird." That image had strong appeal for many customers who would never have been satisfied with a two-seater.

Unlike the limited editions and other personal cars before it, the four-seat Thunderbird was fresh from the ground up, created specifically for its market. It was intended not just to build showroom traffic but to sell in high volume. Its

success was not lost on the competition. Chrysler soon added four bucket seats and a center console to its high-performance "letter series" 300s. A bit later, General Motors launched a squadron of "personal" or "performance" models from its various divisions, beginning with the luxurious, bucket-seat 1961 Oldsmobile Starfire. Except for Cadillac's Eldorado Brougham, however, none of these was really a separate model in its own right or a direct T-Bird competitor. It wasn't until 1963 that GM responded with the elegant Buick Riviera, conceived expressly by styling chief Willam L. Mitchell with the Thunderbird in mind.

Studebaker, too, emulated the Thunderbird product package in its 1962–64 Gran Turismo Hawk. This was a beautiful car, cleverly created out of Studebaker's then nearly 10-year-old hardtop bodyshell by designer Brooks Stevens. With a roofline obviously inspired by the Thunderbird's, the GT Hawk could be equipped with four-speed gearbox, disc brakes, and supercharged V-8 engine. But Studebaker was in dire financial straits by the early '60s, and the Hawk did not sell as well as it deserved.

The swift, solid sales success of the four-seat Thunderbird combined with continuing buyer interest in sports cars to suggest a new market segment in the early '60s—the sporty, low-priced compact. The first of these was the Corvair Monza, introduced late in the 1960 model year as a trim option for Chevrolet's new rear-engine economy car. The most advanced of the Big Three compacts, Corvair was simply too unconventional for an economy car, and did not sell well against Ford's ultra-simple Falcon. Chevy quickly realized its mistake, and brought out the front-engine, live-axle Chevy II for 1962 to compete with the Falcon after suffering two years of disappointing Corvair sales. But the Monza had vinyl bucket seats, full carpeting, and snazzy close-coupled looks, and was seen by many as sort of poor man's Thunderbird. As such it sold like hotcakes. Priced at about $2200, it cost $1500 less than a T-Bird and some $500 less than a Triumph TR-3. Successful beyond even GM's projections, the Monza singlehandedly kept Corvair alive for the next nine years.

For 1961, Chevy offered an optional four-speed gearbox, which only added to the Monza's appeal. Compared to about 12,000 units built in what was left of the 1960 model year, Monza production soared to 143,000. Body style

The success of the 1958 T-Bird inspired other companies to copy the personal-luxury concept. One of the imitators was the 1962 Studebaker Gran Turismo Hawk (above). But the introduction of domestic compacts in the early 1960s spurred interest in another type of car that hinted at a market for the Mustang: small and sporty, with a lot of verve on the road. The Dodge Lancer GT (left) was a sports variant of a compact line. The unconventional Corvair couldn't match sales of the Ford Falcon, but the sporty Monza models (opposite page) were more fun to drive.

choices were expanded for 1962, and included a new convertible. Sales shot up past the 200,000 mark. For the really serious driver there was the 150-bhp turbocharged Monza Spyder, another new addition to the '62 line. This later evolved into the 1965–66 Corsa. Spyders and Corsas were rapid, good-handling cars of a size and character Chevrolet had never built before. And over a winding road, a well-driver Spyder could give fits to an MG driver.

So, the Corvair proved successful not as an economy car as Chevy had intended but as a sporty, fun-to-drive compact. Even more important, though, it revealed the existence of a brand-new market. Quite naturally, Monza was not alone for long. For 1962, Chrysler jumped into the fray with bucket-seat versions of its compact Plymouth Valiant and Dodge Lancer. That same year also saw the Chrysler Windsor replaced by a sportier "non-letter" 300 series. Priced at around $3500, it sold well by combining a milder, though still powerful, engine with the styling of the legendary letter series cars.

But public interest and the sales battles centered mainly on the sporty compacts. Rival GM divisions were quick to follow Chevy's lead with the Buick Special Skylark, Pontiac Tempest LeMans, and Oldsmobile F-85 Cutlass. Studebaker chimed in with the Lark Daytona for '62, offering the obligatory bucket seats plus complete instrumentation and options like disc brakes, four-speed gearbox, and perfor-

mance V-8s of up to 300 bhp.

Ford Motor Company was not about to be left out of this money-making picture. Its immediate answer to the Monza was the Falcon Futura, which arrived in the spring of 1961 as a spiffed-up two-door sedan with bucket seats and deluxe trim. It sold well, and continued with few changes through 1963. More exciting was the Sprint, first offered in the spring of that year in convertible or hardtop form as a special version of the Futura. The Sprint was available with what would turn out to be a significant new engine— Ford's 260-cid small-block V-8 with 164 bhp. This powerful, efficient engine coupled to an optional four-speed gearbox gave the Sprint truly vivid performance. And, the car had all the features that symbolized performance in the '60s: bucket seats, console, and extra instruments including a 6000-rpm tachometer.

Inspired by the success of the Corvair Monza, other GM divisions offered sport coupe versions of their compacts, like the 1961 Olds F-85 Cutlass (top) and 1962 Buick Special Skylark (above). Ford countered with the Falcon Futura (opposite page), which had bucket seats and deluxe trim. Later, Ford's small-block V-8 was offered in a Sprint version.

The Sprint continued through the Falcon's first restyle for 1964 and the second for 1966. By then, Ford had increased the small block's displacement to 289 cid. For 1967, the "Stage 2" engine with four-barrel carburetor offered 225 bhp. Mercury's Falcon-based Comet S-22 and Cyclone were similar in concept and performance to the Futura and Futura Sprint.

But anyone could see by the sales figures that the bucket-seat Falcons and Comets were not sufficiently competitive with the Monza. Whether it was because of the Corvair's novel rear engine and four-wheel independent suspension or superior promotion by Chevrolet, buyers were not as attracted to Ford's offerings. For example, Ford built 73,000 Futuras and S-22 Comets for 1963 and 118,000 of the '64s while Chevrolet cranked out a whopping 350,000 Monzas in the same period. If Ford was going to beat Chevy in this race, it would need a brand-new product. Like the four-seat Thunderbird, it would have to be designed from the ground up especially for its market.

It is important to realize that, in the years immediately before the Mustang appeared, Ford was in an ideal position to create such a car. A succession of able managers had come to Dearborn since 1945, and a once-ailing company had become a mighty colossus. In the early 1950s, it had overtaken Chrysler as the number-two producer, and during that decade, Ford Division actually outproduced Chevrolet on several occasions. In the early '60s, Ford experienced continuing sales growth. In 1964, for example, Ford Division produced nearly 1.8 million cars, a figure exceeded at that time only by 1923 in the make's history.

The decision to launch a new, sporty, and personal—but by no means limited-edition—model occurred in 1961. Yet such a car would not have been possible without consistently strong sales in the regular product line. Had the 1961–64 Fords sold poorly—or had the company created another Edsel—we might not have seen the Mustang until 1968 or 1969, if then.

The reason Ford Division did so well in the early '60s is due largely to McNamara's successor as general manager of

that period. McNamara had been an able leader, but he was not a car man. His replacement was: a hard-working salesman who had both astute business sense and an enthusiast's appreciation of automotive design. As everyone knows now, that man was Lee Iacocca.

Iacocca's father, Nicola, had emigrated to America from southern Italy at the age of 12. As a teenager, he had scraped together enough cash to buy a secondhand Model T, which he rented out from time to time to acquaintances in and around Allentown, Pennsylvania. Within eight years, his rental business had blossomed to 33 cars, most of them Fords. Soon he had branched out into real estate. Before the Depression, the family's holdings reached a net worth of over a million dollars, a fortune they even managed to keep largely intact through those hard times.

Wrote *Time* magazine in a 1964 cover story on Nicola's son at the time of the Mustang's introduction: "Lee Iacocca never wavered from early youth in his desire to go into the auto business—with Ford. For him, it was something like wanting to join the priesthood. 'I suppose it was partly because my father had always been greatly interested in automobiles,' he says, 'and because I was influenced by family friends who were Ford dealers.'"

Lee breezed through high school with excellent grades, received his bachelor's degree from Lehigh University, then got a master's degree in mechanical engineering from Princeton on a scholarship. Next, he whizzed through a scheduled 18-month Ford marketing course in only half that time and, soon afterward, found himself with an offer to become a transmission engineer in Dearborn. He decided that wasn't for him, so instead he took a job at a tiny Ford sales outpost in Pennsylvania. He did exceedingly well, and began climbing the ladders of various regional sales offices. In 1956, he came to the attention of division manager McNamara, who took a sales scheme Iacocca had dreamed up for Pennsylvania and applied it to the whole country. This was the "$56 a month for a '56 Ford" plan, and it worked. McNamara later said it helped sell an additional 72,000 cars. From there, promotions came thick and fast as the cigar-puffing Iacocca worked sales magic on any car or truck he ever touched, even though Ford often didn't build them the way he would have liked.

Iacocca had a habit of keeping little black notebooks that he used to chart and plan his career. At one point, he wrote that he intended to become a Ford vice-president by age 35. Those black books soon became a topic of dinner conversations all over Dearborn. One of the stories told about Iacocca in those days concerned an incident where he had run into flak from subordinates who resented so young a man telling them what to do. As the story goes, he passed out little black books to them, asking them to write down what they expected to accomplish over the next few years and in what order of importance. Then, every three months, Iacocca would grade his staff against their own goals. When some of the older men groused about this rating method, he told them, "Get with it. You're being observed. Guys who don't get with it don't play on the club after awhile." One staffer sniffed, "He really knows how to whipsaw his men with that notebook."

Iacocca's 35th birthday came and went without a vice-presidency. Later, he told a *Newsweek* magazine reporter, he was so disappointed he thought to himself, "Hell, that's the end." But 18 days later, Henry Ford II called Iacocca into his office and asked him if he'd like to be a Ford vice-president. One year after that, in 1960, Iacocca took McNamara's place as Ford Division general manager.

The Mustang was an entry in Iacocca's personal black book. It was an idea that sprang from his hunch that there must be a market out there looking for a car. That hunch was backed up by several important facts. For one thing, people were still writing to Ford, begging the company to revive the original two-seat Thunderbird. They missed its "personal" character. Meanwhile, Chevrolet had found an unexpected mini-bonanza with the Corvair Monza, and import sports cars like Jaguar, MG, Triumph, and Austin-Healey were selling at a brisk 80,000 units a year despite fairly high prices. Also relatively expensive, but much admired and talked about, were the Corvette and Studebaker's Avanti. Iacocca reasoned that if the flashiness and performance of costlier cars like these could be stuffed into

an inexpensive car for the masses, it would sell like crazy.

So here was the glint of a trend, and Iacocca had scribbled it down in his black book. He was thinking of the sort of car he himself might want, but the idea was still pretty hazy in early 1961. The car didn't yet have a name, of course, nor was it defined as having two seats or four; a front, rear, or center engine location; or a metal or fiberglass body. Those decisions would come later.

For the moment, Iacocca was still trying to change the somewhat lackluster image Ford Division's cars had acquired under McNamara. A good administrator, McNamara had left the Division in beautiful financial shape. But his steadfast refusal to build anything—no matter how exciting—if it didn't sell in high volume had cost Ford the sporty image it had begun to acquire in the '50s with the two-seat Thunderbird. *Time* magazine commented that his cars were . . . "like McNamara himself, [with] rimless glasses and hair parted in the middle."

Once installed as general manager, Iacocca started sprucing up various Ford models. He arrived too late to do much about the 1961–62 lines, which were already approved. But he was able to jazz up the mid-year 1963½ offerings considerably. It was Iacocca who dropped the first V-8 into the Falcon, put fastback roofs on some of the big Fords, and plunged the division back into racing in a big way. With the blessing of Henry Ford II, the company reentered NASCAR competition, and was very successful on the big Southern tracks. By 1965, Ford had won Sebring and Indianapolis, and had almost won Le Mans. It was all part of Iacocca's "thinking young."

Iacocca first broached the subject of a youth-oriented sporty car at a 1961 meeting of the Fairlane Group, an informal eight-man committee composed of top Ford executives plus members of the Ford Division ad agency. The group got its name from the Fairlane Inn Motel on Michigan Avenue in Dearborn, where its meetings were held each week. The committee decided the idea might be worth pursuing, and did so under project code T-5. (Much later, production 1965 Mustangs were sold in Germany under that designation.)

The 1963 Falcon Sprint (opposite page) and Mercury Comet S-22 (above) had some of the basic ingredients for a car like the Mustang with V-8 punch in a lightweight package, but neither model generated enough sales to catch the still popular Corvair Monza. The thinking at Ford was that they would need a completely new car, the way the Thunderbird was redesigned in 1958.

Two additional groups now became involved: market research, under the direction of marketing manager Chase Morsey, Jr., and a team of young engineers and designers headed by Donald N. Frey, who at that time was Iacocca's product planning manager. The role for market research, of course, was to either prove or disprove Iacocca's hunch. Product planning's mission was to come up with a car to fill the market void—if indeed there was one.

Morsey's research came up with some very encouraging conclusions. First, members of the postwar baby boom were just reaching car-buying age in 1960. Further, the number of young people aged 15–29 would increase by about 40 percent between 1960 and 1970 while population in the 30–39 age bracket would actually decrease by nine percent during that decade. Second, buyers between 18 and 34 were expected to account for more than half the projected increase in new-car sales from 1960 through 1970. Third, research showed that car styling in the '60s would need to reflect the preferences and tastes of this new, younger buyer group, not the older generations. Young people had clear ideas about styling and performance. The study concluded: " . . . 36 percent of all persons under 25 liked the 'four on the floor' feature. Among those over 25, only nine percent wanted to shift gears. Bucket seats were a favorite feature among 35 percent of young people, as against 13 percent in the older groups . . . " Fourth, buyers were becoming more educated, more sophisticated, and more willing to spend cash for what the study termed "image extensions." And finally, more families would have more money. The number of families with incomes of $10,000 and up was expected to rise 156 percent between 1960 and 1975. Thus, more households would be able to afford second and even third

One of the earliest ideas for a sporty personal car was the Mustang I, a styling study created in 1962 with the help of Ford engineer Herb Misch (left) and styling chief Eugene Bordinat. Mustang I was a two-seater with all-independent suspension that had adjustable springs and shocks, tubular frame and integral roll bar. One of the unusual features was that the bucket seats were fixed, but the pedals were adjustable for reach.

or fourth cars. Women and teenagers especially were the family members who most wanted cars of their own.

So, a potential and sizable market definitely existed. It was a young, affluent group, big enough to create substantial demand for the right kind of new car—something distinctive and sporty, but not too expensive. The question faced by the T-5 product planners was what should that car be?

One of the first alternatives considered was the mid-engine Mustang I, an experimental exercise for a two-seat sports car aimed more at the Triumph/MG market rather than the Corvette/Jaguar class. It was the product of an inspired triumvirate: an engineer, a stylist, and a product planner. The engineer was Herb Misch, who had come to Dearborn from Packard when former Studebaker-Packard President James Nance was named to head Edsel Division. The stylist was Eugene Bordinat. The product planner was Roy Lunn, formerly of Aston Martin and later a member of Ford's Product Study Vehicles Department. It was Lunn who laid out the basic design.

It was deemed necessary to start from the ground up, so the Mustang I was carefully considered. As a challenger to Triumph and MG, it was planned around a wheelbase of 85 to 90 inches and an engine of 1.5 to 2.0 liters mounted centrally in a multi-tubular frame covered by an aluminum body. Since it was impossible to build a prototype body very rapidly in Detroit, Ford contacted a special body builder in Los Angeles, Trautman and Barnes. T&B built the frame from one-inch steel tubing. The stressed-skin body was made up of aluminum panels only .06-inch thick,

with an integral roll bar and seat structure for added rigidity. Being fixed, the seat did not adjust, but pedals and steering wheel did. The pedals were mounted on a sliding box-member that allowed their position to be adjusted to suit any driver.

Lunn and Misch devised the Mustang I's four-wheel independent suspension, an uncommon feature in Detroit, land of the solid rear axle. Upper wishbones and lower triangulated arms coupled to radius rods were used at the rear, with attachment points widely spaced so that stress would be evenly distributed throughout the body/frame structure. Up front were wishbones, splayed coil springs, and Monroe telescopic shocks. All shocks and springs were adjustable for ride height and firmness. Steering was by a rack-and-pinion unit similar to the one used for the Ford Cardinal prototype, which later evolved into Germany's production Taunus 12M. The steering was geared to provide just 2.9 turns lock-to-lock and a turning circle of 30 feet.

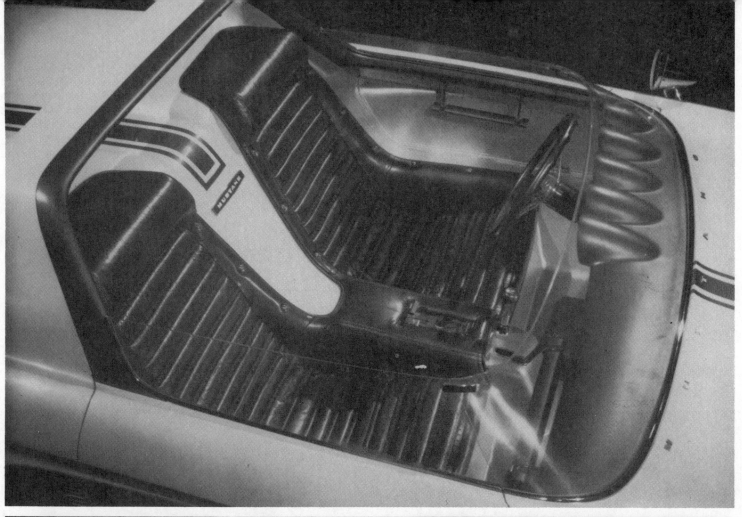

The Mustang I's engine was placed behind the cockpit ahead of the rear wheels. It was derived from the power-plant developed for the Cardinal project, a program begun in 1959 to design what we would now call a subcompact that would slot in below the Falcon in Ford's U.S. lineup. The Cardinal was unusual for its day in projecting the use of front-wheel drive. Its engine was also unusual: a 60-degree V-4 displacing 1927cc (90 × 60mm bore and

stroke). For the Mustang I it was tuned to produce 90 bhp at 6500 rpm breathing through a small, single-throat Solex carburetor. A competition version with two twin-throat sidedraft Weber carbs and a crossover manifold was also developed, and produced over 100 bhp. Taking drive to the rear wheels was a four-speed transaxle, also from the Cardinal program, with cable-operated shift linkage. A 7.5-inch-diameter clutch with special linings, adapted from

Another two-seat proposal in the Mustang planning effort was the XT-Bird careated by the Budd Body Company (top). The XT-Bird was a Falcon-based idea that relied heavily on the styling of the 1957 Thunderbird. Fastback styling was considered early in the series of styling studies under the Allegro name. Thirteen Allegros were designed in what Ford termed a "styling experimental car."

the English Ford Consul, was used. Although gear ratios weren't particularly close (4.02, 2.53, 1.48, 1.00), the 3.30:1 rear axle ratio made them suitable for the V-4.

The Mustang I followed accepted production sports car practice in having disc brakes at the front and drums at the rear. The parking brake operated on the rear drums, a less expensive proposition for mass production than one working on rear discs. The front discs were designed to take about 80 percent of total braking load, and were 9.5-inch Girling units borrowed from the English Ford 109E. The car rolled along on 13-inch magnesium wheels, built for Ford by Lotus of England, and shod with Pirelli radial-ply tires.

Dimensionally, the Mustang I measured 154 inches long overall, had a 90-inch wheelbase, and its track was 48 inches front, 49 inches rear. Lightweight construction resulted in an overall weight of less than 1200 pounds, which enabled the V-4 to provide thrilling performance: top speed was approximately 115 mph. The car's low sloping nose left minimal space for a radiator and ductwork, so the engine was cooled by two centrally located, diagonally mounted radiators, one per side, each equipped with a

thermostatically controlled fan. The 13-gallon aluminum alloy fuel tank had a quick-fill neck. The spare tire was stored in the front compartment.

Mustang I styling went from sketch to approved clay model in just 21 days under Gene Bordinat's direction. Thanks to Lunn, the car met Fédération Internationale de l'Automobile (FIA) and Sports Car Club of America (SCCA) regulations for race cars. Even the roll bar was SCCA-legal. So was the racing windshield, although that would obviously have been replaced by a full windshield on a production Mustang I. There was no soft top, but a light folding hardtop was designed for possible production, attaching to the header of a normal windshield. Concern for good aerodynamics dictated use of retracting headlights and even a fold-away front license plate mount. The car was low—less than 40 inches high—though it cleared the ground by nearly five inches.

Interior styling was another rush job by the Ford studio, but it was nicely executed. The instrument panel used a five-pod display containing fuel gauge, speedometer, tachometer, ammeter, and water temperature gauge. Ignition and light switches were mounted to the left in an angled

Convertibles and notchback coupes also were part of the Allegro ideas. The long hood-short deck styling that became an industry standard in the mid-1960s was an integral part of the look being considered. One design in the Allegro series was the Stiletto (left). Notice the sculptured scoop on the fenders (above and top) that later appeared on production Mustangs in much larger form just ahead of the rear wheels.

extension of the driver's armrest, and a passenger grab handle hung from the dashboard on the right. The choke and horn button were mounted on a central console alongside the shifter and pull-up handbrake. A rubber mat covered the floor. In appearance, the cockpit was starkly functional but practical, in keeping with the goal of low production cost.

The Mustang I was first displayed publicly at the United States Grand Prix at Watkins Glen in October 1962, where it was driven around the circuit to the cheers of fans by race driver Dan Gurney. Later, *Car and Driver* magazine tested the 90-bhp version, and found it as fast as Ford claimed. Its 0–60 mph acceleration took about 10 seconds, yet fuel economy was as high as 30 miles per gallon. The handling was excellent: "It reminds us of the first two-seat 1100cc Coventry Climax-engined Cooper more than any other car, and the Mustang seemed more forgiving. It can be braked well into a turn, and with power on its stability is striking." The magazine also praised the beautifully precise rack-and-pinion steering. But the editors felt body modifications would be needed to provide adequate luggage space. The retractable lights would need to have electric servo motors; on the prototype the driver had to get out and hand-crank them into position.

Innovative and exciting though it was, the Mustang I was a false start. While Ford engineers and stylists, Dan Gurney, and the sports car people raved, Iacocca watched public reaction carefully and shrugged. "All the buffs said, 'Hey what a car! It'll be the best car ever built,'" he later observed. "But when I look at the guys saying it—the offbeat crowd, the *real* buffs—I said, 'That's sure not the car we want to build, because it can't be a volume car. It's too far out.'"

Iacocca's conclusion may have been influenced by a prior decision on the Cardinal project. Cost estimates had indicated that if the proposed front-drive subcompact were sold in the U.S., it would have been only marginally profitable for Ford against the VW Beetle and other small imports. Thus, it was decided to build the Cardinal in Europe but not the United States. This effectively ended production hopes for Mustang I. It was designed to share major mechanical components with the high-volume Cardinal, and would have been economically feasible if that car were built here. But without a U.S. Cardinal to borrow parts from, the Mustang I would have been costly to build, and Iacocca realized it just wouldn't generate enough sales volume to offset the high tooling and development expenses.

Similar drawbacks plagued another early-'60s two-seat proposal, the Falcon-based XT-Bird. This was an exercise in production engineering conceived by the Budd Body Company, a long-time Ford supplier, at about the time Mustang I was being developed. Budd had built the original 1955–57 Thunderbird bodies, and still had the dies. The firm's engineers concluded this tooling could be effectively utilized for a new production car combining the chassis and drivetrain of the 1961 Falcon with a modified version of the '57 T-Bird bodyshell.

Budd envisioned using the Falcon's chassis and retaining much of its underbody structure. The 1957 T-Bird styling would be updated by shearing off the tailfins and lowering the front fenders. Ingeniously, Budd even managed to retain the original '57 dashboard and cowl for the XT-Bird. In deference to contemporary tastes, however, Budd reshaped the severe dogleg of the wraparound windshield so that the A-pillar was less angled, and front quarter vents were added. The XT-Bird, like the original '57, had a steel body and a folding soft top that disappeared into a well ahead of the decklid. Unlike the original, Budd's proposal also had a small rear jump seat that could

A variety of front-end and rear-end treatments was tried on Allegro clay models. One front end (far left) had a Thunderbird-like air scoop and emblem over a horizontal grille that recalls the 1960 Pontiac.

hold children or could be folded down to form a luggage platform.

Budd's executives went out of their way to interest Ford management in the XT-Bird, because they knew Iacocca was looking for a new image-builder. They pointed out the extraordinarily high resale value of 1955–57 Thunderbirds, and suggested this indicated a strong, unmet buyer demand for an updated version of that car. Adapting the old dies would allow Ford to keep price attractively low, Budd estimating the finished production XT-Bird could retail for about $2800. "The total tool, jig, and fixture costs for production of the XT-Bird would not exceed $1.5 million," Budd wrote. "We could ship the entire body-in-white for the XT-Bird to the Ford Motor Company for a total unit cost of between $350 and $400 . . . We believe that we could be shipping complete bodies in white for this car six months from the day you authorize us to start on the job." Such low production and development costs were an accountant's dream.

In the end, though, the XT-Bird remained only wishful thinking. Lack of full four-passenger capacity was its main limitation, though its dumpy lines didn't set many hearts pounding, either.

The Fairlane group also passed over two other two-seater designs, an open racer called Median and a sports model called Mina. By 1962, dozens of four-seat packages were in the design stage, some mere paper renderings, others quarter-scale and full-size clay models. Executives reviewed them all, and asked that one, a four-seater dubbed "median sports car," be worked up into coupe and convertible body styles. Its styling captured, they felt, some of the two-seat Thunderbird's personal flavor. Besides a four-seat package, the median sports car was mocked up as a two-seater, as a 2 + 2 with jump seats, and as a 2 + 2 with a set of cramped rear bucket seats.

This exercise led to a second generation of styling studies called Avventura. There were 12 different clay models in this series, one of which became what was called the Allegro X-car, first shown publicly in August 1963. Actually, there were 13 Allegros, each differing slightly in dimensions and interior packaging. Ford as much as admitted that none of them would ever be produced by labeling Allegro a "styling experimental car."

The Allegro was built on a 99-inch wheelbase, stood 50 inches high, stretched 63.5 inches wide, and was 170 inches long overall. These dimensions were chosen partly to accommodate the 144-cid Falcon overhead-valve six. The car's intended drivetrain layout was conventional: a front-mounted engine bolted to a manual transmission, connected by a driveshaft to a live rear axle. Ford was now leaning towards drivetrain components shared with one of its American-made production cars, though the company

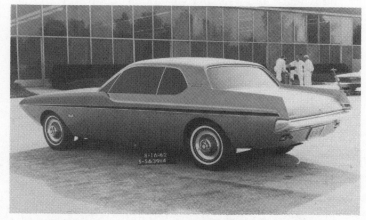

1962 Allegro styling study shows unusual sculpturing on the doors that never made it into production and a grille that bears a strong resemblance to the 1970 Ford Torino.

stated the Allegro "could accommodate the 170-cubic-inch [Falcon] six or the 1200cc or 1500cc V-4s of the [German Ford] Taunus with its front wheel drive." Had the V-4 and fwd arrangements been used, noted *Road & Track* magazine, "it would seem that there is space for four passengers without major body alterations, and the width of the door (for rear seat entrance) bears this out."

As in the Mustang I, the Allegro's seats were fixed and pedals movable to fit the driver. The steering wheel was adjustable up and down. It also swung out of the way as on contemporary production Thunderbirds; a "memory button" allowed the wheel to be returned to a preset position once the driver was seated. The Allegro also featured retractable seatbelts, certainly a portent of the future. Because the seats were fixed structural body elements, the seatbelt housings were attached directly to them, a touch that showed the influence of aircraft design.

The Allegro and its many variations occupied the attention of Ford management for about a year, until midsummer 1962. By that time, though, the theme had been worked over so much it had become stale. Accordingly, Bordinat, Frey, Iacocca, Henry Ford II, and their associates decided in August 1962 to start over with a new series of clays. A new set of dimensions was laid down, and four styling teams were invited to submit competing proposals to fit. The specifications now called for a target retail price of $2500, 2500-pound curb weight, 180-inch maximum overall length, four seats, floorshift, and the use of mostly Falcon mechanical components. The car's character was to be "sporty, personal and tight." Finally, Ford tossed in a marketing brainstorm, probably the key to the whole concept of what would become the Mustang: a long, long option list that would let the buyer tailor the car for economy, luxury, performance, or any combination of these.

The four studios went to work, representing Ford Division, Lincoln-Mercury, Corporate Projects, and Advanced Design. All, of course, were guided by Bordinat, who gave them just two weeks to come up with suitable clays. The four groups produced a total of seven, and on August 16th these were arranged side-by-side in the Ford Design Center viewing area. Of these, one leaped out from the rest. "It was the only one in the courtyard that seemed to be moving," Iacocca said later, and Henry Ford II agreed.

That particular proposal was created by the Ford Division Studio under Joe Oros (later, executive director of Ford and Lincoln-Mercury design). The team included studio manager Gail Halderman and executive designer David Ash. The Oros group had gathered to talk about the assignment at length, before anyone even put pencil to paper. "We said what we would and wouldn't do," said Oros. "We didn't want the car to look like any other car. It had to be unique." They talked so much, in fact, that once they started it took three days to draw the shape that so impressed Iacocca. The proposal looked very much like the eventual production Mustang, but lacked a front bumper. It wore Cougar nameplates, though the name was later changed to Torino or Turino as development work proceeded. Finally, and confusingly, it was dubbed Mustang II. Oros deliberately painted his original clay white so it would stand out at the showing and increase his team's chances of winning this not-so-friendly intramural show-

down. Judging from the reaction of Iacocca and HF II, that strategy—and the styling—succeeded handsomely.

The Cougar-Torino-Mustang II, like the Budd XT-Bird, was designed around the Falcon floorpan. To provide genuine four-passenger seating capacity, wheelbase was pegged at 108 inches, only 1.5 inches shorter than the production Falcon's. Track was 56 inches front and rear, and overall length was 186.6 inches, a bit more than the maximum specified. The car was intended to accept Ford drivetrains up to and including the 289-cid, 271-bhp Fairlane V-8 and four-speed all-synchromesh transmission.

Later, a running prototype based on the Oros car and also called Mustang II was built and displayed around the country. Its first showing was at Watkins Glen before the United States Grand Prix in the autumn of 1963. Although those who saw it didn't realize it at the time, the Mustang II was actually a sneak preview of Ford's forthcoming new sporty compact. Earlier, Iacocca had indicated that if Ford was going to mass-produce any sporty car, the Mustang II had the best chance among any of the experimentals seen to date. "Our preliminary studies," he said, "indicate that a car of this type could be built in this country to sell at a price of under $3000."

Meanwhile, Oros and his staff had one more fling with a two-seater, the last such proposal given any notice before management definitely decided on the four-seat formula. This was the Cougar II, a running prototype first shown in late 1963 and early 1964. It was a fastback coupe with exciting lines not unlike those of the 1963 Corvette Sting Ray split-window coupe. Though Ford didn't mention it, the Cougar II was very close dimensionally to the exciting A.C. Cobra: 90-inch wheelbase; 50.5-inch track front, 52-inch rear; 66.5-inch width; 48-inch height; and 168-inch overall length. The Cougar II had the Fairlane 260 V-8, four-speed all-sychromesh gearbox, and all-independent suspension. Said *Road & Track*: " . . . the aerodynamics look reasonably good and the performance should be excellent, especially with one of the hotter versions of the Cobra-ized Fairlane V-8." In a move that anticipated a future Corvette feature, Oros incorporated a removable roof panel over the passenger compartment. It was a good idea, providing closed GT comfort with a measure of convertible openness. But with the panel removed it was discovered the rear roof/backlight acted as an air scoop. This apparently had some benefit for aerodynamics, but also had an unexpected side effect—a blown-out rear window. Oros accordingly added a "relief panel" behind the seats that opened when pressure against the backlight reached 15 pounds per square inch.

The Cougar II was certainly the closest thing to a genuine street sports car turned out by Ford designers, with the smoothest styling of any prototypes developed in these years. Alas, it had the same problem that weighed against the Mustang I and XT-Bird before it. Ford just didn't think a two-seater would sell in sufficient volume to assure a significant return on the high costs of tooling such a car. The Cougar II also didn't fit Iacocca's idea for a four-passenger personal model, and its overall styling was probably too close to the Corvette's for many at Dearborn to feel comfortable.

On September 10, 1962, the original Cougar, the white

clay model with which Oros had wowed the company brass a few weeks earlier, was "validated" for production. Only at this point did Ford Engineering get involved. This was unusual, because engineers are usually called in at a much earlier stage in a car's development than was the case with the Mustang. The need to keep styling options open was probably the reason. Said Jack J. Prendergast, executive engineer for light vehicles: "Styling kept the engineers out too long, but even so Engineering and Styling worked together very smoothly." Except for routine compromises needed to adapt a styling prototype for mass production

Clay mockup dubbed Torino (below) incorporates appearance features from production Mustang, like side scoops and three-part taillights. In the fall of 1963, a running prototype called Mustang II was shown around the country. Few realized then it was a sneak preview.

(conventional bumpers, round headlights, a less rakish windshield angle), relatively few changes were made to the Oros design. Engineering bent over backward, in fact, to keep its styling intact.

The Mustang was mainly a body engineering job, because its basic chassis, engine, suspension, and driveline were, by design, off-the-shelf Falcon and Fairlane components. At 181.6 inches, its overall length was identical to the 1964 Falcon's. Wheelbase, at 108 inches, remained 1.5 inches shorter. Some thought had been given initially to sharing some of the Mustang's sheetmetal with the Falcon, but that idea didn't last long.

According to Ford Studio manager Gail Halderman, "We had to bend something like 78 Ford Motor Company in-house standards or rules in order to build this car." He was referring to a rulebook used by Ford designers at that time listing specific do's and don'ts for production body engineering. For example, the rules prohibited the production Mustang's radical tuck-under on the rear fenders, the minimal bumper-to-sheetmetal clearance, the die-cast headlight bezels, and the degree of roll-under for its front bumper pan. Where Engineering couldn't make structural pieces fit Styling's lines and curves (as in the case of the

front pan, where there was no room for bumper bracing), the original design was revised as little as possible.

With the many optional engines and different horsepower ratings contemplated, it was essential to have a rigid base. Prendergast recalled, "The platform-type frame, evolved from previous light-car experience, was designed to be really in the middle. All the various chassis components were attached to the under side, and all the body components were installed topside." Heavy box-section side rails with five welded-in crossmembers formed the base. The convertible used heavier-gauge steel and extra reinforcements in the rocker areas. The frames of the first coupes were so stiff that they actually resonated, and were

accordingly softened slightly. Prendergast pointed out that at the time the Mustang was being readied for production, Engineering had learned quite a bit about noise, vibration, and harshness through experience with the Falcon and Comet. The result was better engineering solutions for certain problems, such as choice of suspension components, than on those earlier cars. The Mustang suspension, in fact, drew heavily from the later Falcon Sprint/Comet Caliente/Fairlane family. A running change made to the 1964 versions of these cars anticipated the ponycar's arrival. Because of the Mustang's low hoodline, engineers lowered the air cleaner and countersunk the radiator filler cap on Falcons, Comets, and Fairlanes, components Mus-

Torino model (opposite page, bottom) has profile that is close to the Mustang that debuted a year later. The Mustang II show car that was displayed in the fall of 1963 has racier styling than the production car, but came with fender emblems and the chrome galloping horse in the grille that were trademarks of the early Mustang.

tang would share. In a similar way, all Mustang mechanical parts were in production and even cataloged several months before the car itself debuted.

Meanwhile, there was still the problem of choosing a suitable name. Although "Mustang" had been seriously considered early on, as shown by the Mustang I two-seater, it was some time before it took hold. Different departments had applied a variety of working titles to Iacocca's project, including Allegro, Avventura, Cougar, Turino and Torino, as well as Mustang. Henry Ford II favored "T-Bird II" or "Thunderbird II." Surprisingly, Iacocca had no strong preference.

John Conley, from Ford's ad agency, went to the Detroit Public Library to get some additional ideas. Earlier, he had combed through lists of birds to come up with Falcon for Ford's 1960 compact. (Chrysler, he later learned, had already used it on a 1955 experimental sports car. But a friendly phone call to Chrysler from Henry Ford II netted Dearborn the rights to that name.) This time, Conley searched through names of various horses. Besides Mustang, he also considered Colt, Bronco, Pinto, and Maverick. All four of these were eventually used for cars—Colt by Dodge; Bronco, Pinto, and Maverick by Ford, of course. Mustang, however, was by now the clear choice. In many ways it was a natural. It conjured up visions of cowboys, prairies, movie adventures, the romantic West. It was easy to spell and easy to remember. As one Ford ad man said, "It had the excitement of the wide-open spaces, and it was American as all hell." Thus, the wild, free-spirited horse of the Western plains was carved out of mahogany as a template for the soon-to-be familiar sculpture that graced the grille of the first production prototype.

31

THE REVOLUTION BEGINS

Target date for the Mustang's introduction was April 17, 1964. The place was to be the New York World's Fair, which opened that day. As if the public's appetite hadn't been whetted enough by a series of exciting show cars, Ford decided to whet it some more by "accidentally" baiting the press. On March 11th, Henry Ford's 20-year-old nephew, Walter Buhl Ford II, just "happened" to drive a black pre-production Mustang convertible to a luncheon in downtown Detroit. Fred Olmsted, auto editor for the Detroit *Free Press*, spotted it in a parking lot, and hurriedly called photographer Ray Glonka. Glonka's picture was picked up by *Newsweek* and a number of other publications, giving a national audience its first glimpse of the new Mustang. If anything, those sneak photos only heightened the public's desire to see the car in full.

Time magazine, meantime, had made a deal with Ford that allowed the news weekly to follow the Mustang's development story in pictures. Photographer J. Edward Bailey had been with Oros and Bordinat almost since the beginning of the Mustang II clay. In return, the magazine

had promised not to publish anything about the new car until introduction day. *Time* kept its promise, but despite its hopes for an exclusive, *Newsweek* ran a cover story on Iacocca and his baby's birth the same week. Ford publicists had pulled off a rare feat: in a barrage of media coverage, *Life, Look, Esquire, U.S. News & World Report*, the *Wall Street Journal*, and most business and automotive publications all carried big articles on Mustang just days before the official sales date. On the evening of April 16th, Ford bought the 9 p.m. slot on all three major TV networks, and an estimated 29 million viewers were treated to the Mustang's unveiling without leaving their living rooms. The next morning, 2600 major newspapers carried announcement ads and articles.

Ford invited some 150 auto editors to be its guests for the World's Fair opening and some sumptuous wining and dining. The next day, they were set loose in a herd of Mustangs for a drive from New York to Detroit. "These were virtually hand-built cars," recalls one Ford information officer, "and anything could have happened. Some of

Mustang II show car, displayed in late 1963, was preview of production Mustang styling.

the reporters hot-dogged these cars the whole way, and we were just praying they wouldn't crash or fall apart. Luckily everyone made it, but it was pure luck." The luck paid off in glowing reports in the following weeks.

Mustangs were soon put on display in airport terminals, Holiday Inn lobbies, and dealer showrooms across the country. Everywhere, the car's base price, $2368 f.o.b. Detroit for the hardtop, was boldly advertised. Crowd reaction was tremendous. One San Francisco trucker stared so hard at a Mustang sitting in a dealer's showroom that he drove right in through the window. A Chicago dealer had to lock his doors to keep people from crowding in and crushing his cars—and each other. A Pittsburgh dealer made the mistake of hoisting his only Mustang up on a lube rack. Crowds pressed in so thick and fast he couldn't get the car down until supper time. At one eastern dealership, 15 customers wanted to buy the same new Mustang, so the car had to be auctioned off. The winning bidder insisted on sleeping in it to be sure it wasn't sold out from under him before his check cleared the next morning. It was the same story all over the country: dealers simply couldn't get Mustangs fast enough. All the early cars were sold at or above retail, and with very unliberal trade-in allowances.

Long before introduction, Ford had projected first-year Mustang sales at 100,000 units. As the World's Fair approached, Iacocca upped the estimate to 240,000, and switched over Ford's San Jose, California, plant to Mustang production. Iacocca had been conservative: it took only four months to sell 100,000 Mustangs. For the full 1965 model run—April 1964 through August 1965—a total of 680,989 were sold, an all-time industry record for first-year sales. By March 1966, the one-millionth Mustang had rolled off the line.

A legend had been created overnight. Mustang was an instant hit, and the years of effort and planning that had gone into its concept and design were a big part of that. Mustang proved to be right on target for a vast, hitherto untapped market. By almost any yardstick, it was certainly the start of a revolution. The stampede was on.

Most automotive experts reacted to the new sporty car with qualified enthusiasm. This stemmed partly from the nature of the car itself. Underneath that striking new shape was little more than just another Detroit compact. However, most critics were willing to forgive such humble origins because performance and handling options were available to make Mustang a competent grand tourer. In fact, Ford's vast option list covered virtually every mechanical and physical aspect of the car.

There really was no such thing as a typical Mustang. Perhaps more than with any car before it, the character of any particular one depended on how it was equipped. This chameleon-like ability to take on so many different personalities also accounts for the wide range of press reactions. So, the Mustang's options are worth mentioning, if only to indicate their variety and their importance in the car's appeal to such a wide range of customers. And it was precisely this broad appeal that made the car such a resounding success. Mustang took up the personal-car theme of its predecessors with an option list longer than anything Detroit had ever contemplated—or offered. For less than $3000 you could order a very individual, very exciting

automobile depending, of course, on whether you were willing to wait for your specially optioned dream.

Standard equipment on the "1964½" models included the 170-cid Falcon six, a three-speed manual floorshift transmission, full wheel covers, padded dash, bucket seats, and carpeting. From there, you were on your own. A sampling: Cruise-O-Matic, four-speed manual, or three-speed overdrive transmissions; a choice of three different V-8s; limited-slip differential; Rally-Pac gauges (tachometer and clock); special handling package; power brakes; front disc brakes (from late 1965 on); power steering; air conditioning (except with the "Hi-Performance" V-8); console; deluxe steering wheel; vinyl roof covering; pushbutton radio with antenna; knock-off-style wheel covers; 14-inch styled steel wheels; and whitewall tires. There were also option *packages*: a Visibility Group (mirrors and wipers); an Accent Group (pinstriping and rocker panel moldings); an Instrument Group (needle gauges for fuel, water, oil pressure, and amperes, plus a round speedometer); and a GT Group (disc brakes, driving lights, and special trim). The most expensive single option, air conditioning, listed at only $283, and many of the more desirable extras, like the handling package ($31), front disc brakes ($58), Instrument Group ($109), and Rally-Pac ($71) were well within the reach of most buyers.

Engine options played a big role in determining a Mustang's personality. During the long 20-month 1965 model run, powerplant offerings were shuffled slightly. The original standard engine, the 101-bhp Falcon six, was dropped after September 1964 (considered the accepted break between "1964½" and the "true" 1965 models). Its replacement was a 200-cid six with 120 bhp. The 200 was an improvement on the 170 because of its higher compression, redesigned valvetrain, and seven (instead of five) main bearings. The new six also featured an automatic choke, a short-stroke cylinder block for longer piston and cylinder wear, hydraulic valve lifters, and an intake manifold integral with the head. The smallest V-8 initially offered was the 260-cid small-block with 164 bhp. Derived from it was a 289 that produced 195 bhp with two-barrel carburetor or 210 bhp with the optional four-barrel carb. A "Hi-Performance" (HP) version of the 289 four-barrel delivered 271 bhp. After September 1964, the 260 was discontinued and a two-barrel 289 with 200 bhp became the base optional V-8. Output of the four-barrel unit was then boosted to 225 bhp, while the "hi-po" version was left unchanged. The four-barrel 289 cost $162 extra, the 271-bhp mill $442.

These small-blocks were classic V-8s—light, efficient, and powerful. Advanced thin-wall casting techniques made them the lightest cast-iron V-8s on the market. They featured short-stroke design; full-length, full-circle water jackets; high turbulence, wedge-shaped combustion chambers; hydraulic valve lifters; automatic choke; and centrifugal vacuum advance distributor. The four-barrel engines achieved their extra power by increased carburetor air velocity matched to the engine's performance curve. They also had different valve timing compared to the two-barrel engines, plus a higher compression ratio that demanded premium fuel. The Hi-Performance 289 developed .95 bhp per cubic inch, and offered 312 pounds-feet of

torque at 3400 rpm. It featured a high-compression head, high-lift camshaft, free-breathing induction system, free-flow exhaust, solid lifters, low-restriction air cleaner, and chrome-plated valve stems.

Although the HP 289 seemed to be the answer to every dragster's dream, there were ways to improve its performance even more. For about $500 and a visit to your friendly Ford parts counter you could get an impressive amount of "Cobra equipment." This included such items as special camshafts, heads, and intake manifolds; dual four-barrel carburetion; and even Weber carbs. All these goodies were considered factory-stock, even though none of them were actually installed at the factory. Said *Road & Track:* "The Cobra equipment will do a fabulous job if you set it up right, and you don't have to switch basic engines. You just bolt it onto your standard V-8. Also, this equipment will now be legal in the FX classes at the dragstrip." The $73 Cobra cam kit consisted of solid lifters and a 306-degree-duration cam with .289-inch lift. The $222 cylinder head kit comprised two stock HP heads with extra-large intake and exhaust valves and heavy-duty valve springs and retainers. Matched pistons, combined with the cam and head kits, made up the $343 engine performance kit. Then there were carburetors and manifolds. A single four-barrel carb and big-port aluminum manifold cost $120. With dual four-barrels it was $243, and with triple two-barrels the price was $210. As a final touch, a dual-point centrifugal distributor was available for $50.

Even now, it's unclear exactly how much horsepower could be wrung out of a Mustang engine with Cobra equipment. Ford tested a stock HP 289 with four-barrel carburetor on a dynamometer, and recorded only 232 bhp at

This page, above: The 1965 2+2 with the GT Equipment Group and styled steel wheels. Below: Hardtop was the best-selling '65 Mustang model. Opposite page: Three pre-production 1965 prototypes.

5500 rpm, which was hardly the advertised 271 bhp at 6000 rpm. However, that test was run will all normal hardware installed; a stripped engine had been tested to get the advertised figure. An unstripped 289 fitted with special distributor, hot heads, triple carbs, and special non-Cobra headers recorded a dyno reading of 314 bhp at 6500 rpm, so 350 or more might not be too much to claim for a full-house Cobra-equipped engine. "You'll be able to feel that on the street," commented one engineer.

A four-speed gearbox was mandatory with the Hi-Performance 289. The HP was also the only engine offered with optional "short" rear axle ratios (3.89:1 and 4.11:1) so beloved by the dragsters. Standard ratios were 3.20:1 with the six, 2.80 for the two-barrel V-8, 3.00 for the four-barrel

34

V-8, and 3.50 with the HP. It could be argued that ratios like 2.80:1 made the milder Mustangs overgeared, but this appealed to those customers who preferred economy and smooth highway cruising over lightning-quick getaway.

Front disc brakes were offered beginning late in the 1965 model year as a $58 extra, and were well worth the money. Built by Kelsey-Hayes, they were cast-iron units of one-piece construction with a disc diameter of 9.5 inches. A radial rib separated the two braking surfaces, and each pad was actuated by two cylinders. Discs were a valuable option, because the Mustang's ordinary front drums were not noted for their fade resistance.

Ford added a snazzy fastback body style to the Mustang line in the fall of 1964. It was called the "2+2" in the brochures, and for a good reason: its rear legroom was scanty, even less than in the hardtop or convertible. However, the fastback made up for that with a rear seat that folded down and a partition between it and the trunk area that could be dropped forward. With seat and partition lowered, the long platform could accommodate items like skis or fishing rods. The sleek-looking fastback lacked rear quarter windows. Instead, its roof pillars had little air vents that were ostensibly part of a flow-through ventilation system.

Long-hood/short-deck proportions were the Mustang's most singular styling distinction. It set the pattern for what came to be known, in Mustang's honor, as the "ponycar"; in other words, a low-priced personal car of similar shape.

Above: Ford publicity photo issued at the start of the formal 1965 model year emphasizes the new 2+2 fastback. Left (from the bottom): the mid-engine Mustang I and the Mustang II show car pose with the production 1965 hardtop and Carroll Shelby's first GT-350.

Competitors reacted as quickly as they could to the new theme, but it took time. It wasn't until 1967 that Chevrolet and Pontiac brought out the Camaro and Firebird. Ford's sister division, Lincoln-Mercury, also needed two years to ready its Mustang-based Cougar. American Motors moved fairly rapidly by bringing out its Javelin for 1968. Chrysler, on the other hand, had introduced the Plymouth Barracuda, a "glassback" derivative of the compact Valiant, at about the same time as the Mustang, but it didn't really have the same kind of style until it was handsomely overhauled, also for '67. So, Mustang had the ponycar field all to itself—and enjoyed a minimum two-year head start on the competition.

Upper left: Smooth-winding Ford small-block V-8 made the '65 Mustang a lively performer. Above and left: The 1965 convertible, now the most desirable first-year Mustang. Lower left: Mustang paced the 1964 Indy 500, only a month and a half after the car's April launch.

Model Year Production
April 1964–August 1965

No.	Model	1965
63A	Fastback, standard	71,303
63B	Fastback, deluxe	5.776
65A	Hardtop, standard	464,828
65B	Hardtop, deluxe	22,232
65C	Hardtop, bench seats	14,905
76A	Convertible, standard	94,496
76B	Convertible, deluxe	5,338
76C	Convertible, bench seats	2,111
	TOTAL	680,989

Models		Prices/Weights
07	Hardtop, I-6	$2372/2445
07	Hardtop, V-8	2480/2720
08	Convertible, I-6	2614/2669
08	Convertible, V-8	2722/2904
09	Fastback, I-6	2589/2495
09	Fastback, V-8	2697/2770

General Specifications	1964½	1965
Wheelbase	108.0	108.0
Overall length	181.6	181.6
Std. Trans.	3-sp. man.	3-sp. man.
Optional Trans.	Overdrive	Overdrive
	4-sp. man.	4-sp. man.
	3-sp. auto.	3-sp. auto.

Engine Availability

Type	CID	HP	1964½	1965
I-6	170	101	Std.	—
I-6	200	120	—	Std.
V-8	260	164	Std.	—
V-8	289	200	Opt.	Std.
V-8	289	225	Opt.	Opt.
V-8	289	271	Opt.	Opt.

Although it was certainly attractive, the Mustang was not an exotic or earthshaking piece of design. Despite generally clean lines, it still showed traces of gingerbread. The "scoops" ahead of the rear wheel openings were not functional; the shallow, high-set grille looked awkward; and detail execution around the headlights and the rear of the body was not faultless. Space utilization, given the 108-inch wheelbase, was not very efficient. A Mustang really wasn't suitable for four passengers on a long trip, and trunk space was as limited as rear legroom. Poor space utilization was characteristic of all ponycars, the price of their racy proportions. This may partly explain why ponycar popularity declined in the '70s as buyers became more attuned to space-efficient engineering from Europe and Japan.

The enthusiast car magazines had other criticisms. *Road & Track*, in particular, was not happy with the driving position, citing a deep-dish steering wheel set too close to the driver's chest, too little leg space between the clutch and the nearest interfering object (the turn indicator lever), sparse standard instrumentation, and bucket seats only marginally effective in holding occupants in place. The Mustang's low list price, *R&T* decided, was responsible for such lapses. But the editors admitted that the car was carpeted, trimmed, and finished "in a manner that many European sports/touring cars would do well to emulate."

On the standard suspension a Mustang was anything but a grand tourer in the European mold. "The ride is wallowy, there's a tendency for the car to float when being driven at touring speeds, and the 'porpoise' factor is high on an undulating surface," *R&T* noted. "There's just nothing different about it in this respect . . . there seems little excuse for such frankly sloppy suspension on any car with the sporting characteristics which have been claimed for the Mustang." In straight-line performance, *R&T*'s 210-bhp/four-speed car did about what the editors expected: 0–60 mph took nine seconds; the standing quarter mile was reached in 16.5 seconds at 80 mph; top speed was 110 mph. Fuel consumption was 14–18 mpg. *Road & Track* applauded the car's good looks and low price, but regretted that it was otherwise little different from "the typical American sedan."

Once *Road & Track* laid hands on a properly optioned Mustang, however, its opinion changed dramatically. The test car, with the 271-bhp Hi-Performance V-8, delivered much improved acceleration and top speed. The 0–60 mph time fell to 8.3 seconds.

More interesting for the editors was the effect of the optional and inexpensive handling package. This consisted of stiff springs and shocks, a large-diameter front anti-sway bar, 5.90 × 15 Firestone Super Sports tires, and a quicker steering ratio (3.5 turns lock-to-lock). "The effect is to eliminate the wallow we experienced with previous Mustangs, and to tie the car to the road much more firmly, so on a fast run the point of one's departure into the boondocks is delayed very considerably," *R&T* wrote. "There is a certain harshness to the ride at low speeds over poor surfaces, but this is a small price to pay for the great improvement in handling and roadholding." There was a marked degree of oversteer present in this car, even though 56 percent of its weight was on the front wheels, but its hard suspension, *R&T* said, inspired more driver confidence. The editors now cheered the HP Mustang as "a big step in the right direction." But they looked forward to the advent of disc brakes and independent rear suspension.

A collection of 1965 Mustangs (clockwise from top left): the GT 2+2 fastback, the hardtop with optional fog lights, the standard 2+2, and the convertible. Sporty styling, attractive pricing, and a bevy of options helped Mustang set a first-year sales record.

Until then, *R&T* summed up, it would be "reluctantly unconquered." The discs showed up as an option within months, but irs never materialized.

As a voice for what Iacocca called "the sports car crowd, the real buffs," *Road & Track* was perhaps the harshest of all the car magazines in its judgment of the Mustang. By contrast, *Motor Trend*, a magazine whose tastes have traditionally favored Detroit products, liked all versions of the new car, and the HP in particular. *MT* scored 7.6 seconds in the 0–60 mph sprint, and ran the quarter mile in slightly less time than *Road & Track*. It was obvious that, with the right options, Mustang could be quite an automobile indeed.

An even more enthusiastic endorsement of the HP Mustang came from no less an expert than Dan Gurney. Writing in *Popular Science*, he stated: "This car will run the rubber off a Triumph or MG. It has the feel of a 2+2 Ferrari. So what *is* a sports car?" Gurney's Mustang did 123 mph maximum, and consistently beat a similarly equipped Corvette in quarter-mile acceleration runs. If Ford hadn't created a true sports car in the HP Mustang, it had certainly come close.

With Mustang sales roaring along as the 1966 model year approached, Ford product planners saw little reason to tamper with success. To the casual viewer, the 1966 Mustang looked like a carbon copy of the '65, but there were definite detail changes. Up front, the honeycomb grille texture was replaced by thin bars, and the thick horizontal chrome bar was discarded, leaving the galloping horse to float in its chromed rectangular frame. Mustang GTs kept the grille bar, however, with auxiliary driving lights mounted at its ends. At the rear was a restyled fuel filler cap. Along the sides, the simulated rear wheel scoop was decorated with three windsplits, front fender nameplates and emblems were revised, and GTs got an additional plaque. Finally, the stock wheel covers were redesigned.

Several more important changes were made inside. The original Falcon-like instrument cluster was replaced by the five-gauge arrangement previously reserved for the GT. The Rally-Pac combination tachometer and clock, mounted on the steering column, was still an option.

Running gear changes included upgrading six-cylinder models from 13- to 14-inch wheels and reworking engine mounts for all models to reduce vibration. Engine offerings remained at four: standard 200-cid six and the three optional 289s. The option list was extended to include a stereo cartridge tape system and deluxe seatbelts with reminder warning light.

Total 1966 sales were down compared to the 1965 model year, which was longer than usual due to the Mustang's

Styling changes were few for '66. Smart 2+2 (top) offered little trunk space (above left), but fold-down seat option helped. Base '66 hardtop (above right) displays new grille and wheel covers.

early introduction. But for comparable 12-month periods, 1966 sales actually ran ahead by 50,000 units. Mustang still had no direct competition, and romped along at close to half a million hardtops, 70,000 convertibles, and 35,000 fastbacks.

Ford promoted the six-cylinder Mustang quite vigorously for '66. "We felt there was a need to emphasize the economy aspect at that time," one Ford executive remembers. "Also, the six-cylinder coupe was by then the only Mustang selling for less than Mr. Iacocca's original target figure." (It listed at $2416, attractive indeed.) Though it looked like its V-8 counterpart, the six-cylinder Mustang was considerably different under the skin. Its wheels had only four lugs, while V-8 models had five. Sixes came with nine-inch-diameter drum brakes; V-8s had 10-inchers. The six-cylinder cars also had a lighter rear axle and a slightly narrower front track than the V-8s, and their spring rates were somewhat lower to keep an even keel; they would have looked tail-heavy had they used the heavier V-8 sus-

pension. The standard drum brakes, though, were quite effective with the six, capable of slightly shorter stopping distances from 60 mph than a V-8 car's discs, though they were susceptible to fade on hard application. The Mustang six performed reasonably well for a car of its class. *Motor Trend's* automatic-equipped model ran 0–60 mph in 14.3 seconds and averaged 20 mpg on regular gas.

Most criticisms noted in Mustang road tests of the period concerned minor irritations such as lack of rear-seat ashtrays and armrests or the absence of dashboard-level interior lights. But there was one consistent gripe—lack of interior room. "Five passengers can fit," wrote *Motor Trend,* "but the fifth one usually sits on the other four's nerves." However, *MT* summed up the Mustang as "safe and roadworthy, easy to handle, and fun to drive" in spite of its size limitations.

As mentioned, the Chevrolet Camaro and Pontiac Firebird appeared and the Plymouth Barracuda got a major redesign, all for 1967. Ford took on this new herd of pony-

A major restyle for 1967 gave the 2+2 a full fastback roof to replace the earlier notched style. The car shown carries the optional GT Equipment Group, ribbed back panel, and styled steel wheels.

cars by giving Mustang a thorough going-over. The big news that year was availability of a larger V-8, the 390-cid (bore and stroke 4.05×3.78 inches) four-barrel unit with a rousing 320 bhp. This engine was standard on the Thunderbird, and was an option on the big Ford and intermediate Fairlane as well as Mustang. Dealers usually recommended that Mustang buyers order the 390 with "SelectShift" Cruise-O-Matic transmission, an automatic that could be manually held in any one of its three forward gears for maximum acceleration. The 390 extended the total of Mustang power teams to 13.

The 390 certainly made the Mustang potent, but it came with a built-in front-end weight bias—58 percent of the total—so these cars understeered with merry abandon. The standard F70-14 Firestone Wide-Oval tires helped reduce the understeer somewhat, but almost anybody who drove a 390 said the 289 made a far better-handling Mustang. Customers were also well-advised to order the competition handling package with their 390. This consisted of stiffer springs and front stabilizer bar, Koni adjustable shocks, limited-slip differential, quick steering, and 15-inch wheels. Also available with the HP 289, it improved handling at the expense of ride. Of course, the big payoff for the 390 customer was straight line performance. Typical figures were 0–60 mph in 7.5 seconds, a standing quarter-mile of 15.5 seconds at 95 mph, and a top speed of close to 120 mph. If this wasn't the fastest car you could buy in 1967, it was certainly right in there with the top five percent of production automobiles.

Besides the burly new engine option, other features added to the 1967 Mustang's appeal. There was shapely new sheetmetal from the beltline down, and fastbacks got a sweeping new roofline that did away with the earlier, slightly notched effect. The restyle featured a concave tail panel, a couple of extra inches in the nose, and the loss of the gill-like impressions on either side of the grille opening. Width bulged by 2.5 inches, track by 2.0 inches. Engineers also paid attention to reducing noise and vibra-

The 1967 hardtop and convertible were restyled mainly from the beltline down. Ragtop's bendable tempered glass rear window can be seen in the bottom photo. It was one of several new extras that year.

Mustang sales fell markedly in the 1968 model year, but it wasn't for lack of sex appeal, as this convertible shows. The by-now familiar styling and a crowded ponycar field were the main reasons. Top power option that year was the big 427 with 390 horsepower.

tion with new rubber bushings at suspension attachment points.

That change in track width was an important one. It was made largely to provide adequate room in the engine bay for the bulky big-block V-8, but it also benefited handling. Front springs were relocated above the top crossmember, as in the Fairlane. The upper A-arm pivot was lowered and the roll center raised, a change picked up from Carroll Shelby's GT-350. The effect was to decrease understeer by holding the outside front wheel exactly perpendicular to the road. Since this change didn't require stiffer spring rates, ride didn't suffer.

Against its new rivals, the '67 Mustang compared quite favorably. Its economical six-cylinder engine was more miserly than those in the Barracuda or Camaro, yet it still provided decent performance because Mustangs were gen-

erally lighter. Ford also offered a wider selection of V-8s than either of its competitors, although the Camaro's optional 375-bhp 396 had the edge on any other ponycar in straight line performance. Mustang was less roomy and had a smaller trunk than the Barracuda, though the fastback versions of both had a fold-down back seat and trunk partition. The Mustang rode a bit harder than the Camaro, and was noisier than either Camaro or Barracuda. On the other hand, it offered a new option the others didn't: the swing-away steering wheel straight from the T-Bird. Also, Mustang convertible tops had a rear window made of articulated glass, which was superior to plastic. All three cars were nice-looking, so buyer preference was largely a matter of individual taste.

Competition from Big Three rivals—including corporate cousin, Mercury Cougar—naturally hurt Mustang in

Left top and center: Prototype for the Shelbyesque "California Special," a 1968 limited edition that may have been inspired by Shelby's Trans-Am Mustang notchbacks. Bottom left and below: Optional C-stripe sets off 1968 GT fastback's smooth contours.

Model Year Production

No.	Model	1966	1967	1968
63A	Fastback, standard	27,809	53,651	33,585
63B	Fastback, deluxe	7,889	17,391	7,661
63C	Fastback, bench seats	—	—	1,079
63D	Fastback, del. bench seats	—	—	256
65A	Hardtop, standard	422,416	325,853	233,472
65B	Hardtop, deluxe	55,938	22,228	9,009
65C	Hardtop, bench seats	21,397	8,190	6,113
65D	Hardtop, del. bench seats	—	—	853
76A	Convertible, standard	56,409	38,751	22,037
76B	Convertible, deluxe	12,520	4,848	3,339
76C	Convertible, bench seats	3,190	1,209	—
	TOTAL	607,568	472,121	317,404

Prices/Weights

Models		1966	1967	1968
01	Hardtop, I-6	$2416/2488	$2461/2568	$2602/2635
03	Convertible, I-6	$2653/2650	$2698/2738	$2814/2745
02	Fastback, I-6	$2607/2519	$2592/2605	$2712/2659

General Specifications

	1966	1967	1968
Wheelbase	108.0	108.0	108.0
Overall length	181.6	183.6	183.6
Overall width	68.2	70.9	70.9
Std. Trans.		3-sp. man.	3-sp. man.	3-sp. man.
Optional Trans.		4-sp. man.	4-sp. man.	4-sp. man.
		3-sp. auto.	3-sp. auto.	3-sp. auto.

Engine Availability

Type	CIA	HP	1966	1967	1968
I-6	200	120	Std.	Std.	—
I-6	200	115	—	—	Std.
V-8	289	195/200	Opt.	Opt.	Opt.
V-8	289	225	Opt.	Opt.	—
V-8	289	271	Opt.	Opt.	—
V-8	302	230	—	—	Opt.
V-8	390	320/325	—	Opt.	Opt.
V-8	427	390	—	—	Opt.

model year sales, down approximately 25 percent from 1966. Much of the loss was suffered by the best-selling hardtop. The convertible and fastback exchanged places in popularity; the former dropped to only about 45,000 units, while the latter moved up to over 70,000 by virtue of its slick new styling. But 472,121 sales was hardly a bad record for any car made by any company, and Mustang's success story continued for '67 as it had since the car's introduction.

As if to answer the question of some Ford planners ("Why change a good thing?"), Mustang sales plummeted for 1968. On paper the losses were difficult to explain. It was a year of improving sales for the industry in general and Ford Division in particular, and Mustang offered the widest selection of engines and convenience options in its brief history. The likely answer was continued competition, now rougher than ever. Besides GM and Chrysler, American Motors was a threat with its new Javelin and AMX. Also, Mustang prices were up from the year before. The convertible now had a base list price of over $2800, for example. A handful of options could run that to over $4000, quite a sum in that year.

Competition from other Ford products was also a factor. The Mustang fastback, with sales plunging to about 40,000, had a major rival in the Ford Torino, the new top-line series in the intermediate Fairlane line and the 1968 replacement for the Fairlane 500XL and GT as Ford's muscle car. Besides a notchback hardtop and a convertible, the lineup included a slick new fastback in Torino GT and Fairlane 500 trim. It was visibly larger than the Mustang (201 inches in overall length compared to 184), and it had a genuine rear seat because of its 116-inch wheelbase (eight inches longer than Mustang's). The mid-size fastback's sleek lines were quite similar to the Mustang fastback's, as were rivals like the Dodge Charger and Plymouth Barracuda. The Torino GT version accounted for over 74,000 sales in its debut season, and it's reasonable to suggest that a healthy portion of those would have otherwise been Mustang fastbacks.

Another factor in the sales decline may have been familiarity. Since a fairly major facelift had been carried out for '67, Mustang wasn't substantially altered for 1968. The same three body styles—hardtop, convertible, and fastback—returned. New rear quarter panels had the trademark simulated air scoops just ahead of the rear wheels, but these were integrated with the side sculpture for the first time. Crease lines ran back from the upper front fender around the scoop and forward again into the lower part of the door. On GTs, the sculpture was accented by tape striping, which gave a look of forward motion. The grille was more deeply inset, with an inner bright ring around the familiar galloping horse. GTs still carried fog lamps within the grille opening, and other equipment was essentially unchanged. The GT package also included dual exhausts with chrome-plated "quad" outlets, a pop-open fuel filler cap, heavy-duty suspension (high-rate springs plus HD shocks and front sway bar), F70-14 whitewall tires on six-inch rims, and styled steel wheels. Wide-Oval tires were also available.

Some of Mustang's broadest-ever array of engines had to be detuned for '68 to meet new federal emission standards, which applied to all 50 states for the first time that year. The compression ratio of the basic 200-cid six was lowered from 9.2:1 to 8.8:1, and output dropped slightly to 115 bhp from the previous 120 bhp. The two-barrel 289 V-8 had a similar compression drop, now rating 195 instead of 200 bhp. Interestingly, horsepower on the big 390 was actually increased to 335. The middle engine was a considerably changed version of the small-block, stroked out to 302 cid (bore and stroke 4.00 × 3.00 inches) for a rated 230 bhp. It was a tractable, reasonably economical compromise V-8, and cost only about $200. At the top of the chart, at a whopping $755, was a mighty 427 V-8 with 10.9:1 compression and a conservative 390-bhp rating. Standard transmission was still the three-speed manual all-synchromesh gearbox. The four-barrel 271-bhp 289 was dropped. The 427 was available only with Cruise-O-Matic.

Safety features made news for 1968. Some were added at Ford's discretion, but most were required by the government. These consisted of: energy-absorbing intrument panel and steering column, front and rear retractable seatbelts, standard backup lights, dual-circuit brake system, hazard warning flashers, side marker lights, energy-absorbing seatbacks, front seatback catches, positive door lock buttons, safety door handles, double-yoke door latches, padded sunvisors and windshield pillars, double-thick laminated windshield, day/night rearview mirror on a breakaway mount, outside rearview mirror, safety-rim wheels, and load-rated tires. The specifications included corrosion-resistant brake lines and a standardized shift quadrant for automatic transmissions. To meet government standards for glare, Ford put a dull finish on windshield wiper arms, steering wheel hub and horn ring, rearview mirror, and windshield pillars. Among features continued from previous years were reversible keys and 6000-mile lube and oil change intervals. Another popular item was the 5/50-24/24 warranty. The powertrain, suspension, steering, and wheels were warranted for five years or 50,000 miles, whichever came first; other components were warranted for 24 months or 24,000 miles. A second

owner could assume any unused portion of the guarantee for a fee not exceeding $25.

The 427 option was intended only for very serious drivers, hence its high price. This was an enormous engine for a car as light as the Mustang. While it could easily deliver 0–60 mph times of only six or seven seconds, it also brought very pronounced oversteer, a handling trait not all that familiar to the average motorist. For most buyers the 390 was much more flexible and practical. It could be teamed with three- or four-speed manual transmission as well as automatic, and could yield over 15 mpg in conservative driving. It was tractable in traffic, idled smoothly, and was mild-mannered at low speeds. Although it added extra weight to the front end compared with smaller Mustang engines, this wasn't usually noticeable unless you poked your foot to the floor.

The 390-equipped cars for '68 benefited by the addition of floating-caliper power front disc brakes as a new extra-cost item. These provided more stopping force than the '67 discs with the same amount of pedal effort. The floating caliper design was also said to promote longer brake life because it used fewer parts. Ford recognized the need for front discs in big-engine Mustangs by making them a man-datory option for all cars equipped with the 390 or 427.

At over 300,000 units for 1968, Mustang sales were good but hardly great. And this was far below the heady period of 1965–66 when Iacocca's brainchild had earned over one million sales. Meanwhile, Ford was about to take a new direction with its ponycar.

The 1969 Mustang arrived after Semon E. "Bunkie" Knudsen became president of Ford in early 1968. Under Knudsen, Ford vigorously emphasized racy styling and high performance. Mustang reflected his emphasis with a new breed of grand touring and luxury models: Mach I, Grandé, and Boss 302. All models retained the basic body package and 108-inch wheelbase from previous years, but were changed in almost every other dimension. The '69 was generally more roadable than its predecessors, and some versions were very quick. The Cobra Jet Mach 1 and Boss 302 would be the fastest production Mustangs other than the Shelby GTs, and were Ford's response to the challenge of the Camaro Z/28 and Firebird Trans Am.

When Bunkie Knudsen left General Motors as executive vice-president to join Ford, Detroit gasped in astonishment. There probably hadn't been such a startling shift since Bunkie's father, William S. Knudsen, left Ford after an

Far left and left: Racy Mach 1 was the performance version of the completely redesigned '69 Mustang, and sold well. Bottom left: Mach 1 cockpit featured standard high-back bucket seats. Below: Luxury Grandé hardtop was another new offering for '69.

argument with the elder Henry and went to Chevrolet. In the 1920s, "Big Bill" had built Chevrolet into a Ford beater, and now his son was trying to make Ford more competitive with Chevrolet for the '70s. Rumors about a drastic shakeup in Ford management began flying almost as soon as Bunkie arrived in Dearborn. Although some staff changes were expected, he didn't instigate a wholesale cleanout, and he certainly had Ford looking a lot more competitive within a few months.

Knudsen's presidency meant a renaissance for the performance Mustang. He wanted lower, sleeker cars, with particular emphasis on the fastback. In fact, Knudsen said that while "the long-hood/short-deck concept will continue . . . there will be a trend toward designing cars for specific segments of the market." While he denied Ford had any intention of building a sports car, he did hint that an experimental mid-engine car was being developed. (This turned out to be the Mach 2, a design exercise begun in 1966 making liberal use of off-the-shelf Mustang components wrapped up in a curvy two-seat coupe package.) He also assured the press that Ford's efforts in stock car racing would continue. Knudsen was sanguine about the Mustang's market prospects, and the car's declining sales since 1966 didn't bother him. "We are comparing today's Mustang penetration with the penetration of the Mustang when there was no one else in that particular segment of the market. Today [that market is] much more competitive."

One of Knudsen's more productive raids on his former employer resulted in the hiring of stylist Larry Shinoda to head Ford's Special Design Center. Shinoda was assisted by a talented crew that included Harvey Winn, Ken Dowd, Bill Shannon, and Dick Petit. Together with engineers like Chuck Mountain and Ed Hall, Shinoda's department conceived such eye-opening cars as the King Cobra, a racing Torino fastback. Shinoda's arrival at Ford was also good for the Mustang. Since the early '60s, he had designed wind-cheating shapes like the original Sting Ray, Corvette Mako Shark, Monza GT, and Corvair Super Spyder for GM's William L. Mitchell. Shinoda favored the use of aero-dynamic aids like spoilers, low noses, air foils, and front air dams. Many of these features would later appear on Mustangs and other Ford models.

Styling for the 1969 Mustang was mostly completed by the time Shinoda arrived, with dimensions that marked a complete departure from the original ponycar concept. The new car was four inches longer, most of it in front overhang, and was also slightly wider and lower. The grille continued the familiar motif, but had two extra headlights added at its outer ends in place of the optional but mostly ineffective fog lights of previous models. The recessed side sculpture of past years was erased. Taillights were still vertical clusters, but were no longer recessed in the tail panel, which was now flat instead of concave. Driving range was increased by enlarging the fuel tank from 17 to 20 gallons.

Dimensional increases were evident on the inside, too. The 1969 Mustang had 2.5 inches more front shoulder room and 1.5 inches more hiproom than previous models

Opposite page: Mach 1 looks were enhanced by "Shaker" hood with matte-black paint and stock-car-style hood tiedowns. All '69 Mustangs featured a four-headlamp front end. This page, above and left: Hot Boss 302 was the street version of Ford's Trans-Am racer. Rated horsepower was a nominal 290 bhp, but actual output was close to 400. Lower left: Grandé came with wire wheel covers, bodyside pinstripes.

due to a reduction in door thickness. A modified frame crossmember under the front seat allowed rear legroom to be increased by a significant 2.5 inches. Trunk capacity was enlarged "13 to 29 percent," according to bubbly Ford press releases, but actually this wasn't much of a gain because there wasn't much space to begin with. A Mustang trunk could still only just manage a two-suiter and not much else. As before, there were three basic body types— hardtop, fastback, and convertible—but there were several new permutations. Two appeared at the beginning of the model year, the third at mid-season.

Taking careful aim at the personal-luxury ponycar represented by Cougar and Firebird, Ford released the six- and eight-cylinder Mustang Grandé hardtop. Priced at about $230 over the standard hardtop, it offered a vinyl-covered roof with identifying script, twin color-keyed outside rearview mirrors, wire wheel covers, a two-tone paint stripe just below the beltline, and bright wheel well, rocker panel, and rear deck moldings. Its dash and door panels were decorated with imitation teakwood trim, a very good copy of the real thing, and its body was hushed by some 55 extra pounds of sound insulation.

47

This page, left: The running horse emblem as it appeared on 1970 models. Below and bottom: Pre-production 1970 Grandé prototype has upper-bodyside gills that were deleted from actual production cars. Opposite page: Mach 1 was mildly restyled for 1970, as were other Mustangs. Twist-type hood locks, grille-mounted running lamps, and broad hood striping were exclusive to Mach 1 that year. Ford's 428-cid Cobra Jet V-8 was the top power option; a 351 was standard.

A much more exciting newcomer was the Mach 1 fastback, with a $3139 base price. As an intruder into Shelby territory, it featured simulated rear-quarter air scoops, decklid spoiler, and a functional hood scoop, nicknamed "The Shaker" by Ford engineers. Attached to the engine air cleaner, it stuck up through a hole in the hood, and earned its name by vibrating madly, especially at high revs. Though its dimensional differences were slight compared to other Mustangs, the Mach 1 was definitely the raciest of the new breed. Its broad, flat hood and sweeping roofline combined with NASCAR-style hood tie-downs and that aggressive scoop to create the aura of genuine performance. And with a standard 351 cid V-8 and 250 bhp, it didn't disappoint.

Engine options proliferated for 1969, extending even to the six-cylinder cars. For $39 you could order a larger 250-cid six with 155 bhp. Ford greatly improved six-cylinder smoothness that year with "center percussion" (forward located) engine mounts. Competition manager Jacque Passino was optimistic about the six: "We've been putting out Mustang sixes kind of artificially since '64 to fill up production schedules when we couldn't get V-8s. I think there is a real market for an inexpensive hop-up kit for the 250-cubic-inch engine." But he was whistling in the wind. A kit never materialized, nor did a fuel-injected six he also predicted, though both probably should have.

Mustang V-8 offerings began with the 220-bhp 302-cid unit and ran to the top-line Cobra Jet 428, available with or

1970

Model Year Production

No.	Model	1969	1970
63A	Fastback, standard	56,022	39,470
63B	Fastback, deluxe	5,958	6,464
63C	Fastback, Mach 1	72,458	40,970
65A	Hardtop, standard	118,613	77,161
65B	Hardtop, deluxe	5,210	5,408
65C	Hardtop, bench seats	4,131	—
65D	Hardtop, deluxe bench seat	504	—
65E	Hardtop, Grandé	22,182	13,581
76A	Convertible, standard	11,307	6,199
76B	Convertible, deluxe	3,439	1,474
	TOTAL	299,824	190,727

Models		Prices/Weights	
		1969	1970
01	Hardtop, I-6	$2635/2690	$2721/2721
02	Fastback, I-6	$2635/2713	$2771/2745
03	Convertible, I-6	$2849/2800	$3025/2831
04	Grandé, I-6	$2866/2765	$2926/2806
01	Hardtop, V-8	$2740/2906	$2822/2923
02	Fastback, V-8	$2740/2930	$2872/2947
02	Boss 302, V-8	$3588/3210	$3720/3227
03	Convertible, V-8	$2954/3016	$3126/3033
04	Grandé, V-8	$2971/2981	$3028/3008
05	Mach 1, V-8	$3139/3175	$3271/3240

General Specifications	1969	1970
Wheelbase	108.0	108.0
Overall length	187.4	187.4
Overall width	71.3	71.7
Std. Trans.	3-sp. man.	3-sp. man.
Optional Trans.	4-sp. man.	4-sp. man.
	3-sp. auto.	3-sp. auto.

Engine Availability

Type	CID	HP	1969	1970
I-6	200	115/120	Std.	Std.
I-6	250	155	Opt.	Opt.
V-8	302	220	Std.[1]	Std.[1]
V-8	351	250	Opt[2]	Opt.[2]
V-8	351	290/300	Opt.	Opt.
V-8	390	320	Opt.	—
V-8	428	335	Opt.	Opt.
V-8	428[3]	335	Opt.	Opt.
V-8	429[4]	375	Opt.	Opt.

[1]290 hp std. Boss 302   [3]with Ram Air
[2]Std. Mach 1   [4]Boss 429

without ram-air induction. The 351-cid Mach 1 powerplant was an option for lesser Mustangs and, indeed, most other Ford products except the Falcon. Though derived from the 289/302, the 351 was really a new engine. Its greater deck height and combustion chamber design differed from those of the earlier small-blocks. It was also heavier than the 302, but much lighter than the big-block mills.

For all-out performance the Cobra Jet was king. Developed by Ford's Light Vehicle Powertrain Department under Tom Feaheney, it made the Mach 1 one of the world's fastest cars. For this application it was thoughtfully combined with a tuned suspension designed by engineer Matt Donner. Donner used the 1967 heavy-duty setup, but mounted one shock ahead of the rear axle line and the other behind it to reduce axle tramp in hard acceleration. Result: a street machine that handled like a Trans-Am racer. The big-engine Mustang still exhibited final oversteer, but the rear end was easily controllable with the accelerator.

"The first Cobra Jets we built were strictly for drag racing," Feaheney said, "The '69s had a type of the competition suspension we offered in '67. Wheel hop was damped out by staggering the rear shocks. It was not a new idea but it worked. Another thing was the [Goodyear] Polyglas tire. I really can't say enough about this . . . In '69 every wide-oval tire we offered featured Polyglas construction." All this talk of handling may obscure the matter of straightline performance. The Cobra Jet Mach 1 would run

the quarter mile in about 13.5 seconds, as quick as the fastest four-seater in production at the time.

With styling help from Larry Shinoda, Ford released an even more exotic Mustang in early 1969, the Boss 302. This car was created primarily to compete with the Camaro Z/28 in SCCA's Trans-Am series. To qualify it as a production racer, Ford had to build at least 1000 copies, but actually 1934 of the '69s were constructed. Despite its limited numbers, the Boss brought people into Ford showrooms like the original Mustang had back in 1964. Knudsen knew what grabbed the public. Among its design touches were front and rear spoilers, effective at any speed over 40 mph. The four-inch deep front spoiler was angled forward to divert air away from underneath the car. The rear spoiler was an

Ford regained the Trans-Am championship in 1970 with the Boss 302. Production version (above left and right) featured standard "sports slats" on rear window. Option was extended to all 1970 "SportsRoof" fastbacks (lower right). Posh 1970 Grandé (left) shared new two-headlamp grille with other models.

adjustable, inverted airfoil. Matte-black rear window slats, like those of the Lamborghini Miura, did nothing to enhance airflow but looked terrific. The aerodynamic aids resulted in a gain of perhaps 2.5 seconds per lap at Riverside Raceway in California with no increase in engine power.

Of course, there *was* an increase in power—a big one. The Boss 302 V-8 was said to produce 290 bhp at 4600 rpm, but estimates of its actual output ranged as high as 400 bhp. It had "Cleveland" heads with oversize intake valves and huge 1.75-inch exhaust valves, which were inclined in the big ports to improve fuel flow. Other engineering features were an aluminum high-rise manifold, Holley four-barrel carburetor, dual-point ignition, solid lifters, bolted central main bearings, forged crankshaft, and special pistons. To help prolong engine life, Ford fitted an ignition cutout that interrupted current flow from the coil to the spark plugs between 5800 and 6000 rpm, thus preventing accidental over-revving.

Boss 302 hardware also included ultra-stiff springs, staggered shocks, four-speed gearbox, 11.3-inch power front disc brakes, heavy-duty rear drum brakes, and F60 × 15 Goodyear Polyglas tires. Ford hadn't missed a trick: even the wheel wells were radiused to accept extra-wide racing rubber. On the street, the Boss was unmistakable, with matte-black center hood section and grille extensions plus special striping with "Boss 302" lettering. It was the ultimate 1969 Mustang.

Boss 351 became the hottest standard model for '71 (top).
Emissions standards spelled the end of the high-winding 302 V-8, though
a Boss 302 prototype was built (lower left and right).

Mustang's expansion into both the luxury and performance ends of the ponycar field showed interesting results. Out of 184,000 cars delivered in the first half of 1969, only about 15,000 were Grandés but close to 46,000 were Mach 1s. On cue, division general manager John Naughton predicted "heavy emphasis on performance" for what he (or his press writers) saw as the "Sizzlin' '70s." Said Naughton: "We're going to be where the action is, and we're going to have the hardware to meet the action requirements of buyers everywhere." The Mach 1, he continued, would be Ford's big gun in the performance race. The Boss 302 and the even hairier Boss 429 (which started coming off the line in very small numbers in mid-1969) were intended for the outer fringes of the market—

and the Trans-Am. Two Boss styling features, backlight louvers and adjustable rear spoiler, proved so popular that they were extended to any 1970 Mustang "SportsRoof" (fastback) as options. Ford, said Naughton, was going to "make it happen in 1970."

And in a way, Ford did. The 1970 Boss, as *Motor Trend* put it, was "even Bossier." Unique side striping identified

it; a well-engineered suspension cornered it; and hotter-than-ever engines powered it. A new item was a Hurst competition shifter with T-handle shift knob, the first Hurst linkage in a production Mustang. Further up the price scale, at around $4000, was the Boss 429 with Ford's Cobra Jet NASCAR engine. Even more potent than the other big-inch V-8s, it had cast magnesium rocker arm covers and semi-hemispherical combustion chambers. Valves were set across from each other for a crossflow cylinder head, and ports, intake passages, and oval exhausts were all enormous.

Mach 1 engines for 1970 ranged from the standard two-barrel 351 up to the 428 four-barrel with ram air. The Cleveland engine was further improved by canted-valve

Standard fastback (upper left) and Mach 1 got near-horizontal roofline for '71, plus new dash (upper right).

cylinder heads and larger intake and exhaust ports. Mach 1 handling was helped by addition of a rear stabilizer bar that allowed the use of more moderate spring rates for a better ride. Mach 1 also got its own special grille with driving lamps.

The luxury Grandé returned with either six or V-8 power. Like all 1970 Mustangs, it inherited the Mach 1's high-back front bucket seats, which added greatly to interior comfort. A landau-style black or white vinyl roof, twin racing-type mirrors, special identification, and bright wheel lip moldings completed the package.

There were still "basic" Mustangs in 1970 available with standard six or 302 V-8 in hardtop, convertible, and Sports-Roof fastback body styles. Like other models, they boasted new front-end styling marked by a return to single headlights. Rear appearance was revised with recessed taillamps. Prices hadn't climbed much since the Mustang's early days. The six-cylinder coupe still listed at only a bit more than $2700, and a V-8 convertible could be had for as little as $3126. Convertibles, though, were on the wane: production dipped to only about 7700 for 1970. Continu-

Below: Gutsy Boss 351 is probably the most desirable '71 model today. Center and bottom right: The 1971s would be the biggest Mustangs in history. Grandé (shown) and standard hardtops acquired bulgier sheetmetal and new "tunnel" type roof styling. Bottom left: The 1971 convertible, actually a pre-production prototype bearing a Mach 1-style hood not offered on standard models.

ing buyer preference for air conditioning and closed coupes had conspired to reduce the popularity of convertibles, including the Mustang.

Despite its diverse model lineup, Mustang dropped by another 100,000 units in the 1970 production totals. Fastbacks slipped 40 percent, and hardtops declined 35 percent. While the Mach 1 accounted for a solid proportion of fastback sales, it was not a high-volume seller by the standards of the mid-'60s, and couldn't make up for continuing strong opposition by other performance models from Ford and rival manufacturers. The Boss 302 remained strictly a limited-production Trans-Am special with low sales potential: output was just 6318 units for 1970.

After just two years as Ford Motor Company president, Bunkie Knudsen was summarily dismissed in 1969. Said chairman Henry Ford II: "Things just didn't work out," but never elaborated on that statement in line with his long-time motto "never complain, never explain." Insiders suggested that, like his father before him, Knudsen had accumulated, and was wielding, too much power. "Knudsen moved in and started doing things his way," wrote prominent Detroit analyst Robert W. Irvin. "Knudsen was almost running the company and [some said] he had alienated many other top executives. Others said Knudsen's departure was an indication of how the Fords don't like to share power." (Irvin wrote those words in July 1978, as a comment on the firing of Lee A. Iacocca.) To soften the impact of Knudsen's dismissal, Henry Ford II announced

The 1971 Mustang reflected the influence of new Ford president Bunkie Knudsen and his comrade from GM, stylist Larry Shinoda. Mach 1 featured standard twin-scoop hood and color-keyed urethane front bumper.

there would now be three presidents: R. L. Stevenson for International Operations, R. J. Hampson for Non-Automotive Operations, and Iacocca for North American Operations. But that lasted only a year: Iacocca became overall president in 1970.

By late 1969 it had become clear the ponycar was losing its appeal. Mustang sales had been sliding since 1967. Camaro and Firebird sales had held up, but were not improving. The AMC Javelin was a mild success, but no blockbuster. Neither were the rebodied 1970 Plymouth Barracuda and new Dodge Challenger, its stablemate, which did not bring in the pile of orders Chrysler had expected. By 1971, compacts like the Ford Pinto and Maverick, Chevrolet Vega, and AMC Gremlin were cutting into ponycar sales, which were down to almost half of what they had been in their best-ever year, 1967.

Given the auto industry's normal lead time, the '71 Mustang was really shaped by the events of 1968–69. Iacocca didn't have much to do with it as Knudsen influenced most of the new design. By 1970, however, there was one cold hard fact staring Ford product planners in the face, and it was hard to ignore: "Total Performance" was no longer appealing to buyers, at least not in really high volume. Also, the effect new government regulations would have on future car design was still unknown and still being debated. The idea that the world might soon run low on oil was not yet taken seriously by many people. Product planners saw lack of sufficient interior space as the reason why

ponycars started trailing compacts in sales, so the decision to make the next Mustang generation larger, roomier, and heavier was perfectly logical in the context of the late '60s.

Ford's racing heritage would still be seen in the new design, though nobody would have predicted in 1969 that the company would be out of racing only a few months after the '71s were announced. (In late 1970, Ford abandoned most of its efforts in Trans-Am, USAC, NASCAR, and international competition.) That's why a sweeping, almost horizontal, roofline inspired by Ford's GT racers showed up on the 1971 Mustang SportsRoof, as well as a full-width grille and Kamm-style rear deck like those of the Shelby GTs. The advent of color-coordinated, polyurethane-covered bumpers enabled stylists to shape a more interesting and better integrated front end for the '71. Larry Shinoda accompanied Bunkie Knudsen in departing from Ford, but not before he had given the new Mustang more muscular body contours, a more acute windshield angle, and hidden wipers, all of which reflected his GM background.

More stringent 1971 emissions standards took their toll on Mustang engine offerings. The Boss 302 powerplant was replaced by the Boss 351 Cleveland V-8 with four-barrel carburetor, 11:1 compression ratio, and 330 bhp (gross) at 5400 rpm. It was more tractable than the Boss 302 and, since it wasn't as high-revving, more durable. On other Mustangs, the standard V-8 was a 302 with two-barrel carb and 9:1 compression yielding 210 bhp at 4600

rpm. The standard six was now the 250-cid unit with 9:1 compression and 145 bhp at 4000 rpm. There were three other optional V-8s—a two-barrel 351 with 240 gross horsepower, a four-barrel version with 285, and the four-barrel 429 Cobra Jet rated at 370 bhp.

Mach 1 was one of two performance models in the '71 lineup, but could be ordered with air conditioning ($407) and automatic transmission ($238). In fact, it could be outfitted with a whole host of convenience features more appropriate to a luxury car: power steering, tilt steering wheel, "sport deck" rear seat, AM/FM stereo, and intermittent wipers. Other extra-cost items were sports interior ($130), power front disc brakes ($70), center console ($60), and an instrument group ($54). Liberal use of the option book could raise the Mach 1's $3268 base price to well over $5500. Standard equipment this year included high-back bucket seats, integrated front spoiler, honeycomb grille, dual exhausts, auxiliary lamps, and racing-style door mirrors. The 429CJ engine cost $436 extra, and made the Mach 1 undeniably quick. So equipped, the car would do 0–60 mph in 6.5 seconds, 0–75 in about 9.0 seconds, and the quarter-mile in 14.5 seconds. With automatic transmission and 3.25:1 final drive ratio, it had a top speed of about 115 mph and returned 10–11 mpg. "It is a decent mixture for those who want good performance and some comfort," wrote Chuck Koch in *Motor Trend* magazine, "but it still remains a little unwieldy for city traffic."

A new Boss 351 model took over from the Boss 302 as the

racer's delight for '71. Koch also tested it, and found it handled better than the Mach 1 thanks to its standard "competition" suspension. This consisted of uprated coil springs and hydraulic shocks up front, staggered rear shocks, and front and rear stabilizer bars. Koch also discovered the Boss 351 was quicker than the Mach 1 429. It did 0–60 mph in 5.8 seconds and the quarter-mile in 13.8 seconds. But with a short 3.91:1 rear axle ratio, it would only reach about 100 mph flat out.

By contrast, the 210-bhp 302 was no match for these very powerful V-8s. Its typical figures were 0–60 mph in 10 seconds, the quarter-mile in 17.5 seconds, and a top speed (with 2.79:1 axle ratio and automatic) of only 86 mph. Yet this was hardly sluggish, and the 302 delivered decent gas mileage (up to17 mpg). All things considered, the 302 was probably the best all-around powerplant offered for '71.

With the perspective of hindsight the 1971 Mustang doesn't seem like a bad car, even though it got a lot of bad press at the time. It was larger because buyers didn't like cars with cramped interiors. It was the thirstiest Mustang yet because, with gas still selling for only 30 cents a gallon in those days, most buyers weren't too concerned about fuel economy. Yet the '71, especially with the competition suspension, rode and handled better than previous Mustangs. Understeer was greatly reduced, and roadholding was improved. Optional variable-ratio power steering gave it better road feel than in the past, despite the gains in weight and size. The low, flat-roof fastback was racy-

Top: Only about 6000 of the 1972 Mustang convertibles were sold. Body style would be gone for 10 years after 1973. Above left and right: You have to look hard to spot the appearance differences in this 1972 Grandé from its 1971 counterpart.

looking and attractive in an era of uninspired styling.

But a good car does not necessarily mean sales success, as Ford Motor Company knew all too well. If Mustang wasn't losing customers to the Camaro, Firebird, and Barracuda, it was definitely being outsold by the Maverick, Plymouth Valiant, Dodge Dart, and Chevrolet's Nova. And even though it was all-new, Mustang once again sagged in sales for '71. Model year production totaled less than 150,000 units, with hardtops dropping to 83,000, the convertible capturing a bit more than 6000, and the fastback holding at about 60,000.

There is nothing to do with a one-year-old design in Detroit except live with it, so Mustang was little changed

for 1972. To meet the year's even stricter emission standards, Ford detuned the standard six and eight as well as the three optional 351 V-8s. All horsepower figures were now expressed in SAE net, rather than gross, ratings. The 250-cid six was thus rated at 95 bhp net at 4000 rpm and the 302 at 136 bhp net at 4600 rpm. Output for the 351 engines ranged from 168 to 275 bhp. Ford promoted new colors and fabrics, the prettiest of which was the Sprint decor option, available for hardtop and Sportsroof models. It could be combined with mag wheels, raised white-letter tires, and competition suspension. On the outside, Sprints were usually painted white and had broad, blue Shelby-style racing stripes edged in red. Complementary colors were

Sprint Decor Option (top) was a mid-1972 dress-up package with white paint and blue and red accents. Normal '72 front end (above) could be exchanged for a Mach 1-style treatment (right) with color-keyed bumper, honeycomb grille, and running lights.

used inside. "Control and balance make it a beautiful experience," the ads read. Nevertheless, sales dipped again, this time by about 20 percent. Only the convertible, which by now didn't account for much of the yearly total, maintained its previous level.

By this time, Ford was well along with development of a totally new Mustang, a car more faithful to the spirit of the original. Typically, the real push for a total redesign came from Lee Iacocca. "I've said it a hundred times and I'll say it again: the Mustang market never left us, we left it," he would remark later. "We kept the 460 out of it, but we had all the other engines in it." Echoed design vice-president Eugene Bordinat: "We started out with a secretary car and all of a sudden we had a behemoth."

For one more year, 1973, Mustang remained its hefty self, and sold a bit better than the previous season. The convertible scored the largest percentage sales increase (up 100 percent to nearly 12,000 units) because Ford had announced the body style would be discontinued the next year. The 1973 Mustang convertible was thus the last ragtop Ford would build for the next ten years.

Meanwhile, the federal government had issued its impact standards for bumpers, which would now have to sustain low-speed front and rear shunts without damage. To meet this requirement, many automakers, including Ford, designed some awful-looking cowcatchers. Mustang

fared better than most as its '73 bumper stuck out only a little more than the '72 and didn't look too bad. The bumper consisted of an I-beam mounting bar inside a box-section bracket. This assembly was attached to two longitudinal rubber blocks that gave way on contact, then bounced back to their original position. An optional color-keyed rubber cover was available to clean up appearance even more.

The influence of federal requirements was evident elsewhere, too. The 1973 dash was bereft of sharp knobs and other projections that might cause unnecessary injury in a crash, and got extra padding. Bigger brakes were fitted, as were larger calipers for cars with non-power discs. Flame-retardant interior trim materials were adopted to meet the government's "burn rate" of four inches per minute. Emission control was handled by crankcase ventilation and

exhaust gas recirculation. The latter routed gases from the exhaust manifold through a vacuum valve into the carburetor, where they were diluted by the incoming fuel/air mixture. This permitted leaner carburetor settings for lower emissions.

Except for the front bumper, the 1973 Mustang was visually little changed from 1971–72, but was the only Ford that year offered with a new 351 High-Output V-8. Prices, which had been cut to spark sales the year before, remained fairly stable. The base six-cylinder hardtop listed at $2760 while the V-8 convertible was the most expensive at $3189. The Mach 1, which came with a 168-bhp (net) 351 as standard, sold for $3088.

Nine years after the Mustang's debut, the old marketing technique of offering a wide range of options was still important. The '73, Ford said, was "designed to be de-signed by you." The optional vinyl top now came in six colors. It covered the whole roof on hardtops and the front three-quarters on fastbacks. A hood with lock pins and matte silver or black center section was available. Also on the list were forged aluminum wheels, "metallic glow" paint, and decorative side striping. Convertibles and hardtops could be ordered with Mach 1-style black-finish grilles containing auxiliary running lights. An electric rear window defroster was available for hardtops and SportsRoofs.

Thus ended the third-generation Mustang. Though its basic shape, sporty styling, and long option list had endured, Ford's ponycar had grown into something completely different from the 1965 original. Everybody knew that, and by 1973 most agreed this wasn't the way to go. But Ford was readying an entirely new product, a concept that would begin a second revolution.

Opposite page: The 1973 Mach 1 retained its basic 1971 appearance, but was well down on power. Handling was still good, however. New slot-style road wheels were added to the option list that year. This page: Vertical parking lights mark the last of the "fat" Mustangs from the front. Again in '73, buyers had a choice of front-end styling, the traditional grille with framed horse (top) or the optional Mach 1 type that was included with the two-tone hood option (above). Sales rose slightly for the year.

Model Year Production

No.	Model	1971	1972	1973
63D	Fastback, standard	23,956	15,622	10,820
63R	Fastback, Mach 1	36,499	27,675	35,440
65D	Hardtop, standard	65,696	57,350	51,480
65F	Hardtop, Grandé	17,406	18,045	25,674
76D	Convertible, standard	6,121	6,401	11,853
	TOTAL	149,678	125,093	134,867

Prices/Weights

Models		1971	1972	1973
01	Hardtop, I-6	$2911/2937	$2729/2941	$2760/2995
02	Fastback, I-6	$2973/2907	$2786/2908	$2820/3008
03	Convertible, I-6	$3227/3059	$3015/3051	$3102/3126
04	Grandé, I-6	$3117/2963	$2915/2965	$2946/3003
01	Hardtop, V-8	$3006/3026	$2816/3025	$2897/3085
02	Fastback, V-8	$3068/2993	$2873/2995	$2907/3098
02	Boss 351, V-8	$4124/3281	—	—
03	Convertible, V-8	$3320/3145	$3101/3147	$3189/3216
04	Grandé, V-8	$3212/3049	$3002/3051	$3088/3115
05	Mach 1, V-8	$3268/3220	$3053/3046	$3088/3115

General Specifications

	1971	1972	1973
Wheelbase	109.0	109.0	109.0
Overall length	187.5(6)		
	189.5(8)	190.0	194.0
Overall width	75.0	75.0	75.0
Std. Trans.	3-sp. man.	3-sp. man.	3-sp. man.
Optional Trans.	4-sp. man.	4-sp. man.	4-sp. man.
	3-sp. auto.	3-sp. auto.	3-sp. auto.

Engine Availability

Type	CID	HP	1971	1972	1973
I-6	250	145 (gross)[1]	Std.	Std.	Std.
V-8	302	210 (gross)[2]	Std.	Std.	Std.
V-8	351	240 (gross)	Opt.	—	—
V-8	351	285 (gross)	Opt.	—	—
V-8	351	280 (gross)	Opt.	—	—
V-8	351	330 (gross)	Std.[3]	—	—
V-8	429	370 (gross)	Opt.	—	—
V-8	351	168 (net)	—	Opt.	Opt.
V-8	351	200 (net)	—	Opt.	Opt.
V-8	351	275 (net)	—	Opt.	—

[1]rated 95 hp (net) 1972–73   [2]rated 136 hp (net) 1972–73   [3]Std. Boss 351 only

RESHAPING A LEGEND

The smaller and lighter Mustang II opened a new chapter in the Mustang story, and it couldn't have been better timed. It arrived in Ford showrooms almost simultaneously with the Arab oil embargo of 1973–74, and people came in droves to see it. With 385,993 units in its first year, Mustang II came within 10 percent of the original Mustang's 12-month production record of 418,812 cars. Lee Iacocca was behind it—again—and those first-year sales made him look pretty good—again. Of course, Mustang II was in the works for some time before the Arabs decided to put the squeeze on oil supplies. That they did this so soon after the car was introduced was mere coincidence.

Market changes that had occurred since the original Mustang appeared were already being reflected by Dearborn's more recent products. The Maverick, introduced in 1970, was dimensionally close to the 1965 Mustang, and in its debut year topped the Mustang's first-year record with over 450,000 sales. But the Maverick was not the sporty car the first Mustang was. Mustang II was designed to fill that role.

While Iacocca had only guessed that a market for the original Mustang existed, he knew in advance there would be strong demand for the Mustang II. Sporty 2+2 import coupes with luxury trim, bucket seats, and four-speed gearboxes were becoming increasingly popular in the early '70s. Ford's European Capri and GM's Opel Manta from Germany, both "captive imports," and cars like the Toyota Celica were all selling well. In 1965, cars like this accounted for less than 100,000 units, but were up to

Below and opposite page: This series of Ford styling photographs from July and August 1969 indicates the initial thinking for the Mustang II program was simply an extension of 1971–73 concepts, reflecting the influence of the Knudsen regime. The workout here owes a lot to the "Breadvan" Ferrari GTO, and appears to have very good aerodynamics.

300,000 by 1972. Projections for 1974 put sales at over 400,000. Part of the Mustang II's mission was to capture a big slice of the "mini-ponycar" pie.

Ford design vice-president Eugene Bordinat gave full credit for the Mustang II concept to the first Mustang's father: "Iacocca was the first guy to come along who had the feeling for cars that had existed in General Motors for some time." Said Iacocca: "When I look at the foreign car market and see that one in five is a sporty car, I know something's happening. Look at what the Celica started to do before the two devaluations [of the dollar] nailed it! Anyone who decides to sit this out just ain't gonna dance!"

Once again, Dearborn's mighty army of stylists and engineers worked from an idea Iacocca had clearly defined: "The new Mustang must be small, with a wheelbase between 96 and 100 inches. It must be a sporty notchback and/or coupe—the convertible is dead and can be forgotten. It must come as standard with a four-speed manual gearbox and a four-cylinder or small six-cylinder engine. Most important, it must be luxurious—upholstered in quality materials and carefully built." Ben Bidwell, who handled Mustang II product planning, said Iacocca took a personal interest in the quality control aspect: "He will be out there in the showroom and he'll run his finger around the molding, and if it so much as scrapes him some poor son of a gun will get it."

The Mustang II's flashy interior was created by David Ash of Ford Design, who said he was partly inspired by Jaguar, Rolls-Royce, and Mercedes. To give his prototype interior the feel of a real automobile, he ordered a complete mockup, unusual in the design business. It even had exterior sheetmetal and all four wheels attached. "It was a time-consuming thing to build," Ash said, "but it served its purpose very well. We didn't have to go through an elaborate series of meetings to determine everything. It was all approved right here. We were on a crash basis to get it done, and it was very enthusiastically received . . . We put everything in that we could conceive of that connotes restrained elegance plus the get-up-and-go that says Mustang—something of a fire breather . . . It's a kind of a mini-T-Bird."

The Mustang II dash was marked by a large oblong panel, placed squarely in front of the driver, housing all controls and instruments, which surprisingly included a tachometer, temperature gauge, and ammeter as standard. Seats were covered in pleated cloth, vinyl, or optional leather—very plush. There was no seatback rake adjustment, sad to say, but the seats themselves were definitely

This page: More early proposals for the "third-generation" Mustang, beginning with a fastback version of the compact 1970 Maverick. Car at bottom was styled by Don DeLaRossa, and convinced management to include a notchback in the Mustang II program. Opposite page, top: Another view of the "Anaheim" notchback. Middle: A two-seat proposal from Ghia. Bottom: An early mockup from late 1970, big and fat.

more comfortable than those of any previous Mustang. Rear legroom was limited, because the new car was seen as being used primarily by one or two adults, who would sit in front. There would be room in back only for a couple of small children or for an adult passenger to be comfortable there for a short time.

On the outside, the Mustang's customary long-hood/short-deck proportions were retained but on a reduced scale—smaller than even the original. The real target was the sporty import coupes. Compare measurements, for example, of the 1965 Mustang, the Mustang II, and the 1974 Toyota Celica:

Dimension (in.)	Mustang	Mustang II	Celica
Wheelbase	108.0	96.2	95.5
Length	181.6	175.0	163.9
Width	70.2	68.2	63.0
Height	51.0	49.9	51.6

Against the 1973 Mustang, the "II" was 20 inches shorter, four inches narrower, an inch lower, 400–500 pounds lighter, and its wheelbase was nearly 13 inches less.

At announcement time, some observers suggested the Mustang II was really just a Pinto with a sporty body. Although the two cars did share many components, the Pinto was actually upgraded for '74 to take advantage of some parts and features designed for the Mustang II. Both had unit construction, and both used the same front suspension: independent with unequal-length upper and lower arms and coil springs. For the Mustang, however, the lower arm was attached to a rubber-mounted subframe; on the Pinto it was bolted directly to the main structure. The Mustang subframe carried the rear of the engine/transmission assembly, and was designed to provide more precise steering and a smoother ride than Pinto. Isolating the rear engine mount also reduced drivetrain vibration in the passenger compartment. Because Mustang II was intended to sell for more than a Pinto, company cost accountants approved this more expensive mounting arrangement. Both cars also had rack-and-pinion steering, but the Mustang's steering gear was mounted differently, again to minimize shock. Also, the Mustang could be ordered with power steering, but not Pinto. At the rear, the Mustang's leaf springs were two inches longer than the Pinto's, and its shock absorbers were staggered as in the earlier high performance Mustangs. Spring rates were calculated by computer to match equipment, weight, and body style of each individual car. The Ghia notchback, for example, came with very soft settings, while the optional competition suspension had the stiffest rates, along with a thicker front sway bar, a rear sway bar, and Gabriel adjustable shock absorbers.

9-20-71
S-17451-35

9-23-71
S-17465-17

10-19-70
S-16200-20

Above: Traditional running horse emblem was made less muscular and given a shorter stride for Mustang II, a clue to the new car's lower performance. Above left: Except for an oil pressure gauge, full instrumentation was standard on every Mustang II. Below: Newly named Ghia notchback replaced Grandé as Mustang II's luxury model, reflecting Ford's recent acquisition of the Italian coachbuilder.

Styling for the Mustang II was a collection of ideas taken from several proposals developed independently by the Ford and Lincoln-Mercury studios and the Italian coach-building firm of Ghia, which had then recently been purchased by Ford. The final decision came down to a choice of five clay models, one notchback and four fast-backs. The one selected as the basis for production styling (and surprisingly little altered) was a fastback from the Lincoln-Mercury group. But the design got mixed reception, and some felt the notchback was a hodge-podge. The three-door was considered more handsome, but it was not a "classic" shape like the '65.

For the first time in Mustang history, there was no thought of offering a V-8. In line with Iacocca's instructions, engine offerings were limited to a 2.3-liter (140-cid) overhead cam inline four and a 2.8-liter (171-cid) ohv V-6. The four was the first American-built engine based on metric dimensions, which was not surprising. Originally designed for some of Ford's larger European cars (including the German and British Capri), this unit was actually a bored and stroked version of the European 2.0-liter engine already being used on the domestic Pinto. A novel feature was its "monolithic engine timing." After each engine was assembled, an electronic device hooked into a computer

Above: Lee Iacocca poses with the original Mustang and the then-new Mustang II in a 1974 Ford publicity picture. Left: Still called 2+2, the Mustang II version of the familiar fastback gained added practicality with a lift-up hatch door and standard fold-down back seat. Mustang II styling was developed on this body style by the Lincoln-Mercury studio, and was surprisingly little altered in the translation to production form. Bottom: The performance-oriented Mach 1 remained in the Mustang II line. Shown is the 1974 version. Available only in 3-door form, Mach 1 was powered by the 2.8-liter V-6 as standard.

was connected to two engine sensors, an indicator point at the rear of the crankshaft and an electrical terminal between the distributor and coil. The computer compared readings from each sensor, and then set timing automatically by means of a distributor adjustment. Because the computer could set timing very precisely, this technique was very useful for meeting the increasingly tough engine emission standards.

The V-6 also had a European counterpart, and used the same camshaft, valvetrain, pushrods, and distributor. It was, in fact, the same engine that powered the U.S. version of Ford's European Capri beginning with the 1972 models.

However, it was modified for the Mustang II with a bore and stroke increase to boost capacity from the original 2.6 liters (155 cid) to 2.8 (171 cid). It also had separate instead of siamesed exhaust ports for performance and good thermal efficiency. With standard dual exhausts, the V-6 could be ordered as an option on any Mustang, and was standard on the Mach 1 hatchback. Like the first 2.0-liter Pinto engines, the V-6 was imported from Ford's West German subsidiary in Cologne.

The Mustang II's standard four-speed gearbox was based on the British four-speed unit also used in the Pinto, but was strengthened to handle the Mustang's more powerful engines. The vacuum-assisted brakes were a combination of 9.3-inch discs up front and 9 × 1.75-inch drums in the rear.

In ride and handling, the "cooking" Mustang IIs and the new top-line Ghia notchback (replacing the Grandé as the luxury model) were typically American. The Mach 1, with its standard V-6, radial tires, and optional competition suspension, was more capable. No Mustang II had overwhelming acceleration. The car was heavy for it size (curb weight of 2650–2900 pounds), so a V-6 with four-speed would produce 0–60 mph times only in the 13–14 second range, though top speed was around 100 mph.

Mustang II didn't change significantly during its five-year production life. The four-cylinder and V-6 Ghia as well as the V-6-only Mach 1 were available for the full run, and Ford continued to provide a lengthy list of options for all models. Aside from air conditioning and a variety of radios and tape players, the 1974 roster included a vinyl top, sunroof, and forged aluminum wheels, among other

items. The next year, an extra-cost flip-up glass "moon-roof" (at $454) and a "luxury package" for the already posh Ghia were added. Sales dropped by over half for the 1975 model year, but production held steady after that at about 190,000 annually. This was certainly more desirable and more profitable for Ford considering Mustang sales in the early '70s.

Emission and safety regulations notwithstanding, a small but enthusiastic group of Mustang buyers still craved performance. Ford answered their pleas by reviving the small-block V-8 as an option for 1975. This was the familiar 302-cid unit tuned to deliver 122 net horsepower, which was increased to 139 bhp for '76. Since the Mustang V-8 displaced about 5.0 liters and Chevrolet's Monza 2+2 offered a 4.3-liter (262-cid) V-8, it was natural to make comparisons. The editors of *Road & Track* clearly preferred the Monza. And, despite the subjective judgments involved, they were probably right. Monza was brand-new for '75, a fresh, modern design that seemed smoother and more inte-

grated than the Mustang II. And its comfort, ride, handling, and fuel economy were all judged to be better than the Ford's. *R&T* summed up the feeling of many by saying the Mustang II's styling was "humpy and bumpy, and—in its interior—downright garish" and lacking "ergonomic refinement." Mustang beat the Monza for acceleration by a healthy margin, as one would expect with more displacement, but it also used more gas. The only big advantage the Mustang II seemed to have was in braking. Here are *R&T*'s test results:

	Mustang II	Monza 2+2
engine CID/bhp/rpm	302/122/3600	262/110/3600
0-to-60 mph, sec.	10.5	13.4
¼-mile, speed/sec.	77.0/17.9	72.5/19.5
top speed, mph	106	103
fuel economy, mpg	13.0	17.0

Opposite page, upper left: the 1975–76 Ghia with optional opera window roof treatment. Upper right: Bigger grille eggcrates appeared on post-1974 Mustang IIs (1975 Mach 1 shown) to provide extra air flow for cooling the optional 302 V-8, reinstated as an option for 1975. Bottom: Glass moonroof was a new option for the 1975 Ghia, and was later extended to other Mustang IIs. Note larger rear side windows, adopted as standard after 1974. This page, top and center: Cobra II package was issued for 1976. It was basically an appearance option inspired by the Shelby-Mustangs of the '60s, and could be ordered on the base 2+2 or the Mach 1. It was mechanically identical with the latter. Below: 1976 Stallion appearance package was one of several low-cost dress-up options offered during the Mustang II's production life.

In further pursuit of sport—or what was left of it—Ford offered a boy racer Mustang II for 1976. Called Cobra II, it was basically a trim option available only for the three-door, comprising sports steering wheel, dual remote-control door mirrors, brushed-aluminum appliqués on dash and door panels, and Cobra II door trim. On the outside were a blackout grille, styled steel wheels with trim rings, radial tires, flip-out rear quarter windows with louvered covers, front air dam, rear spoiler, and simulated hood air scoop. A final decorative touch was Cobra II identification on rocker panels, grille, and fenders. The Cobra II was initially offered only in white with blue striping, but was available in other color combinations beginning with the '77s. It was flashy, but a far cry from the Mach 1, Boss 302, or the Shelby-Mustangs.

A special option for the 1977 Ghia was the "Sports Appearance Group," available only with black or tan paint. This included many color-keyed components, including console, three-spoke sports steering wheel, cast aluminum wheels with chamois-color spokes, and a trunk luggage rack with hold-down straps and bright buckles.

For 1978, Ford again tried "paint-on performance" with the King Cobra option. Like the Cobra II, which was continued, the King Cobra ensemble was available only for the fastback, and had every racy styling touch any kid could want. There was a snake decal on the hood and tape stripes

on the roof, rear deck, rocker panels, and A-pillar, around the wheel wells, and on the front air dam that was also part of the package. The words "King Cobra" appeared on each door, the air dam, and on the standard decklid spoiler. A black-finish grille, window moldings, headlamp bezels, and wiper arms plus a brushed-aluminum instrument panel appliqué completed the cosmetics. The King Cobra was fitted with the 302 V-8, power steering, "Rallye" handling package, and Goodrich 70-series raised white letter T/A radial tires. Given all that bold advertising, this was the least Ford could do, and it's probably true that the King Cobra's 17-second quarter-mile time was considered high performance by 1978 standards.

Aside from variable-ratio power steering, electronic voltage regulator, optional "Wilshire" cloth for the Ghia, and a reshuffle of paint and upholstery colors, the 1978 Mustang II was pretty much like the earlier versions, and still sold reasonably well. Model year sales of 192,000 units were second only to the 1974 introduction year. Actually, production would have been higher, but some early '78s were delivered to dealers earlier than usual because of low inventory, and were registered as '77s.

Opposite page, clockwise from lower left: The 1977 Cobra II shows off that year's new T-top option; Fashion Accessory Package was a new 1978 hardtop item. This page, clockwise from upper right: The Cobra II, Mach 1, and Ghia from 1978, Mustang II's final year.

Above and right: The King Cobra option was the ultimate in "paint-on performance" for 1978, though the package included the lively 302 V-8, which made this Mustang II a good performer for the period. Beefed-up chassis, wheels, and tires were also provided. Car shown has T-top, a separate option. Giant "snake" hood decal, front air dam, and rear lip spoiler would be carried over to the 1979 and later Cobra models in the next, all-new Mustang generation. Liberal use was made of matte-black paint for exterior moldings and the like, and the King Cobra was available in just two colors, red or black, both solids. An estimated 500 of these specials were produced. All had standard power steering, the "Rallye" handling package, special wheels, and raised-letter radial tires. Interior appointments included special upholstery and brushed-finish instrument panel appliqué.

Model Year Production

No.	Model	1974	1975	1976	1977*	1978
60F	Standard 2-door coupe	177,671	85,155	78,508	67,783	81,304
60H	Ghia 2-door coupe	89,477	52,320	37,515	29,510	34,730
69F	Standard 3-door coupe	74,799	30,038	62,312	49,161	68,408
69R	Mach 1 3-door coupe	44,046	21,062	9,232	6,719	7,968
	TOTAL	385,993	188,575	187,567	153,173	192,410

*1977 figure includes vehicles produced as 1978 models but sold as 1977 models.

Prices/Weights

Models		1974	1975	1976	1977	1978
02	2-door, I-4	$3134/2620	$3529/2660	$3525/2678	$3702/2627	$3731/2608
03	3-door, I-4	$3328/2699	$3818/2697	$3781/2706	$3901/2672	$3975/2654
04	Ghia, 2-door, I-4	$3480/2886	$3938/2886	$3859/2704	$4119/2667	$4149/2646
02	2-door, V-6	$3363/2689	$3801/2775	$3791/2756	$3984/2750	$3944/2705
03	3-door, V-8	$3557/2768	$4090/2812	$4047/2784	$4183/2975	$4188/2751
04	Ghia 2-door, V-6	$3709/2755	$4210/2819	$4125/2807	$4401/2790	$4362/2743
05	Mach 1, V-6	$3674/2778	$4188/2879	$4209/2822	$4332/2785	$4430/2733

General Specifications

	1974	1975	1976	1977	1978
Wheelbase	96.2	96.2	96.2	96.2	96.2
Overall length	175.0	175.0	175.0	175.0	175.0
Overall width	70.2	70.2	70.2	70.2	70.2
Std. Trans.	4-sp. man.	4-sp. man.	4-sp. man.	4-sp. man.	4-sp. man.
Optional Trans.	3-sp. auto.	3-sp. auto.	3-sp. auto.	3-sp. auto.	3-sp. auto.

Engine Avialability

Type	CID	HP	1974	1975	1976	1977	1978
I-4	140	a	Std.	Std.	Std.	Std.	Std.
V-6	171	b	Opt.d	Opt.	Opt.	Opt.	Opt.
V-8	302	c	—	Opt.	Opt.	Opt.	Opt.

a: rated 85 hp 1974; 83 hp 1975; 92 hp 1976; 89 hp 1977; 88 hp 1978
b: rated 105 hp 1974; 97 hp 1975; 103 hp 1976; 93 hp 1977; 90 hp 1978
c: rated 122 hp 1975; 139 hp 1976–78
d: Standard Mach 1

REVIVING A SPECIAL BREED

Though it had been a modest sales winner, Mustang II never inspired the same degree of enthusiasm as earlier Ford ponycars. But a third revolution was underway in Dearborn. This culminated in an all-new Mustang, introduced (without a Roman numeral suffix) for the 1979 model year. In appearance it was clean and taut, crisp yet substantial. Its surface execution, downswept nose, ample glass area, and lack of ornamentation all displayed the better thinking of American and European stylists. Those who got close enough to see the familiar Mustang nameplate must have been impressed. At long last, Ford had created the kind of restrained, efficient, elegant sporty car it set out to build in the first place. Of course, the '79 inherited some perennial Mustang problems. Handling was still far from perfect, the seats were too low, and the interior still seemed cramped. Also, body construction didn't seem as solid as on European competitors like the Volkswagen Scirocco. Still, no car, especially one selling at such a comparatively low price, can be faultless. By almost any standard, the '79 Mustang was a most attractive buy.

Early-1976 mockup for '79 Mustang program, initially with the "7-X Maverick" working title.

As with its predecessor, the 1979 Mustang's final shape was selected from a variety of proposals. Several styling teams within Ford Motor Company were given the same design parameters, from which they developed sketches, clay models, and fiberglass mockups. Quarter-scale clay models were tested for 136 hours in wind tunnels, because aerodynamics was becoming increasingly recognized as an important element in fuel economy. Finally, finished fiberglass models were shown to top management. The entry chosen was created by a team headed by Jack Telnack, executive director of Ford North American Light Truck and Car Design, the group that had also created the prototype for what went on to become the pretty little Ford Fiesta.

The design brief handed to Telnack's and the other teams was set down in 1976. The new Mustang would use the basic suspension and floorpan from the just-completed Ford Fairmont/Mercury Zephyr compact sedans. This platform could be shortened somewhat and for Telnack's Mustang proposal it was—by 5.1 inches. Mustang II power

units—four, V-6, and 302 V-8—would be retained. As with the original Mustang, curb weight was pegged at a comparatively low 2700 pounds. The interior package size was planned to accommodate two adults comfortably, four in a pinch. Also like the original Mustang but unlike the II, the notchback model was styled first and the fastback developed from it. Several trim versions would be offered: standard, Sport Option, Ghia, and Cobra. The last had blacked-out greenhouse trim, black lower bodysides, color-keyed body moldings, and a snake decal for the hood.

Telnack described the design project to the press in June 1978: "One of the basic themes for this car was 'form follows function'... and we wanted to be as aerodynamically correct as possible before getting into the wind tunnel. In the past we have designed cars and then gone into the tunnel mainly for tuning the major surfaces that have been approved... With the Mustang the designers were thinking about aerodynamics in the initial sketch stages, which made the tuning job in the tunnel much easier. Consequently, we wound up with the most

slippery car ever done in the Ford Motor Company: a drag coefficient of 0.44 for the three-door fastback, 0.46 for the two-door notchback. [Aerodynamics is] probably the most cost-effective way to improve corporate average fuel economy. We know that a 10 percent improvement in drag can result in a five percent improvement in fuel economy at a steady-state 50 mph . . . That's really worthwhile stuff for us to go after."

Telnack's team included light-car design manager Fritz Mayhew, pre-production design executive David Rees, and pre-production designer Gary Haas. The shape they evolved was sort of notchback wedge, very slim in front with the hood tapered from a rather high cowl. The Mustang cowl was actually an inch higher than that of the Fairmont/Zephyr. Telnack said this was to "get a faster sloping hood . . . to pivot the hood over the air cleaner." The shape dictated special inner front fender aprons and radiator supports instead of Fairmont/Zephyr pieces, but everyone agreed this extra expense was warranted. Increased fuel economy was one reward. The front bumper

with integrated spoiler and the slight lip on the decklid were also dictated by aerodynamic considerations. Both body styles were given black-finish slats behind the rear side windows, rather like those of the Mercedes 450SLC. They were too wide for optimum visibility, though, one of the new design's less functional styling features.

Body engineering envisioned use of lightweight materials wherever possible, and plastics, high-strength/low-alloy (HSLA) steel, and aluminum figured heavily. The most significant use of plastics was for the reaction-injection-molded (RIM) soft urethane bumper covers. The number-three frame crossmember and the rear suspension arms were made of HSLA steel. Aluminum was found in the drivetrain and in the bumpers of some models. More weight was saved with thin but strong glass and by thinner door design. The 1979 Mustang thus tipped the scales about 200 pounds lighter on the average than the Mustang II, though the new car was slightly larger in every dimension. In an age of downsizing, this bigger-but-lighter car was a notable achievement.

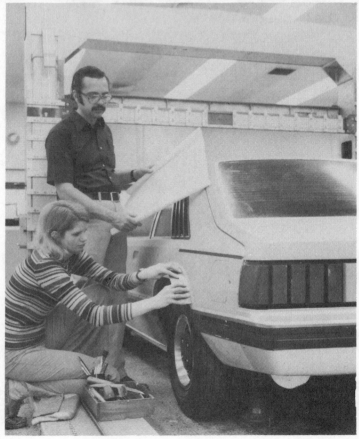

Opposite page: A collection of Ford styling sketches shows the evolution of the '79 Mustang shape. This page: Final design chosen (upper left) was the work of a team headed by Jack Telnack (above). It was the first Mustang styled with aerodynamics in mind, and was subjected to intensive wind tunnel evaluation (upper right). Body surfaces were carefully shaped (left) to minimize turbulence.

75

Equally careful attention was paid to interior design. More efficient use of available space made the '79 far more roomy, comfortable, and convenient than the Mustang II, and sizable gains were made in several key areas. Rear legroom, for example, was increased by over five inches. Overall interior volume was up by 14 cubic feet on the two-door notchback and by 16 cubic feet on the hatchback. Thinner door construction yielded 3.6 inches more shoulder room and 2.0 inches more hiproom in front. In the rear, the gains were 5.0 and 6.0 inches, respectively. Cargo volume was likewise enlarged. The '79 notchback offered two more cubic feet of trunk space and the hatchback an additional four cubic feet compared to the Mustang II.

Some aspects of the '79 interior must have been inspired by European practice. Luxury-trim models were given higher-quality materials, and the '79 Ghia was less flashy than its '78 counterpart. Full instrumentation (speedometer, trip odometer, tachometer, temperature gauge, oil pressure gauge, ammeter and fuel gauge) was standard across the board. Two fingertip stalks mounted on the left of the steering column controlled turn signals, headlight dimmer, horn, and windshield wiper/washer. A third lever was added on the right for the optional tilt steering wheel. Practical convenience options were intermittent wipers, cruise control, and a console complete with a graphic display for "vehicle systems monitoring." This showed an outline of the car in plan view on which warning lights were appropriately placed to indicate low fuel, low windshield washer fluid, and failed headlights, taillights, or brake lights. The display could be tested by a pushbutton. The console also housed a quartz-crystal digital chronometer that showed time, date, or elapsed time at the touch of a button.

As with past Mustangs, the '79 was designed for a broad market spectrum. According to Ford Division marketing plans manager Michael Woods, "Not too long ago we did a concept study on positioning the [imported] Capri and brought in imported car owners, some Capri owners, people who own small specialty cars. We showed them the [new Mustang] and talked to them about strategy. We were pretty gratified that an awful lot of people who were interested in the Capri felt that we had maintained the Capri theme—the functional styling of the car—and that it was consistent with the original car."

Now, the European Ford Capri, especially in its larger-engine forms, was a very competent touring car. If Mustang was to have a similar character its specifications would have to be greatly altered. Capri fans would not be satisfied with merely a plush, short-wheelbase coupe like the Mustang II that weighed too much and handled sluggishly. At the same time, Ford didn't want to lose all those thousands of Mustang II buyers. From the suspension standpoint, therefore, several levels of capability were deemed necessary.

This page: Ford stylists spent considerable time on "formal" themes for the '79 Mustang design, progressing through many variations. Car at top is a late-1973 proposal for a Capri version of the Mustang II. Opposite page: By fall of 1975 there were a number of ideas under development (top and below). The eventual production car (bottom left) broke with tradition in many ways, but was still plainly Mustang.

The main pieces were borrowed from the Fairmont/Zephyr. The front suspension used MacPherson struts instead of conventional upper A-arms. Unlike similar setups still found in many European and most Japanese cars, the coil spring was not wrapped around the shock strut but was mounted between the lower control arm and the body structure. This eliminated the need for an expensive spring compressor when replacing shocks. A front anti-roll bar was standard on all cars, but its diameter varied according to the engine fitted. Rear geometry employed a four-bar link arrangement, also with coil springs, lighter and more compact than the Mustang II's leaf-spring Hotchkiss setup. V-8 models would have a rear anti-roll bar as standard. Since this served more for lateral location than controlling sway, the car's roll center was effectively lowered, and rear spring rates could be commensurately softer.

Product planners decided to offer three suspension levels: standard, "handling," and "special." Each was designed for, and issued with, its own set of tires. The standard suspension came with conventional bias-plys. The mid-level "handling" package used conventional radials. The special suspension was designed around Michelin's recently developed TRX radials with an unusual 390mm (15.35-inch) diameter that required specially sized metric wheels.

The "handling" suspension could be ordered only with 14-inch radials. Compared to the standard chassis, it was tuned for improved handling with higher spring rates, different shock valving, and stiffer bushings. A rear stabilizer bar was also provided when the 2.8-liter V-6 was specified with this package.

The "special" suspension included the Michelin 190/65R390 TRX tires and forged aluminum wheels, a combo Ford first tried on its European Granada. According to Ford, the special suspension was designed "to extract maximum performance from this tire/wheel combination." It featured its own shock absorber valving, high rear spring rates, a 1.12-inch front stabilizer bar, and a rear stabilizer bar.

The 1979 Mustang retained its predecessor's precise rack-and-pinion steering. Power assist was still optional, and the previous variable-ratio rack was also carried over. Housings for both manual and power systems were constructed of die-cast aluminum to save weight.

In addition to the Mustang II's engine offerings, an intriguing new powerplant was offered for '79—a turbocharged version of the standard four. This gave claimed 0–55 mph acceleration of 8.3 seconds with four-speed gearbox, plus fuel economy in the mid-20s. Turbocharging may have been new for Mustang, but the idea had been used for a number of years as a way of improving engine efficiency. The principle is simple. A turbine located in the flow of exhaust gases is connected to an impeller (compressor) near the carburetor. In normal running, the turbine spins too slowly to boost manifold pressure or affect fuel consumption. As the throttle is opened, however, the engine speeds up, which increases the flow of exhaust gases. The increased flow spins the turbine; the impeller speeds up and increases the density (pressure) of the air/

fuel mixture fed to the combustion chambers. The result is more power. To prevent engine damage, maximum boost was limited to 6 pounds per square inch by an exhaust valve that allowed gases to bypass the turbine once that pressure was reached.

Other mechanical highlights for '79 included revisions for the 302 V-8. It was now fitted with a low-restriction exhaust system, used more lightweight components, and featured a ribbed V-belt for the accessory drive. Since the V-6 was in short supply, it was replaced late in the model year by the old 200-cid inline six. There was also a new optional four-speed gearbox developed for the six and V-8. In effect, it was a three-speed manual transmission with an overdrive fourth gear tacked on. Third gear had the direct 1:1 ratio, while fourth had an overdrive ratio of 0.70:1. Final drive ratios were 3.08:1 for automatics, four-speed V-6, and unblown four-cylinder engine, and 3.45:1 for all other drivetrain combinations.

As with previous Mustangs, the performance of any particular '79 naturally depended on the engine/transmission

Opposite page: The 1979 Ghia notchback. Unlike Mustang II, the '79 styling was evolved around the notchback body style. This page: Hatchback was neatly incorporated into the new '79 shape (left and lower left). Broad rear quarter slats weren't as practical, though. Mustang paced the 1979 Indy 500, and some 11,000 replicas (below) were issued. Lovely three-spoke wheels identify TRX package on Cobra (lower right).

chosen. The V-8 was a drag race engine by late-'70s standards: 0–60 mph clocked out at about nine seconds. The V-6's time was in the 13–14 second range, while the turbocharged four took about 12–12.5 seconds with four-speed. Press reaction to the various powertrains was mixed. Some writers thought the V-8 was overpowered and out of step for the fuel-short times. The 2.3-liter turbo got the most attention. As John Dinkel of *Road & Track* put it, "The TRX turbo would seem to be an enthusiast's delight. I just hope that the design compromises dictated by costs and the fact that Ford couldn't start with a completely clean sheet of paper don't wreck that dream . . . There's no doubt the new Mustang has the potential to be the best sport coupe Ford has ever built, but in some respects [it] is as enigmatic as its predecessor."

There was one more enigma brewing as the press previewed the new Mustang in June 1978. A month later, Lee Iacocca was ousted as Ford Motor Company president. Officially, he would take early retirement on October 15th of that year, his 54th birthday. Many insiders had surmised Iacocca would be dumped before Henry Ford II was scheduled to retire as chief executive in 1980 and as chairman in 1982, but the boss didn't say much about it. He reportedly told Iacocca, "It's just one of those things." In removing a strong president, Henry was following a 50-year company tradition. Past presidents Bill Knudsen, Ernie Breech, and Bunkie Knudsen had all been abruptly removed by him or his father.

continued on page 97

Mustang IMSA concept car toured the 1980 auto show circuit, and heralded Ford's return to production-car racing.

Above: The famous Mustang "running horse" logo. *Below:* Prototype 1965 convertible. Note missing grille bar.

Above and below: The production prototype "1964½" hardtop in two early factory shots. Initial $2368 base price plus sporty good looks and a long options list would help Mustang set a sales record its first year.

Above and upper right: The 1965 convertible in top-up guise. This restored example was photographed at Ford's Dearborn Proving Grounds in 1982. *Below:* An early "1964½" hardtop shows classic ponycar proportions.

Left: Mustang was chosen as pace car for the 1964 Indianapolis 500, a neat follow-up to the April, 1964 launch. *Below:* Slick "2+2" fastback was added at the start of the formal 1965 model year. *Right:* The 1966 edition of Carroll Shelby's muscular GT-350, introduced in '65. Early Shelbys command premium prices today.

Far left, below: 1966 standard convertible shows few changes from '65. *Above:* The 1967 convertible. *Below:* GT 2+2 for '67. Big-block 390 V-8 was new option that year.

Above: C-stripe sets off 1968 GT fastback's smooth lines.
Opposite page: Big-inch Shelby GT-500 was replaced for mid-1968 by GT-500KR (middle, top) with 428 Cobra Jet V-8. KR stood for King of the Road.
Below: Burly Boss 302 was created for the 1969 Trans-Am championship. It's shown here in "generic" race trim.

Far left: The 1969 convertible. Bodyshell was all-new that year. *Bottom:* Luxury Grandé was also new for '69. Vinyl top and side striping were standard. *Near left:* Mach I show car of 1968 hinted at '69 production model. *Below:* "Autolite I" Bonneville Speed Record car.

Above: Beautiful Mustang Milano show car of 1970 prefigured later Mustang II hatchback. *Below:* Mach 1 for 1970 sported its own special grille and body trim. *Upper right:* Hot Boss 302 carried Mustang to the Trans-Am Championship in 1970 season.

1970

Below: The 1971-73 models were as big as Mustang would ever get. Mach 1 (shown) and Boss 351 were the raciest of the '71s. *Bottom:* Few changes were made on the '72s, as seen in this Grandé hardtop.

continued from page 80

Iacocca was not bitter, at least not in public. "You just surmise that the Breeches of the world got too big, too soon, and he [Ford] doesn't want strong guys around," he said. "You know, he wants to diffuse and bureaucratize the company as he gets to be 61. I guess that's the only thing I can come up with, because I really don't have a good sound answer myself." Ironically, and as Iacocca carefully noted, June 1978 had been the biggest single month in Ford history. January-to-June had been the biggest six-month sales period ever, and netted the company its largest profit on record. "They probably won't be at this peak again," Iacocca said, "so I guess it's a good time to go."

After 32 years with Ford, Iacocca was a free agent—but not for long. He was too young, too vigorous to retire, and yearned for a new challenge. He found it soon enough: he signed on as president of Chrysler Corporation, which he vowed to pull out of the financial quagmire in which it had been bogged down for so long. A lot of people were pleased by Iacocca's appointment, especially Chrysler stockholders. As *Automotive News* put it, "Any other auto company would be willing to give up three future draft choices to get its hands on that kind of talent." Iacocca, said the editorial, "is a manager, a really professional manager. And he was paid a lot for his services . . . compensation that reached a million dollars a year, figures that defy understanding by mere mortals. Yet, by all standards he earned every penny . . . The job he has done seems to speak for itself."

Below: New 1979 Mustang option was this graphic warning light display, which came with the center console. Right: Newly designed '79 dashboard incorporated full instrumentation and European-style steering column stalks for lights and wiper/washer. Bottom: In the 1980 IMSA show car, steering wheel hub housed most controls, Note special buckets.

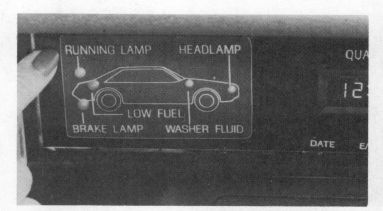

"Improving the Breed" was the theme for 1980 as Mustang celebrated its 15th anniversary. And improved it was. The optional six was now available with four-speed gearbox, a combination offering a good compromise between V-8 performance and four-cylinder economy. A new 255-cid V-8, essentially a smaller-bore derivative of Ford's famed small-block, arrived to replace the 302. Styling changed in detail only. Nobody at Ford was unhappy about the looks of the '79, and neither were customers.

Ford's ponycar had been chosen for pace car duty at the 1979 Indianapolis 500, so it was natural an "Indy Pace Car" replica would appear as a mid-year addition to the line. It did, and went on to inspire the 1980 Cobra package, which gained a similarly styled grille, plus front and rear spoilers, integral fog lamps, hood scoop, and the TRX special suspension. It was offered for the hatchback body style only.

The standard two-door notchback was continued. Highback, all-vinyl bucket seats and color-keyed interior and door trim were standard for all 1980 models, and the previous Sport Option equipment became standard for the hatchback. This comprised styled sport wheels with trim rings, black rocker panel and window moldings, wide

bodyside moldings, striped rub strip extensions, and a sporty steering wheel. Halogen headlights replaced conventional tungsten sealed beams across the board. Ghia models continued as the luxury leaders, marked by color-keyed seatbelts, mirrors, bodyside moldings, and, on hatchbacks, C-pillar trim. Inside the Ghias were low-back vinyl bucket seats with headrests, door map pockets, a visor vanity mirror, thicker pile carpeting, a deluxe steering wheel, roof-mounted assist handles, and a full complement of interior lights. Leather or cloth and vinyl upholstery was available in six different colors.

The Mustang option list was as long as ever for 1980. Tilt steering wheel, speed control, power door locks, remote trunk release, rear window wiper/washer, flip-up glass sunroof, and a wide assortment of wheels, wheel covers, and audio equipment were just a few of the items. New on the slate were Recaro reclining front bucket seats, first offered by the factory on the '79 Pace Car replica. With their infinitely adjustable variable seatback reclining mechanism and adjustable thigh and lumbar support padding, Mustang could no longer be accused of lagging behind its European competition in seat comfort. Other new options for '80

Opposite page: Mustang's Cobra package option was revised for 1980 along the lines of the Indy Pace Car replica. Big changes were a new slat-type grille and deeper front spoiler with built-in fog lights. Inset shows gaudy Cobra hood graphics, offered as a separate extra-cost item. Cobra was available for '80 with either the turbocharged four or the debored 4.2-liter version of the famed Ford small-block V-8. This page, above: McLaren Mustang was created as a "homologation special" for 1980 IMSA and Trans-Am races. Drivetrain and chassis were mostly stock items, but styling was anything but. Only 250 were produced. All had the turbo four. Right: Those who yearned for a Mustang convertible in 1980 had to settle for the new Carriage Roof option on the notchback. This vinyl covering simulated a convertible's top-up appearance, but was no substitute for real open-air driving.

included a roof-mounted luggage carrier, a "window shade" cargo area cover for the hatchback, and accent side tape stripes. An interesting extra-cost dress-up item for notchbacks was the Carriage Roof, a diamond-grain full vinyl roof cover, with black door and quarter window frames and moldings, designed to simulate the top-up appearance of a convertible.

The 1980 drivetrain chart was one of the broadest in Mustang history. The lineup consisted of 2.3-liter (140-cid) ohc four with or without turbocharger, the 3.3-liter (200-cid) ohv six, and the 4.2-liter (255-cid) V-8. The fours came with a conventional four-speed manual transmission, while the six used the manual four-speed overdrive gearbox. Automatic was standard with the V-8 and optional with other engines.

The efficient inline six was a simple, easy-to-service engine, and gave performance similar to the V-6 it had replaced. It featured a seven-main-bearing crankshaft, hydraulic valve lifters, cast iron block, and a one-barrel carburetor. According to Ford's "Cost-of-Ownership" formula, where required maintenance for the first 50,000 miles is averaged according to dealer parts and labor

prices, the inline six cost less to operate than the V-6. The 255 V-8 was the latest in a long line of Ford small-blocks dating from the original Fairlane 221 V-8 of 1962. The rationale for this powerplant was obvious: Ford's need to meet government CAFE (corporate average fuel economy) standards. The 255 gave better fuel economy than the 302 at some loss in performance.

Mustang had been with us for 15 years in 1980, and this brought up the question of how the latest version compared with the 1965 original. Judging by certain "vital statistics," it was tempting to say little had changed.

	1965 Mustang	1980 Mustang
length (in.)	181.6	179.1
width (in.)	68.2	69.1
wheelbase (in.)	108.0	100.4
weight, 6-cyl. coupe (lb.)	2,445	2,516
base six, cid	200	200
base V-8, cid	260	255

Despite their similarity in numbers, the first and the latest Mustangs were really quite different cars. Although the '80 was about the same overall length as the '65 and had the same amount of passenger room up front, it actually had more rear seat room despite a 7.6-inch shorter wheelbase. Ford had obviously learned about space utilization since 1965. While the '80 was burdened with all the mandatory safety features such as reinforced doors and 5-mph bumpers, it weighed hardly more than a comparable '65. Ford had apparently learned something about lightweight materials and construction over 15 years, too.

There were some interesting comparisons in the engine department, too. The 2.3-liter four, of course was not comparable to any Mustang engine of 1965. The six, however, was exactly the same powerplant offered on the '65 (except the early cars that used the 170-cid unit). The 255 V-8 was derived from the 302 which, in turn, was developed from the 289, which itself was enlarged from the original Mustang's 260 V-8. Yet both the six and V-8 got better fuel mileage than their 1965 counterparts.

What the comparisons didn't show was the long, long road Mustang had traveled in 15 years. Along the way, it had become one of the world's fastest four-place production cars. It also became too large, too unwieldy, and too wasteful. That the lighter, more efficient 1980 Mustang so closely resembled the '65 in size and performance was perhaps a coincidence. Then again, perhaps it wasn't. We had a lot of automotive decisions to make in the late 1960s and, looking back, it seems we generally made the wrong ones. Most enthusiasts agree that Mustang changed for the worse after 1970.

But hindsight is cheap and far too easily indulged. Enthusiasts could take heart from the 1980 Mustang. It proved that Americans could build a nimble, handsome, efficient automobile that could be quite entertaining over the twisty bits. After 15 years the original ponycar had come full circle.

During 1980, Ford gave every indication it was about to get its performance act back together and put it on the road. And Mustang would definitely be the star of the show. A

Opposite page: The 1981 Mustang lineup showed few appearance changes from 1979–80, nor did it need to. Drivetrain offerings were shuffled a bit, and a T-bar roof treatment was added to the options list, reviving a feature last seen in 1978. Sales were way down compared to earlier years, a reflection of the country's sagging economy. This page: Ford got back into domestic motorsports in a big way with the advent of its Special Vehicle Operations (SVO) department in late 1980. Mustang was given the emphasis, of course. Shown at right is the specially modified turbocharged 1.7-liter car with 560 bhp designed for the IMSA GT series and other similar events. Below it is the less radically altered Mustang driven by Lyn St. James in the 1981 IMSA Kelly-American Challenge.

tantalizing "concept car," the Mustang IMSA, toured the auto show circuit that season. Powered by Ford's turbocharged four, it sat astride massive Pirelli P7 tires nestled under outlandishly flared fenders. It featured a deep front air dam, a loop rear spoiler, and pop-riveted plastic covers for side windows, taillight panel, and headlamps. In name and appearance, it hinted strongly that Ford was more than just thinking about a return to competition—and about the International Motor Sports Association GT series in particular.

Then in September, Ford announced formation of a Special Vehicle Operations department. Significantly, it was headed by Michael Kranefuss, newly arrived in Dearborn from his post as competition director for Ford of Europe. The purpose of SVO was to "develop a series of limited-production performance cars and develop their image through motorsport." It quickly got down to business with a turbo Mustang to be driven in selected 1981 IMSA GT events by former Porsche pilot Klaus Ludwig. Other Mustangs receiving similar direct factory help were

a Trans-Am car for Dennis Mecham and an IMSA Kelly American Challenge racer for Lyn St. James.

As if to signal its return to the track, Ford debuted the McLaren Mustang in late 1980. The work of designers Todd Gerstenberger and Harry Wykes, it was a heavily modified Mustang with enough built-in potential to make it easily adaptable for race duty. In appearance, the McLaren was quite close to the IMSA show car. It sported a grille-less nose above a low-riding skirt spoiler, functional hood scoops, tweaked suspension (mostly a mixture of heavy-duty off-the-shelf components), bulging fender flares, and delicate-looking BBS alloy wheels shod with broad-shouldered 225/55R-15 Firestone HPR radial tires. Again, the turbocharged four was used, but its was fitted with a new variable-rate boost control. This provided a maximum boost range of 5 to 11 psi, as opposed to the stock engine's fixed 5-psi pressure. At 10 psi, output was rated at 175 bhp @ 2500 rpm, a considerable jump over the stock mill's, which was usually pegged at around 131 bhp (Ford never released official ratings for its turbo-four). Price for

the McLaren Mustang was $25,000 a copy, and only 250 (including the prototype) were built.

All this muscle flexing came too late to affect the 1981 Mustang, however, which was little changed visually or mechanically. Reclining backrests were now standard for the factory bucket seats, and interior trim was upgraded in appearance and completeness. Power side windows and a T-bar roof with twin lift off glass panels were added to the options slate. Cobra buyers could still delete the cartoon snake decal on the hood—a blow for good taste. The turbo engine was now offered only with manual transmission.

A 5-speed overdrive manual gearbox had been announced as an option for both Mustang fours in mid-1980, and this became more widely available for '81. The new gearbox pulled a shorter 3.45:1 final drive (versus the normal 3.08:1 cog) for better off-the-line snap. The overdrive fifth was geared at 0.82:1 for economical highway cruising.

It was just what the base Mustang needed, except for one thing: in adding the extra gear, Ford goofed. As CONSUMER GUIDE® magazine's automotive staff noted in its 1980 test, "Our biggest objections to the 5-speed are its linkage—stiff, yet vague—and its shift pattern. As with the 4-speed unit, 1st through 4th are arranged in the usual H-pattern. But 5th is awkwardly located at the bottom of the dogleg to the right of and opposite 4th, instead of up and to the right . . . Why Ford did it this way is a mystery, but it makes getting into or out of 5th real work. Our guess is that the engineers wanted to prevent inexperienced drivers from accidentally engaging overdrive and needlessly lugging the engine, as well as to prevent confusion with the often-used 3rd. If so, they've succeeded admirably." Apparently, Ford felt most drivers would want to downshift from fifth directly to third, bypassing fourth. At least that's what one transmission engineer said. A more

Opposite page, top: This 1981 Ford publicity photo was issued to show off Mustang's agile handling and the new T-roof option. Bottom: Real performance returned for 1982 in the form of a revived and much-modified 302 V-8, now called the High-Output (H.O.) unit. With near 160 bona fide horsepower and coupled to the standard four-speed manual gearbox, it gave the sporty Mustang GT model impressive 0–60 mph acceleration: close to seven seconds flat by most magazine accounts. This page, above: GT was the sportiest of the '82 Mustangs, replacing the previous Cobra. Flashy tape-and-decal treatment was eliminated, but rear spoiler, front air dam, and other functional styling features remained. Right: A true convertible was announced as a mid-1982 addition to the Mustang line, but actual production was postponed to the 1983 model year.

logical reason was that putting fifth over and up would have entailed excessively long arm reach. The factory's "official" explanation was that the U-shaped shift motion would better emphasize the economy benefits of the overdrive fifth gear. Whatever the reason, the idea just didn't work.

Ford had another idea for 1982, and this one worked just fine. The 5.0-liter (302-cid) V-8 returned as an option for all models, and was modified internally for extra performance. The new hot 302 got a special camshaft adapted from a marine version of the fabled small-block, along with a larger two-barrel carb, bigger and smoother exhaust system, and low-restriction twin-inlet air cleaner. Offered only with the four-speed overdrive manual gearbox, the revived 302 was capable of pushing the Mustang to 60 mph in less than eight seconds—actually closer to seven by most magazine accounts.

Apart from this heartening news, there was little to get excited about. The turbo-four was discontinued after compiling a poor reliability record. Model nomenclature was revised, with L, GL, GLX, and GT in ascending order of price and sportiness. A larger gas tank (up to 15.4 gallons) was adopted for longer cruising range, wider wheels and tires were fitted as standard, and a remote control lefthand door mirror became a no-cost extra. Other drivetrains continued as before, but the optional 4.2-liter V-8 got a lockup torque converter, effective in all forward gears, for its "mandatory option" three-speed Select-Shift automatic. The new GT kept the low-slung front air dam, integral fog lights, and rear lip spoiler from the previous Cobra. It rode a beefed-up chassis featuring stiffer front and rear anti-roll bars, wider 185-section radial tires, and specially calibrated springs, bushings, and shocks.

It's ironic that the best Mustang generation since the

original arrived almost on the eve of what would turn out to be one of the worst sales periods in Detroit history. The market began slumping in mid-1979, and hit new lows in the 1982 model year. That brought hot new competition from GM in the totally restyled, somewhat smaller, third-generation Chevrolet Camaro and Pontiac Firebird. Yet despite these factors, Mustang remained the most popular of the ponycars, according to Ford sales figures. And the return of the 302 V-8 for the '82 Mustang GT signalled that Dearborn was ready to pick up the pace again after a decade in which all Detroit learned to live with government safety, emissions, and fuel economy mandates.

With their 5.0-liter V-8s, tuned chassis, and race-inspired styling touches, the 1982 Mustang GT, Camaro Z28, and Firebird Trans Am were quickly matched up in car magazine comparison tests. While the GM cars won points for their superior handling and arguably more modern styling, the Mustang was conceded to be more practical for everyday use and discernably quicker. *Car and Driver* magazine recorded 8.1 seconds in the 0–60 mph test with its GT against 8.6 seconds for the injected V-8 Camaro with automatic and a comparatively sluggish 10.6 seconds for the carbureted V-8 Trans Am with 4-speed. Writing in the August 1982 issue, *C/D*'s technical editor, Don Sherman,

An all-around look at the 1983 Mustang GT 5.0. Note revised, nearly full-width taillights and discreet chrome exhaust tips.

noted that "... in terms of sheer visceral appeal, [the Mustang] is right up there with the Porsche [928]."

Not all was sweetness and light, however. In testing the Mustang GT's sister ship, the Mercury Capri RS, CONSUMER GUIDE® magazine's staff found the power-assisted rack-and-pinion steering irritatingly vague, overly light, and severely lacking in feel. Wet-weather traction was also a problem because of the V-8's ample torque, 240 pounds-feet developed at a very low 2400 rpm. We weren't able to evaluate handling fully because our test car was delivered during one of the coldest weeks in Chicago history, and test conditions were hardly ideal. Even so, we found it possible to light the back tires easily in a brisk take-off from a stoplight, accompanied at times by rear-end jitter that made us wonder what would happen in hard cornering on bumpy surfaces. C/D's Sherman echoed our concerns: "In left-hand sweepers, the gas pedal acts as a power-oversteer switch . . . That smooth two-step unfortunately turns into a jitterbug in right-hand bends, where power hop conspires to make life difficult."

Despite such faults, Ford's latterday muscle car had much to recommend it. We found its interior roomier and more practical than the Camaro/Firebird's. Though both are hatchback designs, Ford somehow managed to provide

Though '83 facelift was mild, it kept Mustang's classic good looks right up to date. Shown are the GT 5.0 coupe and the new convertible.

a good deal more usable luggage space in its hot rods than GM. We also found the Mustang/Capri 4-speed manual gearbox had a much lighter shift action (and a more comfortably placed shifter) than the truck-like Camaro/Firebird linkage. Our staff was divided on driving position, some preferring the more confined, low-slung stance of the GM cars to the more upright "vintage" feel of the Ford products. Yet most agreed the Mustang/Capri was a far better compromise for those who have to contend with the daily drudgery of stop-and-go traffic, where the manual-shift Camaro/Firebird would prove tiring to drive for any length of time. There was still work to do, but our overall view was that Ford had injected a much-needed dose of pizzazz into its ponycars with the revived 302 V-8.

Somebody at Ford was apparently taking road test criticisms to heart, because a number of changes were instituted for 1983. Chassis refinements for the GT included wider-section tires, including a new optional 220-mm TRX with a broad 55 percent aspect ratio, a slightly larger rear anti-roll bar, softer rear spring rates, stiffer bushings for the front control arms, and revised shock valving. With this special handling suspension came higher-effort power steering for better control. For performance fans, Ford substituted a four-barrel carb for the two-barrel 1982 unit, and adopted an aluminum intake manifold, high-flow air cleaner, enlarged exhaust passages, and modified valve-train. The result, according to preliminary estimates, was an extra 15–20 horsepower over the previous high-output V-8, or something in the region of 170–180 bhp. To answer complaints about the big gap between second and third in the four-speed's wide-ratio gearing, a new five-speed gearbox, made by Borg-Warner, was added.

Mustang came in for other significant changes, too. The most obvious of these was a new nose, good for a 2.5 percent reduction in aerodynamic drag, plus restyled taillights. The 4.2-liter V-8 was dropped from the engine roster, and Ford's 3.8-liter (232-cid) lightweight V-6, introduced for the '82 model year, replaced the 200-cid straight six as the step-up power option. The standard powerplant remained the 2.3-liter four, now with a new one-barrel carburetor instead of a two-barrel, plus long-reach spark plugs for fast-burn combustion, a move aimed at reducing emissions while improving warmup and part-throttle engine response. Available on manual-shift models was a new Volkswagen-like upshift indicator light. This signalled the driver when to shift to the next higher gear for economy, based on the fact that an engine is most efficient running at relatively low revs on wide throttle openings.

Undoubtedly the most glamorous item for '83 was a new

convertible, available only in top-line GLX trim. Since the late '70s, a number of small companies had been doing good business snipping the tops from Mustang notchbacks (and other cars) to satisfy a small but steady demand for top-down motoring. Ford apparently decided it was time to get in on the action, too.

Unlike the Buick Riviera and Chrysler LeBaron ragtops announced at about the same time, the Mustang was a regular assembly line model, the first factory-built convertible from Dearborn since the last soft-top Mustang of 1973. Interior trim and top installation was carried out by a contractor, Cars & Concepts of Brighton, Michigan, but Ford built the rest of it. Unlike the aftermarket conversions, the '83 Mustang convertible featured roll-down rear side windows and a rear window made of tempered glass. It was available with any drivetrain (except the four-cylinder/automatic combination), including the four-barrel H.O. V-8. As the first open-air ponycar in a decade, it added another dash of excitement to an already impressive Mustang lineup.

Other 1983 highlights included revised seat and door trim for all models, a standard roller-blind cargo area cover for hatchbacks, easier-to-read gauge markings, and less interior brightwork. A new sport seat option with mesh-insert headrest replaced the extra-cost Recaro seats, which

had not sold well. Reflecting its new concern with aerodynamics, Ford also deleted the hatchback's liftgate louvers and the notchback's Carriage Roof from the options list. At mid-model year, Ford was scheduled to reintroduce its turbo four as a Mustang option, this time with multiple-port electronic fuel injection and standard five-speed manual shift.

Nearly a generation after the first Mustang rolled out the door, it is pleasant to reflect that the same kind of car is with us today—with the same name and (despite safety, emission, and fuel economy regulations) much the same character. Following the tried-and-true pattern, there's still an options list long enough for you to tailor your Mustang as a mild-mannered runabout, thrilling European-style tourer, or anything in between. Another tradition—the long-hood/short-deck shape, room in back only for occasional riders, and handsome bucket-seat interior—is also preserved. In fact, Mustang never looked better. The current models are clearly more sophisticated and more efficient than the 1965 original, yet have the same spirited youthfulness that long ago infected a generation of car lovers with "Mustang fever." Today, there's a new generation looking for the same kind of excitement. And as has been the case for almost 20 years now, they'll find it in the cars with the Running Horse.

Opposite page: A peek inside the 1983 Mustang convertible reveals few changes to the familiar, well-designed dash, but interior brightwork is reduced. This page: The 1983 GT 5.0 shows off its new, more rounded nose, with distinctive black accent paint and the now-optional hood bulge. Change is claimed to reduce aerodynamic drag by 2.5 percent. Note absence of under-bumper air dam.

Model Year Production

No.	Model	1979	1980	1981
02 (66B)	Base 2-door coupe	143,382	117,015	69,994*
03 (61R)	Base 3-door coupe	108,758	86,569	68,111
04 (66H)	Ghia 2-door coupe	48,788	20,288	11,991
05 (61H)	Ghia 3-door coupe	31,097	17,192	12,497
	TOTAL	332,025	241,064	162,593

*includes 4418 units with "S" (economy) option

Prices/Weights*

Models		1979	1980	1981
02 (66B)	Base 2-door coupe	$4494/2530	$4884/2606	$5980/2601
03 (61R)	Base 3-door coupe	$4828/2612	$5194/2614	$6216/2635
04 (66H)	Ghia 2-door coupe	$5064/2648	$5369/NA	$6424/2665
05 (61H)	Ghia 3-door coupe	$5216/2672	$5512/NA	$6538/2692

*Initial model year retail prices. All figures exclusive of options.

General Specifications

	1979	1980	1981
Wheelbase	100.4	100.4	100.4
Overall length	179.1	179.1	179.1
Overall width	69.1	69.1	69.1
Std. Trans.	4-spd. man. (4-cyl.)	4-sp. man. (4-cyl.)	4-sp. man. (4-cyl.)
	4-sp./OD man. (6-cyl.)	4-sp./OD man. (6-cyl.)	4-sp./OD man. (6-cyl.)
	3-sp. auto. (8-cyl.)	3-sp. auto. (8-cyl.)	3-sp. auto. (8-cyl.)
Optional trans.	3-sp. auto.	3-sp. auto.	3-sp. auto.
		5-sp. man.*	5-sp. man.*

*4-cylinder engines only

Engine Availability

Type	CID	HP	1979	1980	1981	1982
ohc I-4	140	88	Std.	Std.	Std.	Std.
ohc I-4 Turbo	140	131	Opt.	Opt.	Opt.	—
ohv V-6	171	109	Opt.	—	—	—
ohv I-6	200	85	Opt.[1]	Opt.	Opt.	Opt.
ohv V-8	255	117	—	Opt.	Opt.	Opt.
ohv V-8	302	140	Opt.	—	—	Opt.[2]

[1]replaced V-6 option at mid-model year   [2]High-Output version

THE SHELBY-MUSTANGS

To Mustang history could be complete without the story of the Shelby-Mustang, created by former race driver Carroll Shelby. It appeared barely a year after the Mustang, and quickly established itself as one of that elite group, the dual-purpose American production car: brilliant on the street, superbly capable on the track. The impetus for it was Ford's desire to give the Mustang a solid performance image. And what better way to do that than by taking the Sports Car Club of America's B-production championship away from Corvette?

To some, the name Carroll Shelby evokes memories of a disarming country boy with a wide "aw shucks" grin under a black cowboy hat. To more knowledgeable enthusiasts, he was the man who built the Cobra 289 and 427, the fastest sports cars of all time. Shelby's rags-to-riches, back-to-rags, back-to-riches story is the stuff legends are made of. At various times a truck driver, roustabout, ranch hand, salesman, and chicken farmer, Shelby began racing sports cars comparatively late in life. Beginning with MGs in the mid-1950s, he quickly progressed to Ferraris, Maseratis,

The Shelby GT-350 was the ultimate high-performance Mustang in street trim (left) and a Corvette killer when prepared for road racing.

and Aston Martins. He was a good driver, maybe even sensational. But sports car racing was a gentleman's sport in those days. There was no prize money worth talking about, and a driver like Shelby who wasn't independently wealthy had to have a sponsor who would supply the car and pay the expenses of racing it. Shelby had no problem promoting himself or his driving ability, and he delivered on those promises time and time again. By the time he won the prestigious 24 Hours of Le Mans in 1959, he was on top of the world. Then, heart trouble forced him to retire as a driver in 1960.

Shelby settled in southern California and made cars his business. First, he bought a Goodyear tire distributorship, then started the first high-performance driving school in the U.S. He also nurtured a private dream. He would build a car of his own someday—the world's fastest production sports car. But without capital and no firm design ideas, he had only a vision. Then, fate took a hand. Shelby had heard that Ford was developing a small, lightweight V-8, the Fairlane 221 (later enlarged to 260 and eventually to 289 cubic inches). At about the same time, it appeared A.C. Cars Ltd. of Surrey, England, was about to go out of business because it had unexpectedly lost its supplier of engines for its strong, lightweight open sports car, the Ace. Shelby stepped in at precisely the right moment, dropped the Ford small-block into the A.C. sports car, and the Cobra was born.

Cobra and Shelby soon became household words—at least in the households of car enthusiasts—and inextricably linked with Ford's performance program in the early and middle '60s. The reason: Cobras were winning almost every race in sight, including the coveted World Manufacturer's Championship for GT cars, a title that Ferrari had held for 12 years before grudgingly yielding it to Shelby.

The Cobra rub-off onto Ford's regular product line was of enormous value. Dearborn had already discovered the youth market, and had launched the Mustang to capture it. But though initial sales had been higher than anyone at Ford expected, Mustang was seen mainly as a sporty compact, not necessarily as a high-performance machine despite availability of the potent HP 289 V-8. So, Ford asked Shelby to develop a racing Mustang capable of besting the Corvettes in Sports Car Club of America (SCCA) competition. Flushed with the Cobra's success and knowing his way around race tracks and the sanctioning bodies, Shelby had a predictable reply: "Build a hundred of 'em." That was the minimum number of cars that had to be built for a particular model to be qualified (or homologated) as a production-class car.

As a first step, Shelby built two prototypes from a pair of ordinary Mustang fastbacks. A team of engineers and development drivers made numerous changes to transform the soft, boulevard cars into muscular racers that still looked a lot like the production Mustang. After all, if Ford

The 1966 GT-350 (above and top) received a new grille, plexiglas rear quarter windows and a suspension tuned more for street use. The '67 Shelby was larger, heavier than the 1966 model (opposite page).

were going to get any publicity benefit from this exercise, the cars would still need to be recognizable as Mustangs. Another goal for the Shelby program was to come up with a Ford alternative to the Corvette for the street. The Cobra, although sold through selected Ford dealers, was usually regarded by enthusiasts as an A.C. or a Shelby, not a Ford.

Once final specifications had been determined for Shelby's Mustang, a dozen duplicates were built by converting stock units at the Cobra production facility in Venice, California in late 1964. Another 100 white fastbacks ready for conversion were soon shipped from Ford's San Jose, California assembly plant. When SCCA inspectors arrived to approve the model for production racing, they were somewhat surprised to find that more than the required 100 cars had been completed.

For no particular reason, except maybe that it sounded good, Shelby designated his much-modified Mustang the GT-350, though it was often referred to as the Shelby-Mustang or simply Shelby GT. There were two versions planned from the start, a street model and a full-house racer. However, it's important to note that the GT-350 was conceived primarily as a racing car. The street version was simply a less extreme, more tractable derivative of it, and accounted for the vast majority of those actually built. Shelby realized he wouldn't be able to sell many bona fide racing machines, which was one reason why the street version looked so much like the track car. Ford's desire for easy "product identification" between the racing Mustangs and the mass-production models was the other.

What Shelby did to create the GT-350 was never a secret. Ford supplied a white Mustang fastback equipped with all-black interior, the 271-bhp "Hi-Performance" version of the small-block 289 V-8, and Borg-Warner T-10 four-speed all-synchromesh manual transmission with Ford linkage and close-ratio gearing. A beefier rear axle borrowed from the big Galaxie was used in place of the Falcon unit on the stock Mustang to better handle the expected increases in power and torque. This switch gave a heftier center section and larger 10×3-inch drum brakes, which were fitted with metallic linings. Ford also supplied each car with several "delete items," including hood, exhaust system, and rear seat.

On Shelby's small-scale assembly line each car received extensive suspension modifications. The front end got relocated mounting points and the factory's optional disc brakes, made by Kelsey-Hayes. Shelby also fitted a larger front anti-roll bar and a heavy steel tube brace that connected the tops of the two front shock towers to eliminate body flex under hard cornering loads. Trailing arms were added at the rear to provide more secure axle location. Koni shocks were used all around. Wheels were hefty 15×6-inch units made at the Shelby works and shod with Goodyear Blue Dot 7.75×15 high-performance tires. As an option, Shelby offered special steel-rim wheels with aluminum centers supplied to his specification by Cragar. Completing the chassis work was a quicker-ratio steering box to replace the lower-geared stock unit.

Under the hood, the 289 V-8 gained aluminum high-rise manifolds, finned aluminum valve covers and oil pan, and a larger Holley carb. The hood itself was a special fiberglass unit with functional hood scoop. All these changes yielded

an honest 306 bhp. To put that power to the ground, the rear end was fitted with a Detroit "Locker" differential.

The Shelby-Mustang's interior was decked out in true racer style. There were three-inch competition-type seatbelts, a tachometer and oil pressure gauge mounted at eye level on a stock Mustang dash, and a wood-rimmed, flat-dish racing-type steering wheel. Since there was no rear seat, the spare tire was relocated to the empty space for better weight distribution, mounted on a fiberglass shelf. The reason the back seat was left out had to do with the SCCA rulebook, which took account of passenger capacity in classifying a production car. The GT-350 qualified for the sports car classes by this simple measure. Otherwise, it would have had to run as a "sedan."

All 1965-model Shelbys were painted white—no other colors were available. All Ford and Mustang insignias were removed, but blue rocker panel racing stripes displayed the GT-350 name prominently. Most of the early cars also had the optional 10-inch-wide twin "Le Mans" stripes that ran from hood to rear deck over the top, and were also blue (American international racing colors are blue and white).

The most important feature of the R-model racer was the engine. SCCA rules specified that to qualify for production racing, a car could have suspension or engine modifications, but not both. Shelby chose to keep the same sus-

pension components for both street and competition versions so that, under the rules, he could modify the engine. The street mill used a hotter cam, larger carb, and a less restrictive exhaust system than the stock HP 289. The competition engine was advertised as fully dyno-tuned and race-ready. It developed between 325 and 350 gross horsepower from its balanced and blueprinted components, and was, in fact, basically the same engine used in the racing Cobras. Ports were enlarged, polished, and matched to the combustion chambers. Pistons were fly-cut, and a special camshaft was installed. A high-volume oil pump, oil cooler, special tube headers backed by straight pipes, and special valve cover breathers were fitted. The carburetor was a 715-cfm Holley, which gulped air though a spun aluminum plenum chamber mated to the hood scoop. The gearbox was Borg-Warner's T-10 "Sebring" unit sup-

plied with both aluminum and cast iron cases. A steel-plate competition clutch disc was fitted. Every GT-350R was track-tested at Willow Springs Raceway prior to shipment. The racing cars weighed only 2500 pounds, compared to 2800 for the street machines.

The "Competition Prepared" GT-350 had no insulation, carpeting, door panels, or window-winding mechanisms. The only glass it retained was in the windshield, with plexiglas used instead for the door windows (in aluminum frames) and the backlight. A one-piece fiberglass front apron replaced the front bumper and gravel pan. It had a large central cutout that ducted air to the oil cooler and two smaller holes for front brake cooling. The rear bumper was painted white to match the body on early cars, and was later left off entirely. A long-range 34-gallon gas tank with a quick-release cap and a large splash tunnel was installed. American Racing Equipment 7×15-inch five-spoke magnesium wheels were used exclusively on all GT-350Rs.

Even by racing standards, the interior of the competition model was stark. Almost everything was finished in semi-gloss black. All padding, the glove compartment, radio, and ashtray were removed from the dash, which was left with only an ignition switch, light and wiper switches, and a bank of "CS" competition gauges. From left to right, instruments were provided for fuel pressure, oil temperature, speed (0–160 mph), revs (0–8000 rpm), oil pressure,

The '67 Shelbys had a more sculptured, sleeker appearance than the 1966 GT-350s (opposite page, top left). The 1967 models featured a broad hood scoop and high beam headlamps in the grille. Inside, the interior had a genuine roll bar. The brake cooling scoops and air scoops on rear quarter roof panels were functional. The rear was trimmed with a spoiler and wide taillight lenses.

and water temperature. Two lightweight fiberglass racing bucket seats padded in black vinyl were used.

The GT-350 was homologated for SCCA "B-Production," which meant it would compete against small-block Corvettes, Sunbeam Tigers, Jaguar E-Types, and the occasional Ferrari or Aston Martin. A total of 562 Shelby-Mustangs were built as 1965 models, but no more than 30 of these were built to racing specifications. However, since all the special parts were available over the counter, per Shelby philosophy, anyone could turn a street car into the racing model by removing and/or substituting components. Many owners did just that.

The R-model GT-350 listed for $5950, compared to a $4547 list for the street version, both bargain prices even for 1965. That, of course, was part of the Ford philosophy. Since 1962, the company had emphasized a lot of performance for the money in an attempt to enhance the image of its regular models.

The 428-cid Cobra Jet engine became available in the middle of the 1968 model year. Shelbys equipped with that engine had the GT-500KR designation. Convertible versions of both GT-350 and GT-500 models were first offered in 1968.

Not only did the image-making work, but the racing package itself was formidable. On Valentine's Day 1965, Shelby American served notice that the only time a Corvette would see Victory Circle was when there were no GT-350s around. Duly certified, the GT-350 went rapidly to work: it its very first appearance it notched three class wins. However, its dominance of B-Production wasn't quite universal. In 1965, when the SCCA awarded national championships on a divisional basis, one 327-engine Corvette eked out a win in the Southwest region. The rest of 1965—and all of 1966 and '67—saw a Shelby-Mustang parade. Here are the statistics:

B-Production National Champions

1965	Central: Robert Johnson, GT-350
	Midwest: Brad Brooker, Kansas, Corvette/GT-350
	Northeast: Mark Donohue, New Jersey, GT-350
	Pacific: Jerry Titus, California, GT-350
	Southwest: Zoltan Petrany, Texas, Corvette
1966	Walter Hane, Florida, GT-350
1967	Fred Van Buren, Mexico City, GT-350

Because the GT-350 was so visibly successful, it was naturally assumed a lot of them were competing. This was misleading. What the track fans saw were the same cars winning time after time. And since the street cars looked so much like the racers, everyone assumed that they were all alike under the skin. This was, of course, a real ego boost for owners of the street cars, not to mention Ford Division.

Carroll Shelby had arranged to sell the Cobra through a network of performance-oriented Ford dealers, and he again used this tactic to get GT-350s into customer hands quickly. Although touted as "not the cars for everybody," they left showrooms as rapidly as they left stoplights. Demand quickly exceeded the production capacity of Shelby's plant, which was also still building Cobras at the time. By the spring of 1965, the newly named Shelby American Inc. had moved from its Venice facility to two huge hangars on the edge of the Los Angeles International Airport.

The first batch of street GT-350s was made available to the automotive press, and virtually every major publication tested and reported on it. But the Shelby had no obvious competitors, so most journalists could do little more than describe the car and its sizzling performance. The GT-350 may have been loud, rough-riding, and a real effort to drive, but the reward was the car's instant response. Function was the key word. Anything that didn't fit in with the car's purpose—to go fast, handle well, and stop quickly—was either modified or thrown out.

In 1965, the street GT-350 sold for about $1000 more than a standard Mustang and an equal amount less than a Corvette. This pricing put it right in the middle of the performance market. With 0–60 mph times averaging 6.5 seconds, a top speed of 130–135 mph, and race car handling and braking, the GT-350 drew rave reviews. It soon became something of a legend, and began to influence Detroit. Suddenly, scoops and rocker panel stripes began appearing on all sorts of otherwise ordinary production models. While other manufacturers never actually offered a car in the same league, quite a few thought they did.

A lesser-known Shelby-Mustang racing effort was made in the National Hot Rod Association. During May 1965, some members of the GT-350 project began exploring the possibilities of campaigning a car in the NHRA B/Sports Production class. An earlier dragster, the "Dragonsnake," had put the Cobra in the public eye. It seemed logical that a properly set up GT-350 could do the same for Mustang.

The first GT-350 drag car was consigned to noted engine and racing car builder Bill Stroppe for evaluation and development. NHRA approved the engine modifications deemed necessary: machine-ported cylinder heads, 1.63-inch exhaust and 1.88-inch intake valves, heavy-duty valve springs, drag headers, and complete balancing and blueprinting. But it was decided that Shelby's "customer' cars would be sold with the stock 306-bhp powerplant. The full-tilt competition engines would be run in the "factory"

cars, and would be available to private owners. Shelby thought making the street engine "standard" had two advantages: the drag car could be sold at a lower price, and it would avoid hard feelings should a customer blow up an expensive factory-built engine. NHRA also approved a scattershield placed in the trunk, mandatory because the car had solid lifters. A clutch and pressure plate designed for dragstrip duty were also certified. Approval meant that these parts could be installed and sold on the car as it left the factory, saving owners the time and expense of removing the engine or transmission to fit these parts later.

Other modifications developed as the drag racer took shape. Cure-Ride 90/10 uplock shock absorbers were installed on the front, and Gabriel 50/50 downlock shocks were used at the rear. Stroppe also designed a set of ladder-bar torque arms, and specified a Hurst "Competition Plus"

Conversion of 1968 Mustangs to Shelbys was done in Michigan instead of at Carroll Shelby's Los Angeles plant. Shelby was starting to ease out of both racing and the car building business and all promotion and advertising of the '68 models was done by Ford. The cars gained more comfort and convenience features and options, giving them a much milder character than the original GT-350s. While this disappointed enthusiasts, it broadened the market for Shelbys. More Shelbys were sold in the 1968 model year than in any other.

shifter. He checked every loophole in the NHRA and AHRA (American Hot Rod Association) regulations, but some of his proposed modifications just wouldn't fit the rules. These included lengthened front spindles, modified seat tracks, re-radiused rear wheels, and relocated front upper control arms. Stroppe even considered a Weber carburetor-equipped, roller-cam Factory Experimental model, but it never got past the bench-test stage.

The first drag racing GT-350 was completed and sold to a Shelby dealer in Lorain, Ohio in August 1965. A second car was bought and run by Mel Burns Ford of Long Beach, California. The actual number of GT-350 drag cars is not known. Most were officially '65s, but a few 1966s were similarly prepared.

At the time the 1966 Shelby-Mustang was being planned, a lot was happening at Ford. The company's all-out exotic performance car, the mid-engine Ford GT, was faltering in international competition, so responsibility for that program was handed over to Carroll Shelby. Ford had developed the GT to carry its banner to the winner's circle in prestigious international endurance events. Since the company had invested a lot of money and faith in Shelby American, it wanted to see a tangible return on its investment—a competitive Ford GT. Thus, Shelby had a lot more on his mind for 1966 than the GT-350 alone.

Feedback from dealers and customers determined most of the changes made to the Shelby-Mustang. The '65 was good, but without a back seat it was too impractical for the buyer with a family. Also, the noisy, lurching Detroit "Locker" rear end howled and clunked at low speeds, which unnerved most people. The side-exit exhaust system was very loud, and illegal in some states. And the

policy of any color you want, so long as it's white did not appeal to some buyers. From Ford came a demand for something called cost-effectiveness (is the cost of each item or modification justified by potential sales). Meantime, the Shelby people were trying to explain roadability to the accountants.

In effect, the alterations in the GT-350 for '66 were brought about by buyers and company product planners, not Carroll Shelby. In concept and as a finished car, the encore edition was not the sort of thing Shelby would have done had the choice been his alone. Buyers seemed to want performance all right, but they didn't want it at the cost of other automotive virtues. So, starting with the '66, the Shelby-Mustang began evolving away from Shelby's original concept toward something with broader market appeal—a car more like the standard Mustang and less like the semi-tamed racer it started out to be.

Most of the revisions for '66 could have been carried out on Ford's own assembly line. However, Shelby did not always incorporate specific changes with the first car of a new model year, using up parts on hand before ordering new ones. Thus, there is no clear distinction between the 1965 and 1966 GT-350s—appropriate for a limited-production manufacturer like Shelby. The first approximately 250 of the '66 models were actually leftover '65s. They received all the '66 cosmetic touches—a new grille, side scoops, and plexiglas rear quarter windows—but retained the 1965 suspension, Koni shocks, and interior, and were still painted white.

When actual 1966 production began, color choices were expanded to red, blue, green, and black, all offered with white racing stripes. A fold-down rear seat, standard on the Mustang fastback, now became an option. Almost all the 1966 cars had it for an obvious reason: it was easier, and more profitable, for Ford to leave it in during initial assembly than for Shelby to remove it and substitute the fiberglass shelf. For the same reason, the battery was now left in its stock underhood position. Heavy-duty Ford-installed shock absorbers were still used, as were the special Pitman and idler arms that gave the '65 its sharp steering. The '65 and early-'66 cars had rear traction bars that ran from the inside of the car to the top of the rear axle; later '66s were fitted with Traction Master underride bars. The early cars also had lowered front A-arms, which altered the steering geometry for improved cornering. This refinement was determined not to be cost effective, so it was discontinued on later '66s.

Engines and drivelines remained mostly the same. The Detroit "Locker" rear end was made an option, as was automatic transmission. Like the '65s, all '66s had large disc brakes in front and large drums with sintered metallic linings at the rear. Extra pedal pressure was required with these brakes, but they didn't fade. The 15-inch-diameter wheels were now replaced by 14-inch rims, either chrome styled steel or cast aluminum alloy at the buyer's option. All '66s received plexiglas rear quarter windows in place of the stock Mustang fastback's louvers as used on '65 Shelbys. This brought the bonus of improved over-the-shoulder visibility.

While the 1966 GT-350 wasn't quite as loud or fierce as the '65 version, Shelby nevertheless kept it interesting. As

an option, he offered a Paxton centrifugal supercharger. (A special GT-350S model was envisioned but never actually released.) The blown engine was advertised with a horsepower increase of "up to 46 percent."

Increased production was planned for 1966 so every dealer who wanted cars could get them. Shelby also sold the Hertz Rent-A-Car Company on the idea of buying about 1000 specially trimmed units designated GT-350H and finished in black with gold stripes. Hertz rented them at major airports throughout 1966. A good many returned from a weekend's rental with definite signs of competition use. Not surprisingly, Hertz found the GT-350H program a mite unprofitable, and called it off after this one year only.

Shelby-Mustang production for the second model year was 2380, including the 936 Hertz cars and six specially built convertibles that Shelby gave to friends as gifts. No racing cars were constructed, though a few leftover '65s were registered as 1966s. Shelbys continued to race and win that year, although they were essentially the same cars that had run the year before.

Overshadowed by the GT-350's stunning success in SCCA "club" racing in this period was its performance in the Trans-American Sedan Championship. First run in 1966, the Trans-Am was essentially an offshoot of the SCCA's sedan class events. It was intended as a series of "mini-enduros" ranging anywhere from 200 to 2400 miles, two to 24 hours, thus requiring pit stops for fuel and tires. The Trans-Am attracted Mustangs, Barracudas, Falcons, Dodge Darts, and a host of under-2.0-liter cars. By the end of its inaugural season it had become one of the most popular series on the SCCA schedule, due partly to a good many professional factory entries. To make things more interesting, a Manufacturer's Trophy was awarded to the maker whose cars won the most races. Driver ego took a back seat as each factory vied with its rivals to establish or uphold its performance reputation.

Trans-Am rules were based on FIA Appendix J specifications for Series Production Cars (Group 1) or Touring Cars

Big-block engines were the rage among American driving enthusiasts in the late 1960s and the desire for heavy metal under the hood showed in Shelby sales. The 428-cid GT-500 models outsold the small-block GT-350s 2-to-1 in 1968. Since the big V-8 cost only $200 more than the 302-cid engine, the initial price wasn't much different.

(Group 2). The senior class was limited to displacement between 2000 and 5000cc, a maximum wheelbase of 116 inches, and minimal performance modifications. Since only four-seaters were allowed, the GT-350 was not allowed because it was officially a two-seater. In its place, the Mustang notchback hardtop was pressed into service.

The 1966 schedule had seven races, but the winner wasn't decided until the season closer at Riverside, California—the series was that close all year. But it was at Riverside that a huge, blue Shelby American race van appeared with a Shelby-ized notchback Mustang for Jerry Titus, editor of *Sports Car Graphic* and a former GT-350 team driver. Titus took the pole position in qualifying laps, and ultimately won the race, which gave the Manufacturer's Trophy to Ford. But Shelby American's eleventh-hour appearance signaled a change in Ford's racing priorities, probably due to the realization that the 1967 GT-350 would not be as competitive as the 1965 R-models. The factory's Trans-Am effort would now have to be carried out with Mustang notchbacks.

Earlier in the season, Shelby American had permitted Mustang sedan competitors to participate in its race assistance program, because the notchbacks shared virtually all mechanical components with the GT-350s. This support was later withdrawn, because it was felt that there was not enough product identification between the Shelbys and the stock notchback "sedans." Ford took up the slack by offering limited factory support to outstanding non-Shelby teams. By the end of the season, both Ford and Shelby American were committed to besting one another in the Trans-Am.

The production Mustang became larger, heavier, and more "styled" for 1967, which meant the GT-350 would be, too. To keep the car's weight down and its appearance distinctive, Shelby stylists created a special fiberglass front end to complement Dearborn's longer hood. They also put two high-beam headlamps in the center of the grille opening. (Some cars have these lamps moved to the outer ends of the grille to comply with state motor vehicle requirements specifying a minimum distance between headlamps.) The Shelby also used a larger hood scoop and new sculptured brake cooling scoops on the sides. Another set of scoops on the rear-quarter roof panels acted as interior air extractors. The rear end received a spoiler and a large bank of taillights. The result was stunning: the '67 Shelby looked more like a racing car than many racers. There was still nothing else like it.

Because the '67 was heavier than its predecessors, and because customer feedback indicated a preference for a more manageable car, power steering and power brakes were now mandatory options. The newly reworked interior received some special appointments not shared with the production Mustang: a distinctive racing steering wheel, additional gauges, and a genuine rollbar with built-in inertia-reel shoulder harnesses.

Ford offered its big-block 390 V-8 as the top performance option for the '67 Mustang. In typical Shelby style, Carroll went one better by dropping in a 428 to create a second model, the GT-500. It was a highly popular move, and outsold the smaller-engine car by a two-to-one margin. The GT-350 still carried the 289-cid small-block warmed to Shelby specifications, but now without the steel-tube exhaust headers.

All these changes brought about something new for Shelby: performance with luxury. No longer was performance being emphasized above everything else. Since carmakers adopted more conservative horsepower ratings for 1967, mainly to keep the insurance companies happy, the GT-500 was listed at only 355 bhp, although it certainly

had more than that. The GT-350 was rated at its customary 306 bhp. That was odd because, without the headers and straight-through mufflers, output was certainly lower than this. Shelby American made no attempt to race any of its '67 models, of which 3225 were built.

Not wanting to let its 1966 Trans-Am championship seem like a fluke, Ford sponsored a full-fledged, two-car Mustang victory team put together by Shelby American for the '67 campaign. The canary yellow notchbacks with flat-black hoods ran under the banner of "Terlingua Racing Team," an honorary team composed of "sponsors" of Shelby's Terlingua (Texas) Boys' Ranch. But Shelby now had to face a rash of other factory-backed teams running new-model ponycars. A brace of Cougars was fielded by stock car ace Bud Moore. A Camaro prepared by Roger Penske was piloted by a former GT-350 driver, Mark Donohue. Other well-known hotshoes such as Dan Gurney, Parnelli Jones, George Follmer, Peter Revson, David Pearson, Ronnie Bucknum, and Jerry Titus joined the fray. The '67 season was extended to 13 races, and Shelby American's Mustang notchback crossed the finish line often

enough to pick up the trophy for Ford for a second year. Interestingly, most of the factory's attention that season was paid to the Bud Moore Cougars, which got more financial consideration than other Ford teams, plus "trick" parts and drivers Gurney and Jones.

By 1968, Carroll Shelby was beginning to tire of the car business. His GT-350 had dominated SCCA competition, and his Ford GT effort had culminated with wins at Le Mans in 1966 and 1967. He had also seen many close friends lose their lives on the race track. Meanwhile, racing was becoming increasingly competitive and thus expensive, and new technology was making it impossible for all but a few specialists to grasp new principles and apply them successfully. Racing, Shelby decided, wasn't fun anymore: it was business. And building his own cars had lost much of its original attraction because Ford was now calling most of the shots.

At the end of the 1967 model run, Shelby-Mustang production was transferred from Los Angeles to Michigan, where the A. O. Smith Company was contracted to carry out conversions on stock Mustangs. All promotion and

advertising for Shelby cars was handled by Ford. The '68 models were treated to a facelift: a new hood and nose, sequential rear turn signals, and a new convertible body style, available in both GT-350 and GT-500 form. The GT-350 was switched to the new 302-cid enlargement of the small-block V-8, mostly for emission reasons. Luxury options like air conditioning, tilt steering wheel, tinted glass, and AM/FM stereo now outnumbered performance features. At mid-year, the 428-cid engine was replaced by the 428 "Cobra Jet" unit, which had made a name for itself on the dragstrips, and brought a new KR designation (King of the Road) for the GT-500. Again the big-block Shelbys were more popular, outselling the GT-350s by two-to-one. Total production for the model year was 4450.

Shelby American still had its eye on the Trans-Am in 1968. Group 2 rules had become difficult to manage, so SCCA bent them a bit this year. Engines were still restricted to 5.0 liters (305 cid), but a minimum weight of 2800 pounds was set, and wheel rims up to eight inches wide could be used. The schedule again included 13 events. Shelby's Mustangs and Penske's Camaros were

Ford restyled the Mustang for 1969, making it longer and heavier. Shelby's designers modified the front end with a longer hood, fiberglass fenders to reduce weight, and a nose cap also made of fiberglass. The strongest engine was the 428 Cobra Jet introduced in mid-1968. GT-500s no longer received the KR designation that had been used the previous year.

joined by a pair of factory-backed AMC Javelins, while the Cougars bowed out. The Shelby racers were painted blue or red, had flat black hoods, and ran under the "Shelby Racing Co." banner. Titus, still the lead Shelby driver, finished first in the Daytona 24-hour opener. But by the second race, the Penske/Donohue Camaro team was starting to click. They won races 2 through 9 before Titus broke the string at Watkins Glen. By that time there was no catching Camaro, and it went on to take the championship.

By 1969, things were starting to change in the auto industry. The first emission and safety regulations were in effect, and insurance premiums in the region of $1000 were being quoted for 25-year-old males who drove hot cars.

Buyer tastes were changing, too: performance was becoming less important than luxury. Shelby saw the handwriting on the wall. Ever the individualist, he had begun by building the sort of car he himself wanted to drive. He didn't like decisions made by committees, where accountants and lawyers usually overruled engineers and test drivers. And the niche he had created for his cars in the Ford lineup was gradually being taken over by production models like the Mach 1 and Boss 302.

Mustang got a new bodyshell and heavily revised styling for 1969, and the Shelby changed accordingly. To make the heavier, longer, busier production car look considerably more rakish, Shelby's designers extended the hood, fitted a fiberglass front end with a large grille cavity, added reshaped fiberglass front fenders for reduced weight, clipped off the tail, bolted a spoiler on the rear deck, and continued the sequential turn signal feature from the Cougar. The GT-350 received the new 351 "Windsor" engine. The 428

CJ continued for the GT-500, and the KR designation was dropped. Convertibles were still available. As usual, GT-500s outsold GT-350s, and the total number of 1969 cars was 3150. Fuel injection had been considered, as were a moonroof and reclining seats, but these and other ideas never made it to production.

For the 1969 Trans-Am season the rules were changed once more, and now differed even more from those governing Group 2 sedans. Mustang fastbacks were now legal, and Dearborn's new Boss 302 was the hot ticket. Shelby's team prepared a pair of these, for Peter Revson and Horst

The distinctive Shelby touch set the GT-500s apart from regular production Mustangs with a standard roll bar, prominent spoiler bolted to the rear, and unique rectangular tailpipes mounted in the center, just below the bumper. The long row of taillights on the Shelbys also borrowed a sequential turn signal feature from the Mercury Cougar.

Kwech, for the 12-race schedule. A second team fielded by Bud Moore had Parnelli Jones and George Follmer in the driver's seats. Massive factory engineering efforts now produced semi-tube frame chassis (thinly disguised as roll cages), acid-dipped bodies, huge tires, flared fenders, spoilers, wings, and mind-boggling horsepower. The Boss 302 canted-valve engine made an impressive debut in the season curtain-raiser. After a post-race check of lap charts, Parnelli Jones' Mustang was declared the winner. The second race, at Lime Rock, Connecticut, was won by Sam Posey in a Shelby-prepared Boss 302. It would be the Shelby team's only victory that year. At Riverside on October 4, 1969, Carroll Shelby announced his retirement as a racing car developer and team manager.

Shelby also said goodbye to the car business that year. He was no longer a force in the design or production of the cars that bore his name, and competition from other hot pony-cars, including some of Ford Division's own models, had caught up with the softer, slower 1968–69 Shelbys. And on top of all that, his cars weren't even being raced much any more. Ford Division general manager Lee Iacocca saw the end of the road, too, and agreed with Shelby to terminate the program quietly. Cars still in the production pipeline at the end of model year 1969 were given Boss 302 front spoilers, black hoods, and new serial numbers, all mainly for show, and a little over 600 of these 1970 Shelbys were built. Just like that, it was over.

It's somewhat ironic, then, that the Trans-Am reached its peak interest and excitement in the 1970 season. Despite the absence of the Shelby team, there were at least a half-dozen other big league entries: Penske Javelins, Bud Moore Boss 302 Mustangs, Jim Hall's Chaparral Camaros, Jerry Titus' Firebirds, Dan Gurney's Barracudas, Sam Posey's Dodge Challengers, and the Owens/Corning Camaros. Mustang was champion once again, beating all its impressive rivals.

The Shelby GT-350s that debuted in 1965 were race cars first, passenger cars second, building an impressive performance reputation for the special breed of Mustangs. Here a GT-350 leads a pack of sports cars at the start of a race at Elkhart Lake, Wis.

After 1970, the factories began to withdraw their Trans-Am support, possibly because they had created an overwhelming amount of competition. This left the field wide open for many capable independents but, as they quickly learned, the price of being competitive was astronomical. Also, Detroit's ponycars were bigger and heavier than they used to be, and foreign makes like Porsche, Alfa Romeo, and Datsun had started to win races regularly. In a desperate attempt to attract the large crowds of 1970, SCCA allowed A-Production, B-Production, and A-Sedan cars to compete in the 1971 Trans-Am series: Corvettes, Camaros, Datsun Zs—even Cobras and GT-350s—all together. But it wasn't the same. The electricity of earlier seasons had all but disappeared.

Detroit was forced to redefine performance as the '70s wore on. Each succeeding year brought a less inspiring crop of cars with progressively less power and longer 0–60 mph times. Yet it was precisely because of this that Carroll Shelby's very special Mustangs came to be appreciated anew. Astute car collectors began snapping them up as fast as they could, and values started to skyrocket. Today there's quite a good deal of confusion over precisely what a Shelby-Mustang should be worth, but there's no disputing the caliber of any of these cars. They stand as exciting, high-performance *gran turismos*—uniquely American in character, born of a uniquely American passion for pavement-ripping power and blinding acceleration. Yet they also possessed world-class handling and, in later years, levels of luxury and reliability most foreign GTs were hard pressed to match.

Carroll Shelby showed how much depth existed in Ford's basic ponycar package, and he did it with a style all his own. The Shelby GTs were first and foremost one man's idea of what Mustang could and ought to be. Today, as a generation ago, they remain the ultimate ponycars.

Shelby Production by Model Year

Year	GT-350	GT-500	Total
1965	562	—	562
1966	2380*	—	2380
1967	1175	2050	3225
1968	1648	2802**	4450
1969	1279	1871	3150
1970	315	286	601

*includes 936 GT-350H models
**includes 1246 GT-500KR models

Shelby Retail Prices, 1965–69

Year	GT-350 Fastback	GT-350 Convertible	GT-500 Fastback	GT-500 Convertible
1965	$4547	—	—	—
1966	$4428	—	—	—
1967	$3995	—	$4195	—
1968	$4117	$4238	$4317	$4438
1969	$4434	$4753	$4709	$5027

MUSTANG RESTORATION

The Californian who was the first owner of the '65 Mustang that carries the warranty indentification number 5R09T190623 probably wouldn't have recognized the car by the time it arrived in the Chicago area in July 1982. About the only things that hand't changed were that it was still a fastback and it still had a 6-cylinder engine. A car that had started life painted "Rangoon Red" now was a patchwork of colors. The hood, roof, and quarter panels were white; one door was green, the other burgundy. The right fender was covered with a coat of charcoal grey primer and only the left fender was red. The faded fender looked more like Rundown Red than "Ran-

goon Red." The license plates showed that it was last registered in Arizona.

A large dent in the left rear quarter showed where the sheetmetal apparently was pushed in when the car was bashed in the lower left corner. Smaller dents and scratches acquired over 55,000 miles of use and abuse gave the sheetmetal a worn, rippled surface. Inside, red vinyl upholstery, a well-soiled red carpet, and a torn black driver's seat were badly in need of repair. The T-bar handle was missing from the shifter and the throttle lacked a pedal.

It was a clunker, a real beater, like the kind you find in the back rows of used car lots, but it was what we

wanted—an early Mustang, the original ponycar that set sales records and set trends. It was one of 680,989 Mustangs produced in that first, long model year that started in the spring of 1964 and it was an unusual combination of fastback body, 6-cylinder engine, automatic transmission, and power steering. Beneath the weathered paint was a solid body with little rust. The sound sheetmetal could be pounded back into shape without major surgery. The scars of 17 years of service could be covered with fresh coats of enamel. Our Mustang looked rough that day it arrived in Chicago, but it was a diamond in the rough. It was a very restorable Mustang.

When CONSUMER GUIDE® magazine set out to restore an early Mustang, our search for a 1965 or 1966 model started close to home, in the Chicago area. We were quickly reminded of a sad fact of life in the Midwest. The long, snowy winters and the mounds of salt spread on the roads are murder on cars. Most early Mustangs we found had serious rust problems. Lower quarter panels, trunk floor, rockers, and fenders were frequently eaten away by rust, which would make the restoration more difficult and expensive.

We turned to an expert for help, and we think other Mustang enthusiasts should do the same before starting a major restoration. We contacted Don Chambers, owner of Mustang Country, a shop in Paramount, Calif., that specializes in new and used Mustang parts and does partial or complete restorations. We also found that Don buys and sells Mustangs and he pointed out the obvious advantage of buying a car that has compiled all or most of its miles in a warm, dry climate such as Southern California's. The biggest problems from the weather is that the bright sun

Don Chambers (left), who supplied the Mustang and most of the parts for the restoration project, and his assistant, John Hare. Don is the owner of Mustang Country in Paramount, Calif.

fades the paint, which is a lot easier to deal with than repairing the ravages of rust.

Don had a '65 fastback parked behind his shop that was cheaper than anything comparable we had seen around Chicago, even considering the cost of shipping it 2,000 miles by truck. He offered to hang used doors and fenders on the Mustang, advising it would be cheaper than trying to repair the badly damaged ones on the car. We had a deal, with Don agreeing to being our main parts source through the well-stocked shelves of Mustang Country.

When the car arrived, we found a great deal about it just by reading the patent plate. The number on the patent plate (63A J 25 24B 71 2 6) identified it as a standard (as opposed to deluxe) fastback that was painted in Rangoon Red and trimmed in red vinyl when it was built on Feb. 24, 1965. The car had been ordered by a Ford dealer in the Los Angeles district.

The axle ratio was 2.83:1 and the transmission was Ford's C-4 automatic. The first digit of the warranty number (5R09T190623) confirms that this was indeed a '65 model and the "R" means it was built at the San Jose, Calif., assembly plant. "09" is the body code for fastbacks and "T" denotes the 200-cubic inch 6-cylinder engine. "190623" is the consecutive unit number for '65 model cars assembled at San Jose.

For the body repair and painting, we took our Mustang to River Trail Auto Body in Wheeling, Ill., because of their reputation for quality work. Owner Roy Cerino and one of his expert body men, Art Taylor, immediately spotted telltale signs of rust and they became skeptical about the condition of the sheet-

Gus Soto, painter; Roy Cerino, owner; and Art Taylor, body man; of River Trail Auto Body in Wheeling, Ill.

metal. However, after grinding off some paint and pounding a few dents, they were convinced that the metal was sound. We were ready to decide how far to go with our restoration project.

Our first decision was that we would not attempt a complete restoration in which the car is stripped to the bare bones, cleaned to a factory-fresh finish, and reassembled and prepped into show-winning condition. As exciting a proposition as that sounds, we felt it would be beyond the capabilities and financial resources of most of our readers. The tools, facilities, and technical know-how for a complete restoration also would be too much for many people. Finally, a show car is just that, for show only. Our goal was to restore a car that could be driven frequently, if not daily, without worrying about what the judges will find when they go under the car with white gloves.

Clearly, a compromise was in order. We wanted the car to look good inside and out. That meant body repair, paint, new upholstery and interior trim, and new or rechromed brightwork. It also had to run reliably and safely once it was finished, so new tires, a complete engine check, and whatever mechanical repairs were needed had to be done too. We weren't aiming for concours condition, but we wanted people to notice our shiny '65 Mustang when we drove around town, and we wanted it to look smart from up close.

Our goal is to demonstrate to people who have basic tools and enjoy working with their hands what it takes to restore a Mustang to near original condition. That's why we again went to experts. The people who restored our Mustang take cars apart and put

them back together for a living. Their experience in mending bent and broken car bodies will help you put your Mustang into shape. Our step-by-step photos highlight how you should proceed in taking apart, repairing, and replacing body panels, reupholstering the interior, painting, and detailing your car so it will be restored to top condition.

The interior was done by Eckhardt Auto Glass & Trim of Morton Grove, Ill., which does trim work for a large number of body shops and car dealers in northwest suburban Chicago. The men at Eckhardt demonstrated how old pieces can be cleaned and painted to look like new, but they also pointed out where we had to replace parts that we hadn't considered (or didn't

know were missing!). One of the pitfalls of a partial restoration, we learned, is that pieces that aren't refurbished or replaced often stick out like sore thumbs. We ended up needing more parts than we first thought. We also needed a parts source closer to home than Don Chambers' Mustang Country in California. We found one in nearby Bensenville, Ill., at Bob Tessarolo's Mustang of Chicago, a small store that carries a big line of Mustang parts, from body panels and suspension components to engine decals.

Yet, even with two parts suppliers for a car that was originally driveable, we were still missing some small pieces that aren't reproduced or weren't in stock. So off to the local boneyards we went to crawl

The crew at Eckhardt Auto Glass & Trim Ltd. of Morton Grove, Ill. (left to right): Mike Arnott, Danny Kmiecik, Bruce Winner, manager, Rick Fournier, Cesar Solano, Bill Lappa, and Antonio Osorio.

Bob Tessarolo, owner of Mustang of Chicago in Bensenville, Ill., the local parts supplier for the restoration.

Skip Hahn (left) and Gary Radtke of Ye Olde Tunesmith, Ltd. of Skokie, Ill., who did the mechanical work on the Mustang.

inside junked Mustangs in search of rubber hood stops, a gas pedal, shifter handle, molding clips, and other odds and ends. Unless you buy a Mustang that is complete or needs only a few new parts, you'll probably spend some time in the junkyards in your area. Most don't allow customers to take the parts off junked cars themselves, but if you explain that all you need is this little piece, or that small part, they might let you wander back there with some tools. While you're at it, give the Mustangs you find a good looking over. You might spot some other things that will come in handy later.

For engine and mechanical work, we found a couple of craftsmen in Skokie, a few blocks from our editorial offices. The first thing about them that caught our eyes was their name, Ye Olde Tunesmith, Ltd. The next thing that caught our eyes was the 1950 Ford Custom Tudor sedan parked next to the shop. It's owned by Gary Radtke, one of the tunesmiths. Inside we found a 1959 MGA roadster being restored by his partner, Skip Hahn. They both had special affection for older cars. Our kind of people.

Before you start on your restoration, be advised that

the people who did ours have thousands of dollars worth of tools and equipment and many years of experience. The hobbyist working out of his garage with limited facilities is at a distinct disadvantage in trying to accomplish the same things. If you're handy or have some experience with cars, so much the better. If this is your first try at such an ambitious project, take inventory of the tools you have and try to assess what you'll need—at the least, a complete socket wrench set, some hammers and dollies for straightening dents, a variety of screwdrivers, and Allen wrenches. You'll also need jack stands for working under the car (hydraulic jacks also will make your job much easier than regular jacks). Power tools will save a lot of straining (and swearing!). You might be able to rent them if you don't want to buy. You'll need an air compressor for painting. These too can be rented (if you can't borrow one from a friend). Before you start turning wrenches, give the car a good going over to get an idea of how much work will be involved and which parts need to be replaced. Take your time when you work. It's better to work slowly and get it right than to rush through a job and discover you did it wrong. You won't save any time if you have to do it over. As you take things off the car, keep everything together. Drop nuts, bolts, and washers into small plastic bags, for example, and label them so you know where they belong later on. If your memory isn't always reliable, you might also scribble a diagram or a few notes about how you disassembled something. Put the notes into the same bag as the nuts and bolts and you'll have homemade instructions on how to put it together.

Finally, our Mustang originally was red. We painted it white on the advice of our experts at the body shop. "White covers a lot of sins," they told us over and over, and it's something to think about. It's very difficult (sometimes impossible) to pound metal back into original shape. A dark color like red will make it easier to spot the subtle wrinkles and imperfections. Purists will insist on red. We think it looks great in white.

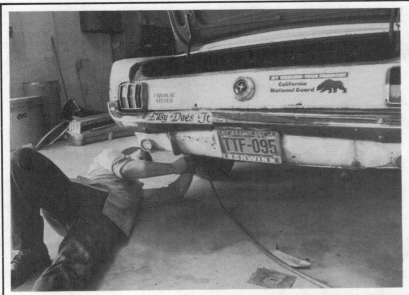

Taking Apart the Exterior

1: Remove the bumper guards first. Rear guards are attached by two bolts; one through the trunk floor and one underneath the gravel pan.

2: The rear bumper is attached to the body by four bolts through the trunk floor. The bolts are located in pairs on either side of the braces welded to the back of the trunk.

3: Pull the bumper off the body. Inner brackets are bolted to bumper and can be removed for cleaning. If your Mustang is like ours, you'll need to have the bumpers rechromed.

4: To remove the rear gravel pan, disconnect the backup light wires and remove the retaining screws that were hidden by the bumper. The pan also has two bolts through brackets in the lower corners that are hard to reach.

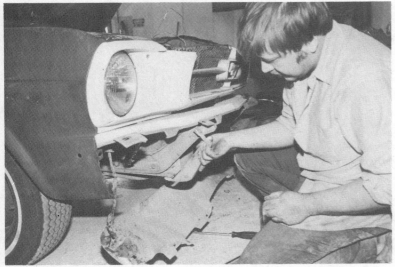

5: Front bumper guards are bolted through upper and lower brackets. Photo shows location of brackets after bumper and gravel pan were removed.

6: Front bumper has bolts on each side into the fender. Reach into the fender well to get at them.

7: Four bolts hold the bumper to brackets in the front of the car. These bolts have special spacers that prevent damage to the chrome by tightening them too much. Save those spacers for when you put the bumper back on the car.

8: Carefully pull the bumper off the brackets and note where the brackets are located so you'll have an easier time putting the front end back together.

9: Front gravel pan has four bolts through the top and one bolt through the bottom corners into the front of each fender.

10: After all the bolts are removed, you can pull the pan out from body and let it hang by the parking light wires.

11: Since the parking light wires are connected to the headlights, you'll have to break down the headlight assembly to disconnect the wiring. The headlight bezel is attached with four screws.

12: Remove the headlights and pull wiring out so you can snap out the parking light wires from connectors and remove the gravel pan.

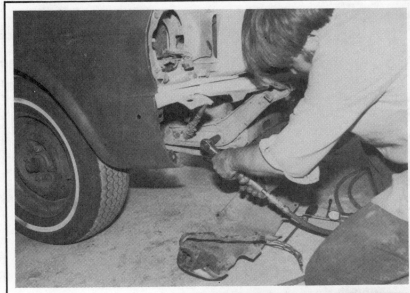

13: Bumper brackets are attached to the frame by two bolts. Two brackets on each side are welded into one piece.

14: The grille has four bolts on the top; two near the center and one on each end.

15: Four more bolts are located behind the grille along the bottom. You'll need an extension on your socket wrench to reach them.

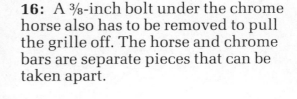

16: A ⅜-inch bolt under the chrome horse also has to be removed to pull the grille off. The horse and chrome bars are separate pieces that can be taken apart.

17: The chrome grille moldings are attached by a screw and spring clips that can be pried off with a screwdriver.

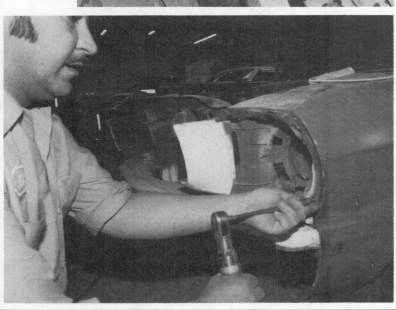

18: Headlight doors have four bolts into the fenders. The headlight buckets are held by two screws. A spring that creates the tension for aiming the headlights is hooked to the doors and buckets; make a note on how it is attached so you'll be able to reassemble it correctly.

19: To remove door locks and handles, you'll have to remove the door panels to disconnect the rod linkage for the locks. The linkage is held by a U-shaped pressure clip and the lock will slide out once the clip is removed.

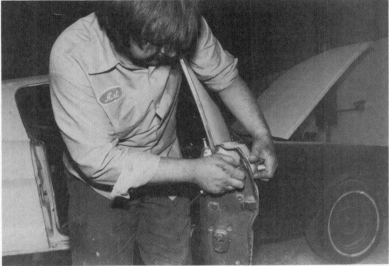

20: The handle is held by a screw near the door edge and a retaining nut inside the door panel.

Remove all chrome trim like "FORD" letters on hood and "Mustang 2+2" emblems on fenders. They are attached with barrel nuts. Pry the letters up carefully with a thin blade screwdriver. You may want to remove the hood and trunk lid for repairs and painting; unbolt them at the hinges, but have somebody help you so you don't drop them while removing the bolts.

Removing Fenders

1: If you're going to replace a fender, chances are the new one won't have holes drilled for fender emblems. Make a template for where the holes should be drilled by taping a sheet of paper to the old fender and poking holes through it from the other side. Tape the template to the new fender and you'll know right where to drill. Reverse the template, and you can use it on the other side.

Another hint: if you buy new fender emblems, the mounting pegs will probably be larger than the originals, so you'll have to drill out existing holes to make them bigger.

2: Early Mustangs have a hidden fender bolt behind the kick panels. With the door removed, it's easy to see the bracket for the hidden bolt (though you don't have to remove the door to reach it).

3: You'll have to unscrew the door sill moldings to remove the kick panels.

4: With the kick panel removed, pull out the rubber fender plug and loosen the hidden bolt.

5: Another bolt is located in the doorjamb above the upper door hinge.

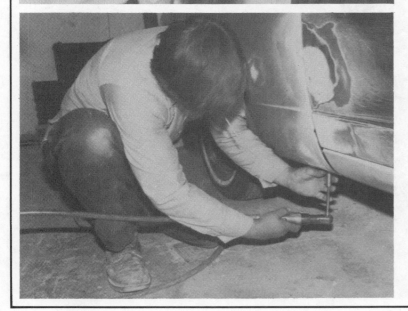

6: The lower fender is bolted to the frame near the rocker panel.

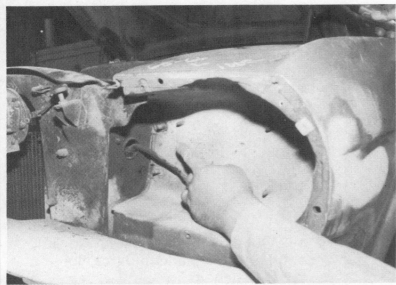

7: Two more bolts through the fender well extend into the headlight housing. Photo shows where they come through, but you'll have to remove them from inside the fender well.

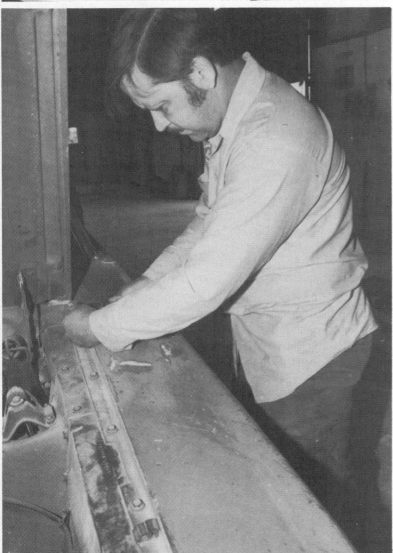

8: Finally, remove the six bolts in a row that attach the fender to the engine compartment. Push the headlight wiring through the hole in the fender and you're ready to pull it off the car.

Hanging Fenders

1: Hanging a fender might require two people to set it in place. Once you've mounted it on the car, loosely attach some of the bolts to the fender compartment so it will hang in place.

2: Make sure first that it fits properly by the door. Pound the fender into place with the palm of your hand. Match lines and corners on the fender with those in the door before tightening the bolts.

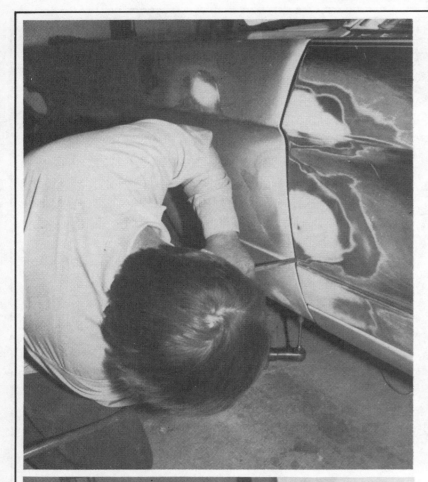

3: With the fender loosely in place, open and close the door a few times to make sure it clears the fender. A screwdriver wedged into the crack between the fender and door will help you maintain proper clearance while you tighten the lower bolt.

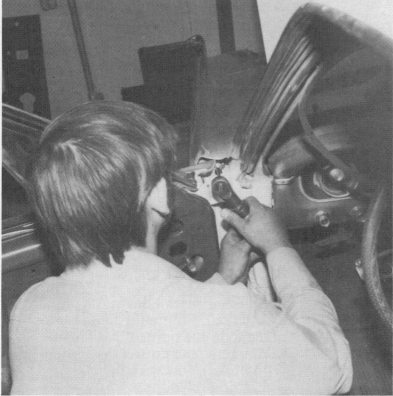

4: Tighten the bolt in the doorjamb and the hidden bolt behind the kick panel. Then loosely attach the two bolts in the fender well, check how the fender lines up, and tighten the rest of the bolts.

Repairing Dents

If you're lucky, your Mustang will have only minor dents that can easily be pounded out or filled in by hand. We weren't so lucky. Ours had a pretty severe dent in the lower left corner, which also resulted in a deep wrinkle further forward on the quarter panel and a bend in the doorjamb that made aligning the left door difficult.

All three problems could have been fixed without the aid of a professional body alignment tool, but we found out some advantages of using the body aligner.

First, it's a lot less work. Swinging a 4-pound hammer gets awfully tiring. If you've got the time, and the strength, to do it all by hand, more power to you. Remember, with the Mustang's unit-body construction, a collision results in a ripple effect. By pulling the dent like we did, you're undoing the ripple effects as well, saving you more work.

We recognize that very few people will have a body aligner in their garage, but we think you could swing a deal with a body shop to pull a major dent like ours and leave the rest of the job to yourself.

1: A hole is pounded in the dent and a chain is shackled to the inside of the dented area.

2: The power body aligner pulls out the dent most of the way and straightens the rest of the quarter panel.

143

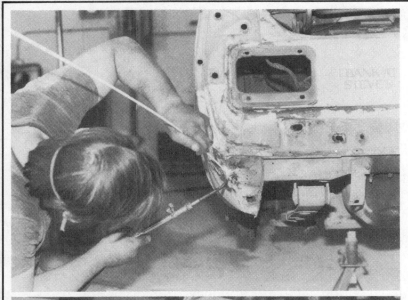

3: Holes from pulling or pounding dents can be plugged with body filler or welded like ours was. Welding the holes gives it greater durability. Smooth out weld spots with a wire brush.

4: The rest of the work has to be done by hand. You'll need different size hammers for different kinds of dents, and dollies and body spoons to help flatten the sheetmetal. Run your hand along the body to find high and low spots; you won't always see them right away.

5: Use a dolly on the other side to help flatten the sheetmetal. In some cases, you can use a hunk of wood like a 2-by-4 to help flatten the body.

Repairing Dents

6: Strategically placed blocks of wood can help square bent lines, as shown on the trunk lid. Also, check how the lock in the lid fits into the plate in the rear panel when you close the lid. The plate on ours was off center, pushing the lid to the right.

7: A 4-pound hammer has a large head for straightening body panels that are supposed to be flat.

8: If you're straightening metal where another panel is supposed to fit snugly, stop periodically and see how well it is lining up.

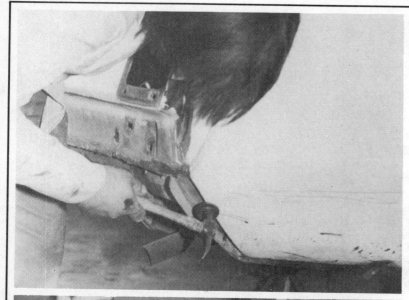

9: Straighten the metal as much as you can. The less body filler you have to use the better. Pay particular attention to corners and edges, where other pieces have to fit. Strive for square lines.

10: After pounding out the dents, grind the paint off to bare metal, taking off all rust. Low spots in the metal will show up as those that still have paint on them as you grind evenly across the panel.

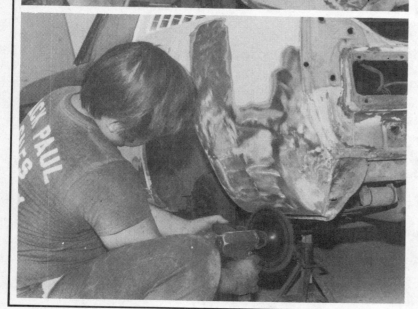

11: You can sand the paint, primer, and rust off by hand with coarse sandpaper (like No. 50), but it will go much faster with an electric drill equipped with a sanding disc. Be careful when grinding not to stay in the same spot too long; you can overheat the steel and push it out of shape.

12: After grinding, mix body filler according to the directions of the manufacturer. Keep in mind when applying that body filler dries much faster on a hot day, so you won't have to use as much hardener when you mix it and you should mix smaller batches.

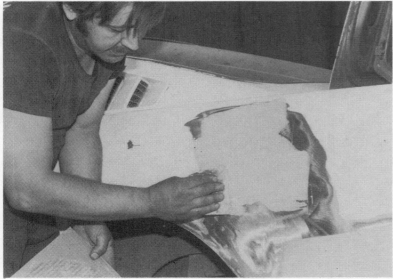

13: Apply the filler as smoothly as possible with a plastic spreader. If it's lumpy, that's more that will have to be filed off. As soon as it starts getting gummy, stop spreading it. It's already too dry to apply evenly.

14: An air file or a hand file is needed to sand the dried body filler down to a smooth surface.

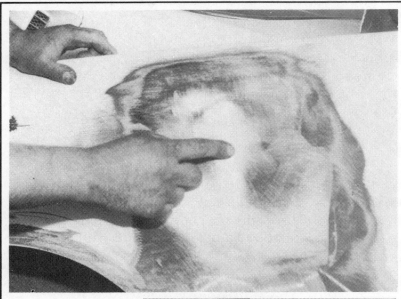

15: After filing it down so it's smooth, you'll be able to see the low spots where filler is left. You'll probably have to go over it again with body filler to get all of the tiny holes and trouble spots.

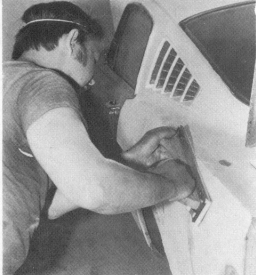

16: When using a hand file, be sure to file up and down as well as across and keep the file as flat as possible to get it back to the original shape.

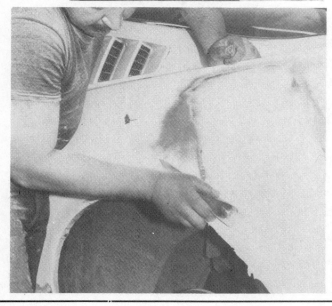

17: On rounded surfaces and edges, wrap fine sandpaper around a piece of pipe, rubber hose, or a broom handle to make a round sanding surface.

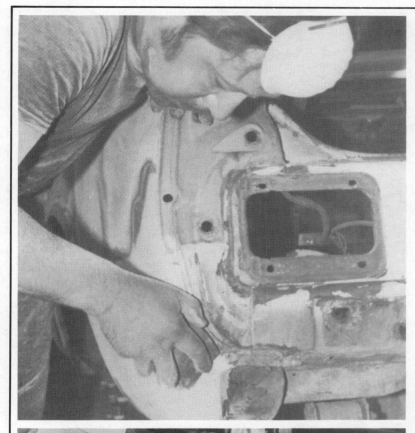

18: Use a wooden sanding block to file the edges so the lines are straight. You'll need smooth edges so body panels fit correctly.

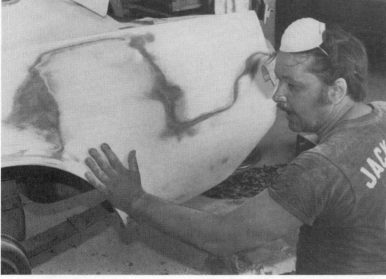

19: Experts don't just look for high and low spots, they feel for them by running their hands across the metal. The smoother the surface, the better it will look when it's painted.

Removing Doors

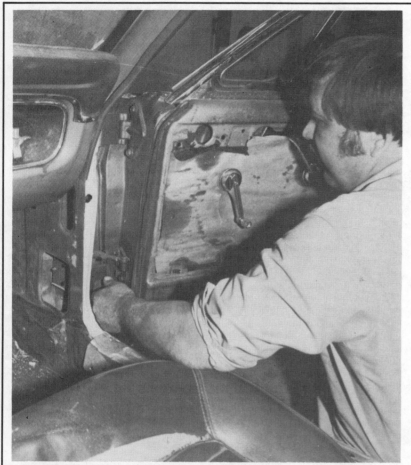

1: If you have to remove a door (we did to repair a rust hole), it can be done by one person. Remove the three bolts in the lower hinge first. Let the rear end of the door rest on blocks or a sturdy crate like the kind used to haul milk cartons.

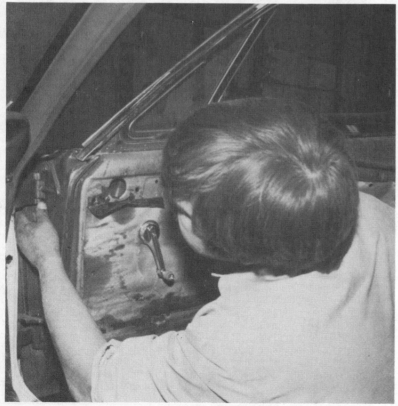

2: Remove the two bolts on the top hinge. Be sure the rear end of the door is securely resting on blocks or a crate so the weight of the door doesn't bend the hinges.

Patching Holes

Very small holes can be plugged with body filler or welded, but we found a pretty-good size rust spot on the front lower corner of the right door that needed to be patched with something more substantial. Some prefer to cut the rusted sheetmetal and weld a new piece in its place. Others recommend a fiberglass bridge patch. Our body man spot welded a small piece of sheetmetal over the hole, saying it was easier than cutting a section of the door and stronger than fiberglass. Before patching a hole, hammer out all the rust so you will be rid of all the moisture and then sand the area around the hole down to bare metal.

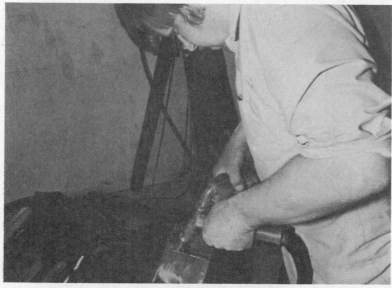

1: Cut a piece of sheetmetal that overlaps the hole about two inches on each side and hold it securely in place while you spot weld it. Instead of welding the patch, you can braise it along the edges with an acetylene torch. If you weld it, do it close to the edges.

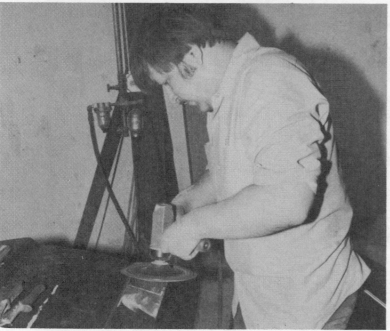

2: Use a wire brush to smooth out the weld burn marks so the body filler you will apply will have a better surface to adhere to.

Patching Holes

3: Apply body filler and file down carefully so you're feathering the edges, trying to disguise where the patch ends. Apply a second coat of filler if needed. Remember though that you can't apply so much body filler that it will leave a bulge in the metal.

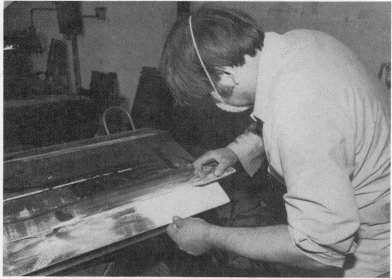

4: Go over the edges with a sanding block to make sure your lines are straight. Sloppy lines will detract from the car's appearance.

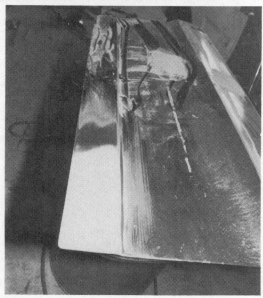

5: The finished patch, now ready for priming. Close attention to detail will result in a neat job like this one.

Hanging Doors

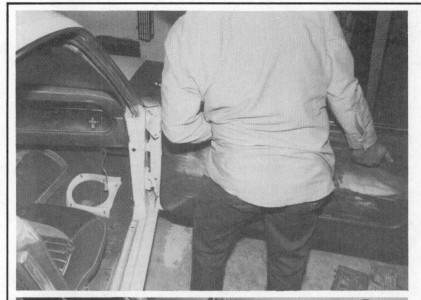

1: It's much easier for two people to hang a door, but one person can do it. Rest the rear of the door on a jack stand, wood crate or other sturdy object that's roughly the same height as the rocker panel. Then rest the front of the door on the rocker panel and line up the hinges with the bolt holes.

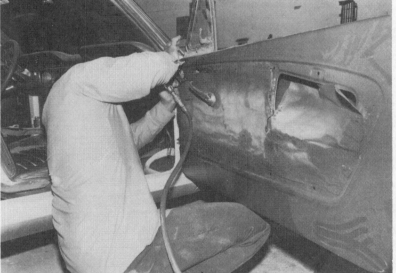

2: Start two of the bottom bolts and the two top ones. Notice how you can use your knee to hold the rear of the door and raise or lower it to fit properly.

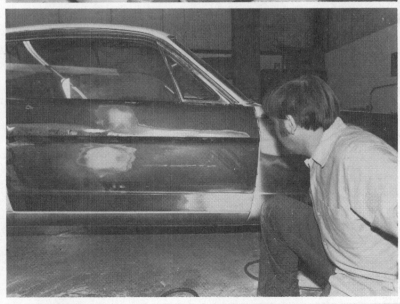

3: With bolts partly tightened, check how the lines on the door match those on the fender and quarter panel.

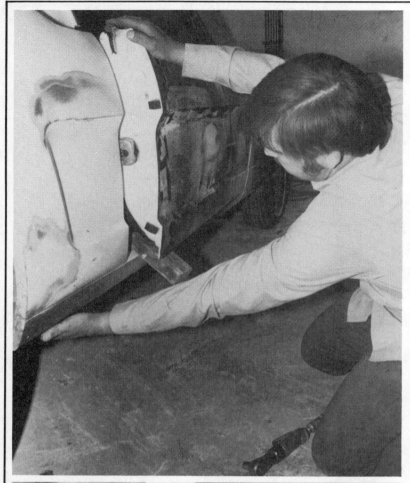

4: If a door is slightly twisted, you might be able to straighten it by wedging a block of wood or a big screwdriver into the doorway and bending it. Also, be sure to line up the door lock with the pin on the striker plate on the doorjamb.

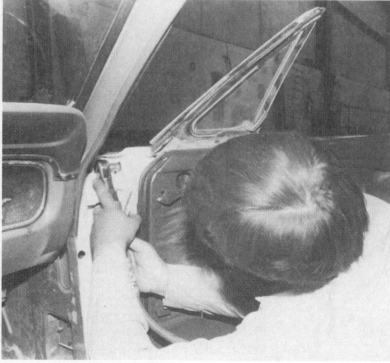

5: Once everything is lined up, you can tighten all the bolts completely. The door should be swinging free when you tighten the bolts.

Metal Preparation

With straight body panels, smooth sheetmetal and several patches of body filler, our Mustang is now ready for the paint shop, though there still was much work to do to prepare the metal for painting. The body on our Mustang was repaired by experienced hands that removed all but the smallest of dings. Body putty and primer filled those in. Be advised, though, that we didn't leave much damage to be covered up by the painter. Putty and primer will cover up only a little; the bulk has to be done by fixing dents and filling in with plastic body filler. Save yourself some grief by doing as much as you can before you get to the painting stage.

You'll need several grades of sandpaper (from No. 80 up to No. 400). An electric sander will be faster than a sanding block. You'll also need body putty, primer, and paint, of course, and a spray gun. Take your time; rushing through it can produce disastrous results. Others might use different materials and techniques, but our Mustang was done by a painter with more than 12 years' experience.

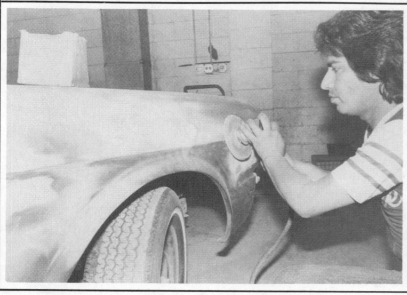

1: Feather edge the surface to be painted with No. 80 or finer grade sandpaper to remove the rough edges left by filing and sanding with coarse paper during the body repair.

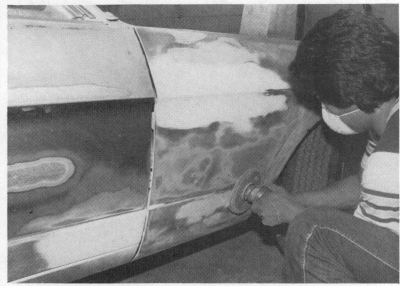

2: Go over it again with finer sandpaper so you're getting most of the paint off and all the scratches. Try to get the metal as smooth as you can; scratches could show through the paint.

Our Mustang had acquired several layers of paint over the years, so it took a lot of sanding to get the metal smooth.

3: After you wipe the surface clean, start masking. Use masking tape to cover edges and spots where paint could drip, such as the door sill and doorjamb.

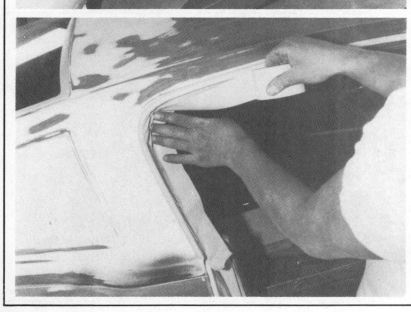

4: Also tape the rubber moldings in doorways, and on the trunk lid. It's easier to pull off tape when you're finished than to remove unwanted paint.

Metal Preparation

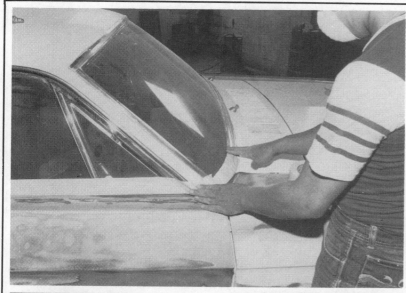

5: A wide strip of tape firmly applied to window moldings will seal out paint from the glass and chrome trim. It's best to remove moldings when painting.

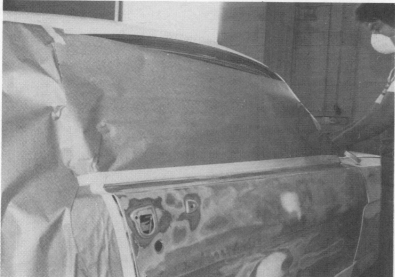

6: Then use newspaper or heavier paper to cover the rest of the areas you don't want painted. Tape the edges securely.

7: On large glass areas, such as the rear window on fastbacks, you can overlap the glass when you attach the paper, then trim it to fit with a razor blade.

Metal Preparation

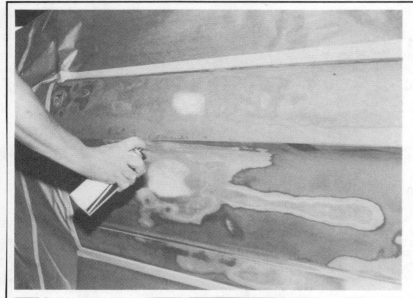

8: Give bare metal a thin coat of acrylic-chromatic primer to prevent corrosion. Cover the wheels with paper, or you can rig a handy cover from heavy cloth attached to wires bent to fit over the tires.

9: Give it a first coat of primer, starting from the bottom and working your way up with even back-and-forth strokes, covering all the metal. Don't hold the paint gun or spray can in the same spot; keep it moving at the same pace so you have an even application.

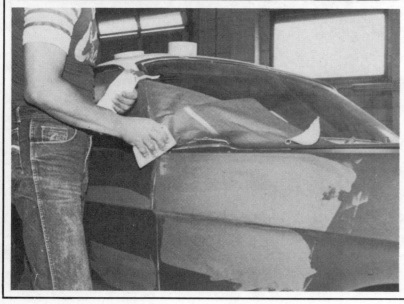

10: After the primer is dry, cover the areas patched with body filler (they'll show through the primer) with body putty. Apply the putty evenly with a plastic spreader. It will fill in scratches and give your car a better finish.

11: Wet sand the putty with No. 220 grade sandpaper wrapped around a sanding block. Dunk it in water frequently to keep it wet. Don't leave much putty; it is just for covering scratches.

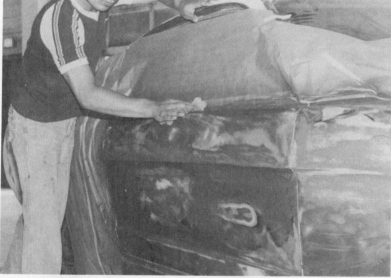

12: Wipe it clean with a wet rag, getting all the residue left from sanding. Let it dry or blow it dry with an air hose.

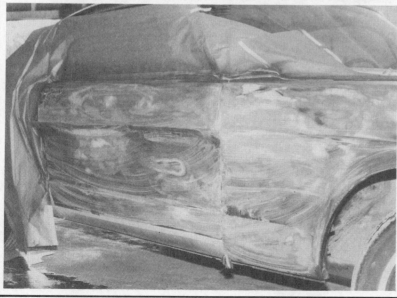

13: Go over the edges and any remaining rough spots with No. 220 sandpaper dry. When you're done, you should have a completely smooth surface. Run your hand over it several times to make sure it's smooth.

14: Apply the second coat of primer. Give it a good coat. Remember to keep moving with a steady sweeping motion.

15: Allow the second coat of primer to dry for about 30 minutes and apply a third one the same way.

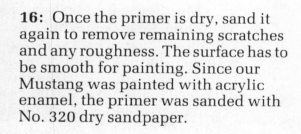

16: Once the primer is dry, sand it again to remove remaining scratches and any roughness. The surface has to be smooth for painting. Since our Mustang was painted with acrylic enamel, the primer was sanded with No. 320 dry sandpaper.

17: Wipe or blow off the dust after you've sanded the entire car. Then wipe it with a clean tack cloth to remove the remaining dust particles. The car is now ready for painting.

Painting

No matter how well you've pounded and filled the body back into shape, or how many new body panels you put on, you can spoil it all with a lousy paint job. It's something everyone will notice. That's why many serious restorers have their cars painted professionally. If you're one who prefers to do it himself (or has to for financial reasons), we have a few words of advice. Rent, borrow, or buy a good paint gun and reliable air compressor. Become thoroughly familiar with how they work before you start. Second, don't practice on your Mustang; get your stroke and technique down before then. Better you should practice on your garage wall than aim a trial-and-error blast of paint at your car. Many restored cars have lacquer (though Mustangs were originally painted with enamel) paint because of its higher gloss. However, new acrylic enamels (used on our Mustang) can be buffed and wet sanded to a glossy finish as well, and enamel is more resistant to chips than lacquer. Bear in mind too that 3–4 coats of acrylic enamel should be sufficient, while lacquer will require many more coats. Clean your painting area thoroughly, sweeping up all debris and washing down the floors and walls with water to get rid of dust that could settle on your fresh paint. Finally, make a last check to be sure that you did a good masking job and covered everything that shouldn't be painted.

Let the paint dry for about three hours before removing the paper and masking tape. Let it bake in the sun for a day before buffing it with a non-abrasive polish to make it shine. If your car has an orange-peel texture that is characteristic of enamel paints, use a very mild rubbing compound or give it a light wet sanding with No. 600 grade sandpaper. Be very careful if you sand; you're just trying to smooth the surface.

1: Use a steady back-and-forth sweeping motion. Many painters start from the bottom and work their way up. Don't hold the paint gun in one spot; keeping it moving will prevent runs.

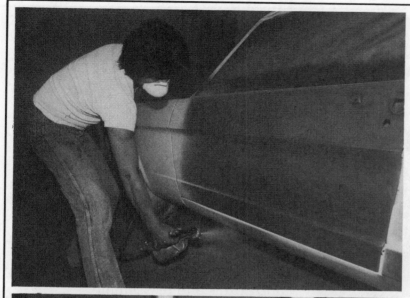

2: Pay close attention to the lower body panels. Find the proper distance you should maintain between the paint gun and the car before your start. Too close and you'll have runs. Too far and you'll have a spotty finish.

3: Be sure to get the edges and partly hidden areas like the wheel lips. If you get runs, you'll have to sand it down and do it over. If you're lucky you'll catch the runs before they dry; wipe them off with paint thinner and paint over it.

4: Looking good after the first coat? Then let it dry for at least 30 minutes before applying a second coat. It's better to apply light coats and do it three or four times than to try one or two heavy coats.

Installing Exterior Trim

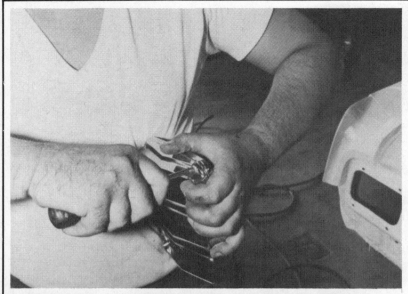

1: Clean or replace taillight lenses and bezels and reassemble.

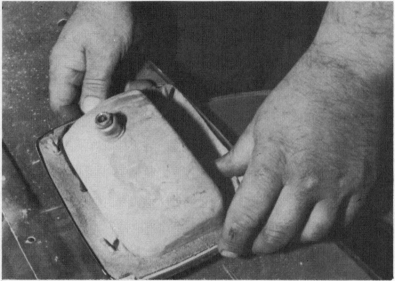

2: Line the inside rim of the taillight assembly with strip cloth or rubber gasket material to seal out water. Do the same for door handles and to plug small holes and cracks.

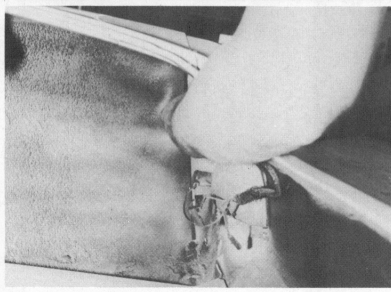

3: Mount in place, tighten nuts, and reconnect wires.

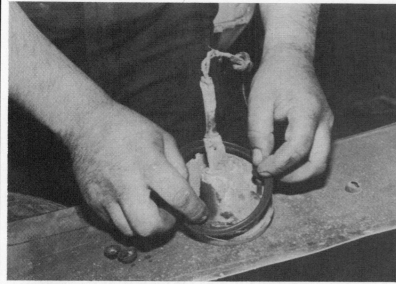

4: Put new gaskets on the inside of the backup lights, again to seal out water. Be sure you have a good seal. Tighten the retaining nuts.

5: Push backup light wires through holes in the body so the wires extend into the trunk, where you will connect them to the taillight wires. Secure the ground wire to a screw or bolt.

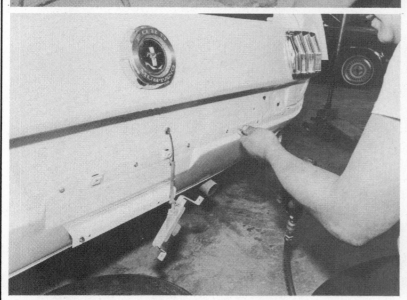

6: Loosely attach the gravel pan to the body with the three center screws and push it into place. Tighten the bolts in the lower corners of the trunk and then tighten the screws.

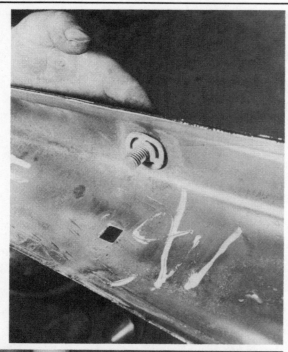

7: Push the chrome-head bolts through holes in rear bumper and place the spacers on the bolts. Those spacers are necessary to prevent damage to the chrome when tightening.

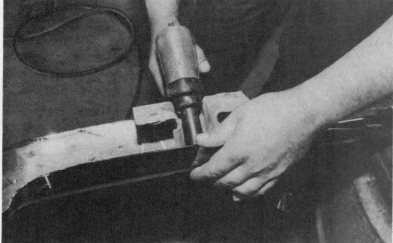

8: Securely attach bumper brackets and mount the bumper on the car, loosely attaching the four bolts in the trunk. Best to have a helper so you don't damage the bumper or fresh paint.

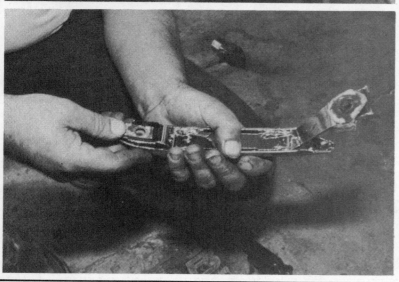

9: Leave the bumper bolts loosely attached so you'll have room to adjust rear bumper guards. Slip cage nuts over the bottom hole of bumper guards and mount on car with bolts.

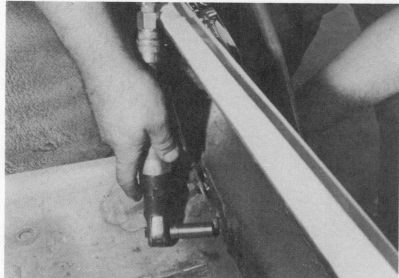

10: Make sure the bumper guards are on straight and then tighten the nuts in the trunk and under the gravel pan. Then tighten the four bumper bolts.

11: Fresh paint, bright chrome, and neatly applied trim add up to a smart-looking rear end.

12: Start reassembling the front by attaching headlight doors, which are held by four bolts.

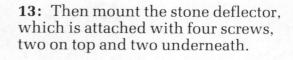

13: Then mount the stone deflector, which is attached with four screws, two on top and two underneath.

14: Slide the clips into channels on underside of chrome grille moldings and line them up so they'll fit into the slots on the stone deflector.

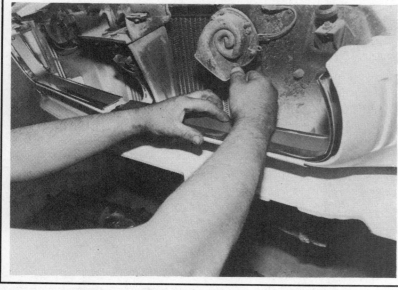

15: Pound the clips into place with your hand. The moldings also have a screw in the corners.

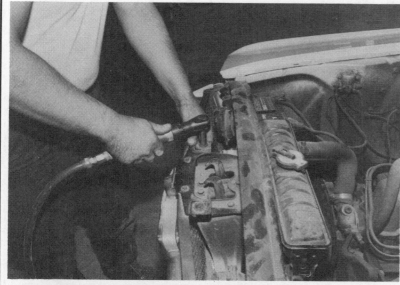

16: Slip the grille into place and attach the two center bolts on top. Line up the bolt holes and tighten the four bolts along the inside at the bottom and the two outer bolts on top.

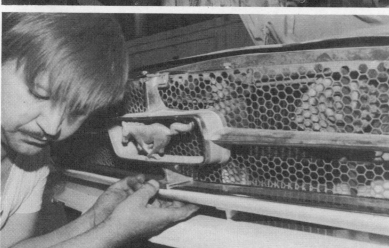

17: Secure the chrome horse and grille bars to the stone deflector with a ⅜-inch bolt.

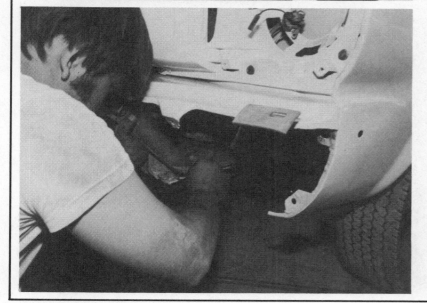

18: Bolt bumper brackets to the frame. Some people prefer to bolt the bumper and bracket together and put them on the car as a unit. We found it easier this way.

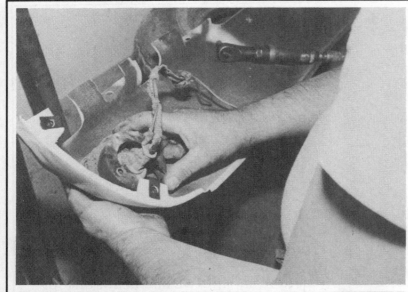

19: Attach parking lights and bezels and slip U-clips over the four bolt holes along the top of the front gravel pan and the hole in each lower corner.

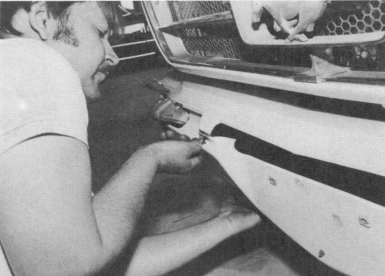

20: Mount the gravel pan, loosely tightening the two center bolts so it hangs in place.

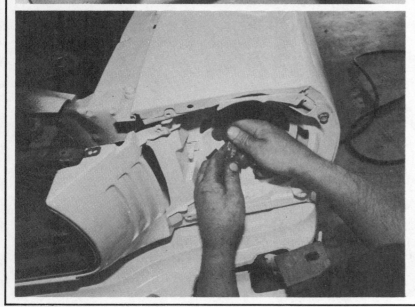

21: Pull parking light wires through the body and reconnect to headlight wires.

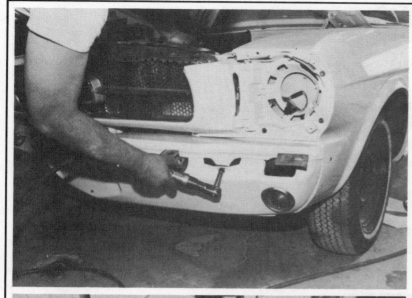

22: Line up the gravel pan and tighten the two hidden bolts under the corners and the four bolts along the top.

23: Before mounting the bumper, place the spacers on the mounting brackets. You can tape the spacers to the brackets to hold them in place. The bumper will hide the tape.

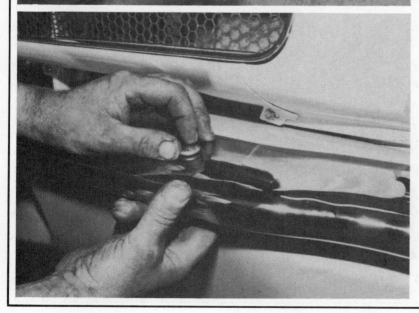

24: Carefully place the bumper on the brackets and insert chrome bolts.

25: Once you're sure it's properly lined up, tighten the four bolts along the front and the single bolts on each side.

26: Slide U-clips over the top bolt holes of the bumper guards and tighten bolt through the bumper bracket. The bottom of the bumper guard bolts to the body under the gravel pan.

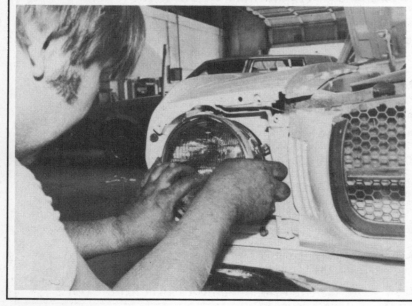

27: Mount the headlight buckets and hook them to the headlight doors with the springs for aiming headlights. Finish it off by mounting headlights and bezels.

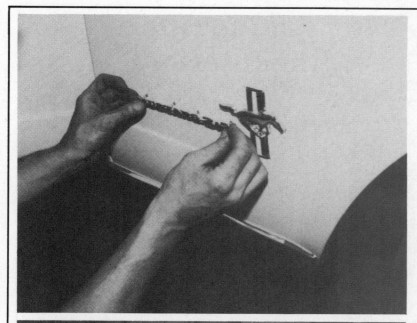

28: Press hood and fender trim pieces into barrel clips to put the final touches on the exterior. Don't use too much force; the emblems are easily bent.

29: A properly done trim job can make your Mustang sparkle.

Taking Apart the Interior

1: Front seats are held in place by four bolts through the floor pan. Remove the rubber plugs from the floor and loosen the nuts. You'll need an extension on your socket wrench to reach the nuts.

2: After you remove the nuts, you should be able to lift the bucket seats out. Notice the four bolts in the seat tracks. Save the metal pads under the seat tracks.

3: On fastbacks, the rear seat cushion isn't bolted down. You just have to push in on the front of the cushion and then pull it out from the top.

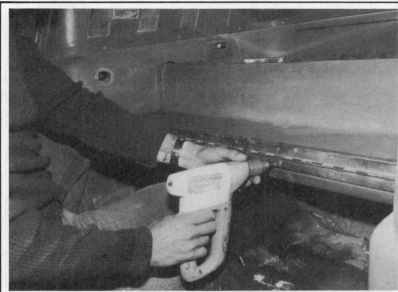

4: The rest of the rear seat assembly comes out in pieces and won't be as easy. Fold the seatback down and loosen the bottom row of screws.

5: You'll then be able to remove the folding panel and go on to the upholstered seatback.

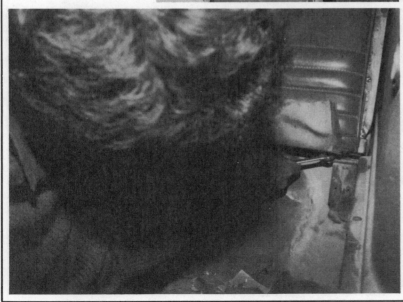

6: The seatback is attached by bolts on each side and screws on the lower molding. Remove those and lift the upholstered panel off the panel behind it.

7: The forward panel comes out separately. Remove the three bolts from each hinge to take out the panel.

8: The remaining panel has two bolts on each end through brackets behind the hinges.

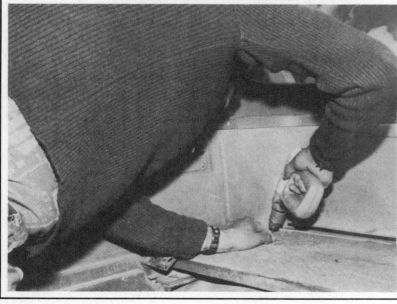

9: Finally, you have to remove two screws near the rear corners of the panel.

10: To remove rear quarter trim panels, start by unscrewing the trim moldings and then the upper vent panel.

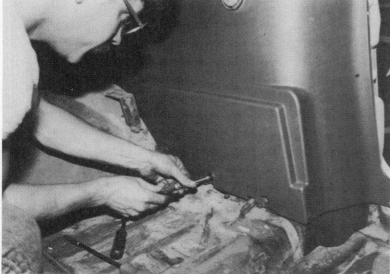

11: Unscrew the door sill scuff plates, pull off the windlace and remove the three bolts holding the trim panel. The panel also is held by screws along the side.

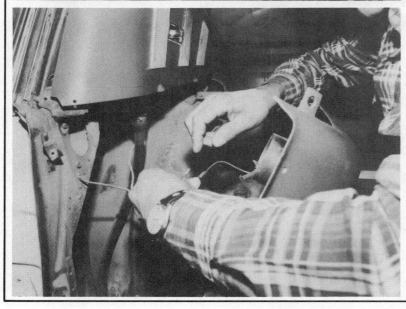

12: Disconnect the rear courtesy lights. Note: the trim pieces in the rear and rear corners of fastbacks are riveted as well as screwed into place. If you remove them, you'll have to rivet them when you re-assemble the interior.

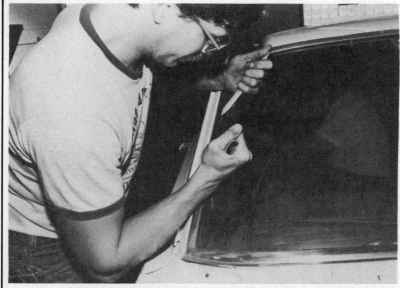

13: To remove the windshield or rear window, pry up the chrome moldings with a knife or screwdriver, loosening the clips that hold them in place. Slide the blade of the knife or screwdriver under the molding to locate the clips.

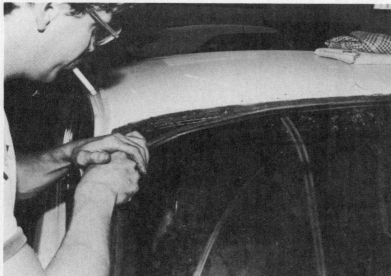

14: Use a flat putty knife to cut through the sealer and pry up the rubber windshield molding. If you're going to replace the rubber, it's easier to cut it.

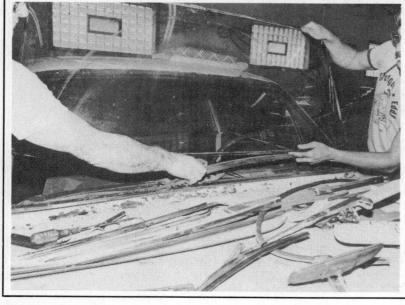

15: With a helper, push the windshield out from the inside and lift it from the window frame. Clean the windshield with a razor while it's off the car.

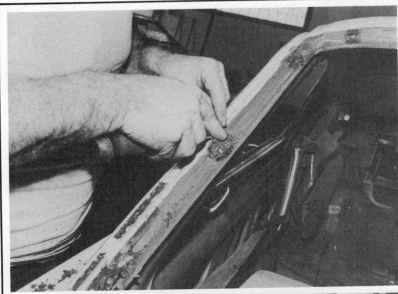

16: Scrape out all the dirt and remaining sealer. You'll need a clean frame for mounting a new windshield or putting the old one back in.

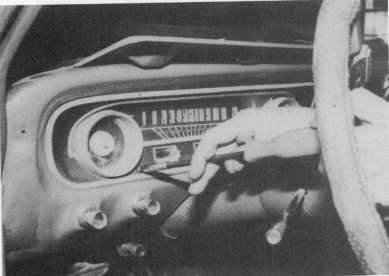

17: It's likely you'll replace the dash pad, so remove the retaining screws and pull it off. Then unscrew the instrument panel, which has two screws at the base and four along the top.

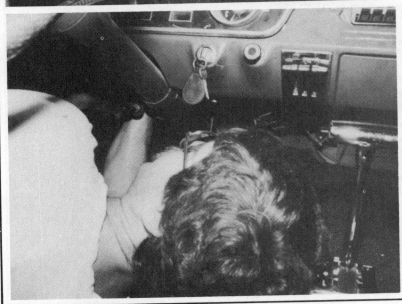

18: Before you can remove the instrument panel, you'll have to reach under the dash to release the speedometer cable, which is held in the center of the panel by a nut.

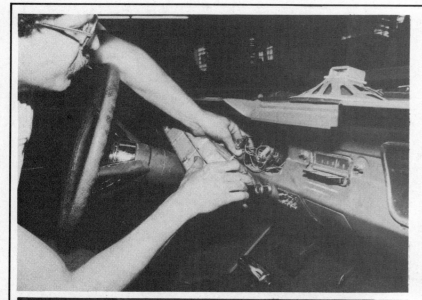

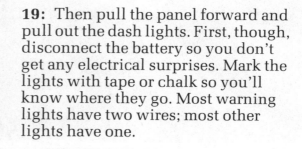

19: Then pull the panel forward and pull out the dash lights. First, though, disconnect the battery so you don't get any electrical surprises. Mark the lights with tape or chalk so you'll know where they go. Most warning lights have two wires; most other lights have one.

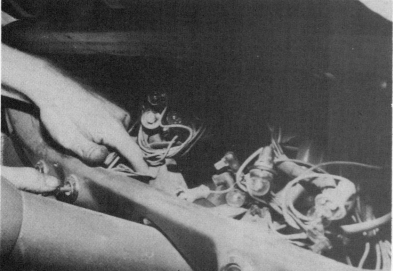

20: The light switch is removed by pulling the knob out to the "On" position and pushing the release button on the switch housing.

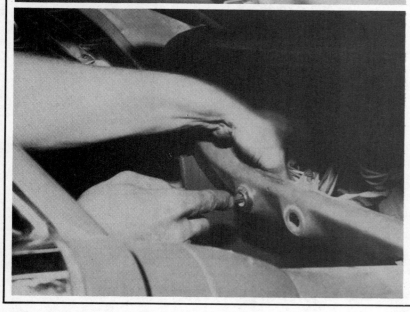

21: The wiper switch is attached with a hex screw at the base. Remove the screw and the switch can be pushed out.

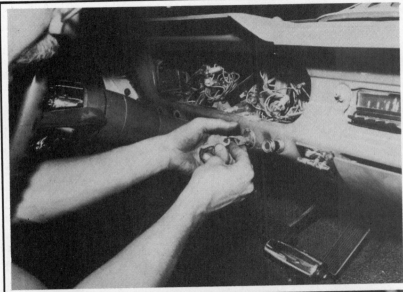

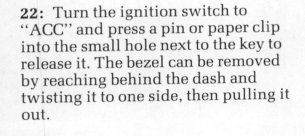

22: Turn the ignition switch to "ACC" and press a pin or paper clip into the small hole next to the key to release it. The bezel can be removed by reaching behind the dash and twisting it to one side, then pulling it out.

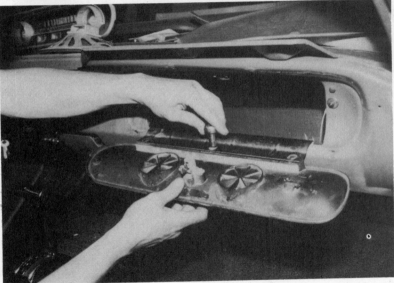

23: The glovebox door comes off by removing the bolts on the hinge. Disconnect the glovebox light and unscrew the glovebox liner, pulling it out from underneath.

Installing New Seat Covers

1: Unscrew the chrome side moldings, pull out the cotter pin that holds the seatback bracket to the cushion, and remove the four large screws that hold the seat tracks.

2: Once the seat tracks are free, you'll be able to remove this spring. You'll also have to remove the adjustment bolt on the backrest and the plate on the cushion. Pry off the backing on the backrest with a screwdriver.

3: The upholstery is held down by hog rings that can be removed with either hog ring pliers or wire cutters. Twist them loose and pull them out.

Installing New Seat Covers

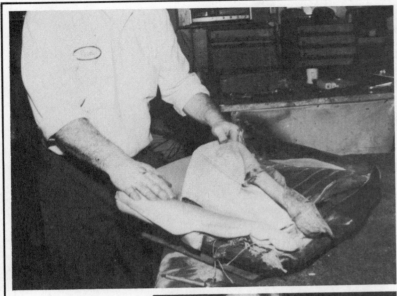

4: Pull the old seat cover off the frame and the foam rubber.

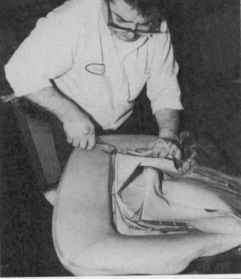

5: The seat covers are held in the center by hog rings around a retaining wire that is fed through a seam. Save the wire; you have to insert it into the new upholstery.

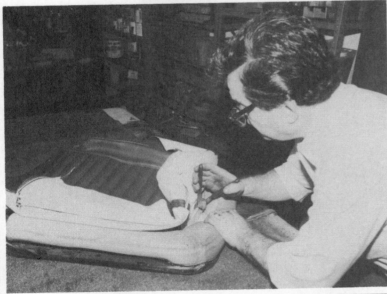

6: Lay the new seat cover on the cushion or seatback and fasten it with hog rings around the retaining wire. You'll need a good supply of new hog rings since the old ones can't be used again.

Installing New Seat Covers

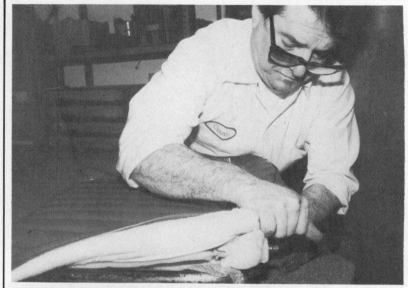

7: Pull the seat cover over the foam rubber and around the frame.

8: Make it snug, removing all wrinkles and checking that the upholstery is on evenly.

9: Turn it upside down and hook the edges with hog rings through holes in the frame.

Installing New Seat Covers

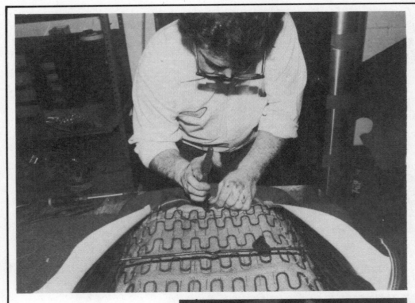

10: On sides that don't have frames, attach the hog rings to the springs.

11: Poke a hole through the upholstery for the mounting stud for the backrest. Wait until you have the upholstery securely fastened before you do this so you only make one hole—the right one.

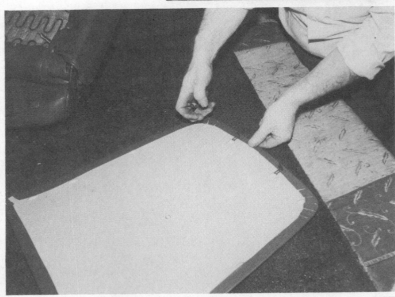

12: Install the panel on the backrest by inserting retaining clips salvaged from the old back panel into slots that are provided.

Installing New Seat Covers

13: Snap the back panel in place by pushing in on the clips.

14: Attach the chrome molding and your newly covered seats are ready to be installed. New seat covers improve the appearance of the interior immensely.

Installing Headliner

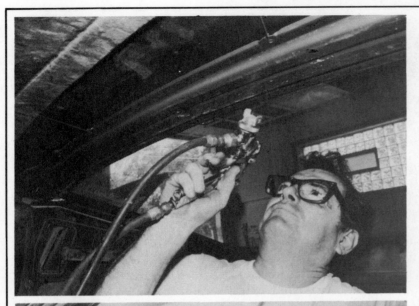

1: Glue the edges of the ceiling where the headliner will attach. You can apply the glue with a brush instead of a gun.

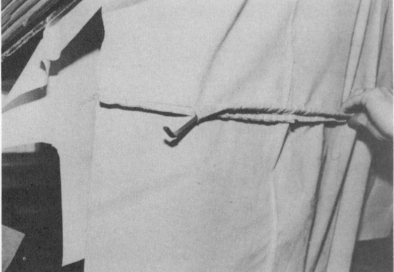

2: Slide the bones from your old headliner into the new one and mount the bones into the slots on the sides of the ceiling. Make sure the dotted center line on the underside of the headliner matches the center spot in the front of the ceiling.

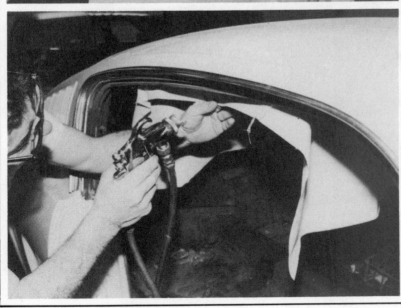

3: Glue the edges of the headliner on all sides where it will attach to the car.

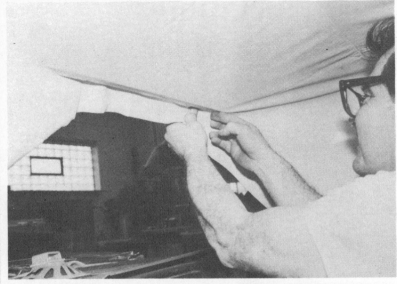

4: Press the fabric securely into place along the edges, pulling it snug so there aren't any wrinkles. Make sure the seams run straight across from side to side.

5: Snip off excess fabric, leaving less than a half inch to be tucked in and covered by the windlace.

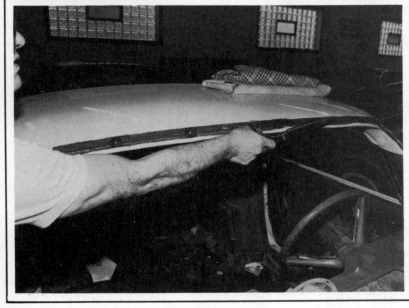

6: It isn't necessary to remove the windshield to install the headliner, but it's easier to do with the glass removed. Leave a half inch or less in front to be glued and hidden under the windshield gasket.

Installing Headliner

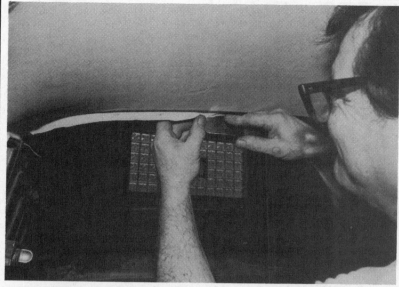

7: If you leave the windshield and rear window in the car, trim the headliner so there's half an inch or less left. Tuck the excess fabric under the rubber gasket with a putty knife.

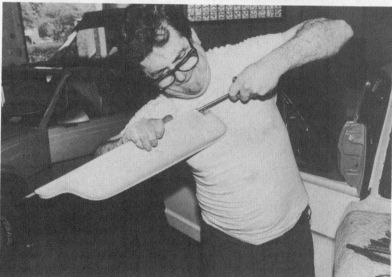

8: Pull out the hardware from your old sunvisors (it can be quite a struggle) and install them in the new sunvisors. Clean the chrome first with steel wool.

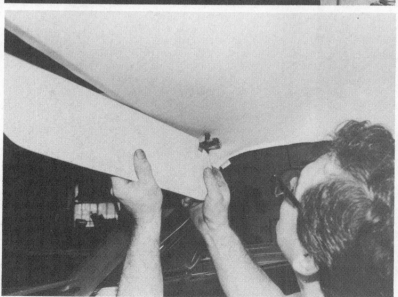

9: Feel through the fabric for the large mounting hole and three smaller holes for retaining screws for the sunvisor. Poke holes in the headliner with an awl and mount the visors. Screw in the rear view mirror to finish the job.

Painting the Interior

Interior trim panels that aren't cracked or badly battered can be made to look like new with some elbow grease and vinyl paint. Keep extra paint on hand for touching up scratches and chips.

1: Remove dirt and grease with a good dose of cleaning solvent to get the panels ready for painting. You can also clean and repaint the windlace.

2: Mask chrome pieces like air vents on fastback trim and spray it with two or three coats of paint. Vinyl paint dries quickly, so you won't have to wait long between coats. When you're done, give it a light sanding with No. 600 sandpaper so it has a smooth finish.

Painting the Interior

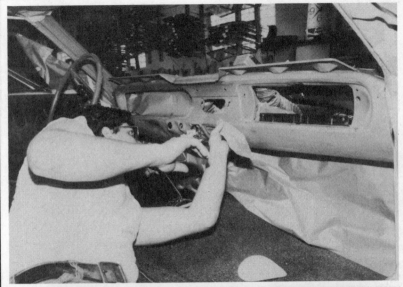

3: If you're going to paint the dash, spend extra time and care masking it. Be careful that only those areas you mean to paint are exposed. Also, keep in mind that some areas, like the top of the dash, will be covered when you put it back together. That way you won't waste time meticulously painting spots that won't show.

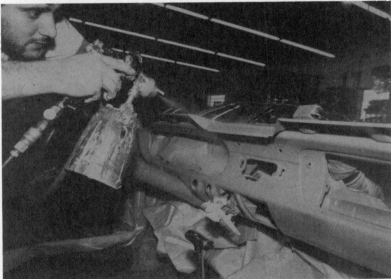

4: Spray carefully, giving it at least two light coats. You should be able to find matching colors through Mustang specialty shops or Ford dealers. Be careful about buying spray cans off the rack in parts stores. The colors may be close, but slightly off. An auto paint store can help you too.

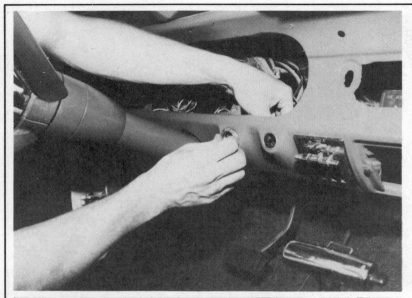

Reassembling Dashboard

1: Putting the dashboard together is essentially the reverse process of what you did when you took it apart. You'll be better off if you made notes (mental or written) on what you did then. Start with the ignition switch, mounting the bezel and turning it so it locks in place.

2: Insert the ignition switch with the key turned to the "ACC" position and push it in until it clicks into place.

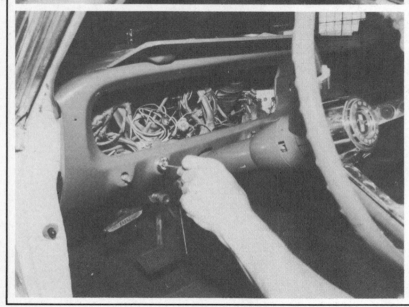

3: Insert the long rod on the light switch until it clicks into place.

continued on page 209

Below: Last year for the Grandé was 1973, also the last year for the "big" Mustangs. *Bottom:* 1973 convertible with optional Mach 1-style hood and grille.

Above and far left: Special red, white, and blue Sprint Decor Option was offered for '72, shown here on the "Sports-Roof" fastback. *Below:* Mock-up for Mustang II logo.

Upper left and left: Mustang II Ghia notchback and new 3-door fastback marked a second ponycar revolution for 1974. *Above:* Cobra II option appeared for '76.

Below: Motortown built this "IMSA Cobra" show car, inspired by Charlie Kemp's Mustang II racer, in 1978. *Far right:* New 1978 King Cobra package was the ultimate in "paint-on performance." *Bottom:* The 1977 Mustang II hatchback with optional T-bar roof.

Mustang became more European with the all-new 1979 design. *Far left:* the notchback coupe. *Above:* 1979 Ghia notchback. *Below:* Turbo 2.3 hatchback with TRX suspension.

Far right, above: Cobra package for 1980 was revised along the lines of the '79 Indy Pace Car replica. Snake decal on hood was a delete option. *Below and far right:* GT replaced Cobra as Mustang's hottest for '82. Revived 302 V-8 was capable of 7.0-second 0-60 mph times.

Above: 1983 saw first big appearance change for the new-generation Mustangs, as exemplified by this GT. New nose improved aerodynamics by a claimed 2.5 percent. *Far left:* Aluminum valve covers dressed up '83 H.O. V-8. New 4-barrel carb cut 0-60 mph acceleration by a full second, keeping Mustang the quickest modern ponycar.

Ford's first convertible in 10 years arrived with the
'83 Mustang GLX. New ragtop could be ordered with
any available powerteam, even the fabled High-Output
4-barrel small-block.

Coming or going, the '83 Mustang GT
looks as fast as it goes. Besides fresh
lines, changes included chassis tuning
and new sports front seats.

continued from page 192

Reassembling Dashboard

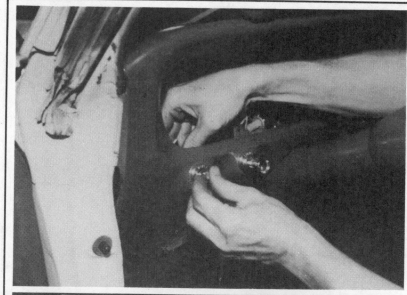

4: Housing for wiper switch screws into the bezel. Then attach the knob with hex screw.

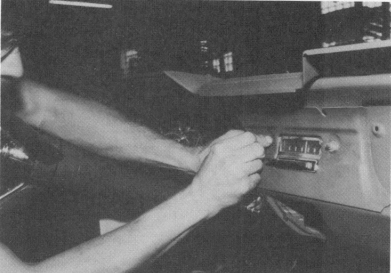

5: A previous owner had carved a piece of the dash out to install a larger radio. We covered it with a plastic adapter plate that was painted the same color as the dash. The edges are covered on top by the dash pad, on the right by the glovebox door, and on the left by the instrument panel. You might want to glue the bottom edge.

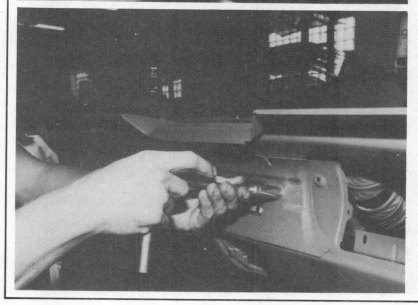

6: Tighten the nuts holding the radio in place after you have the adapter plate lined up.

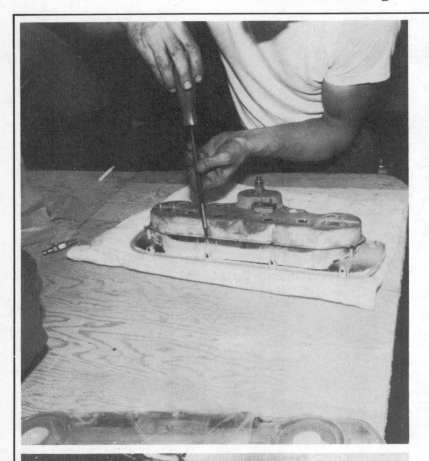

7: If you're replacing the instrument panel bezel and lens, take it apart by removing screws from the rear.

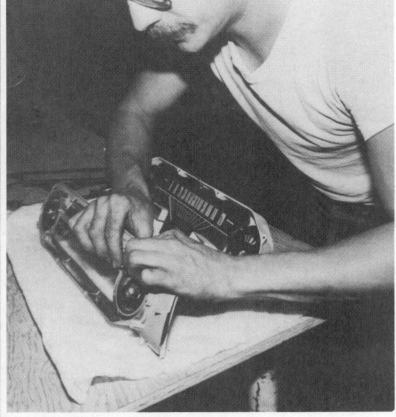

8: Clean any dirt off the face of the speedometer and gauges. Snap new lens onto bezel, being careful not to get any fingerprints on the inside of the lens.

Reassembling Dashboard

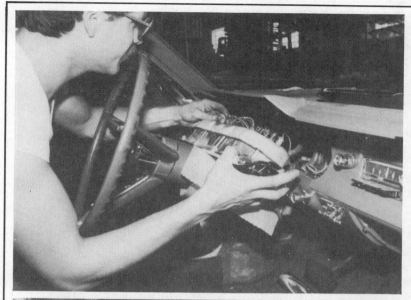

9: Screw the bezel and lens into place and reconnect the dash lights. Make sure all lights work before you screw the instrument panel into the dash. Put a cloth or heavy paper on the steering column so you don't scratch the paint or the bezel.

10: Set the instrument panel in place and tighten the screws securely.

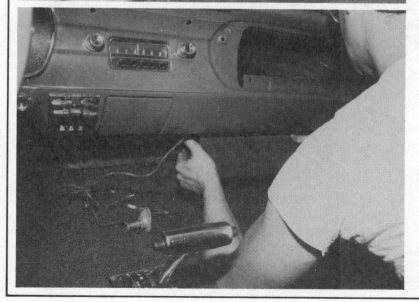

11: The glovebox liner has to be squeezed into place from underneath. It's a tight fit, so be careful that you don't damage it. Screw it down and reconnect glovebox light, making sure it's hooked to the passenger side courtesy light.

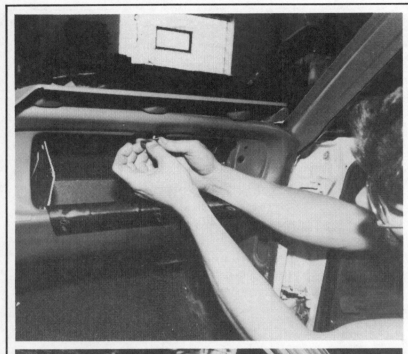

12: Before mounting the glovebox door, loosely attach the striker clip at the top. Leave it loose so you can adjust it to the lock.

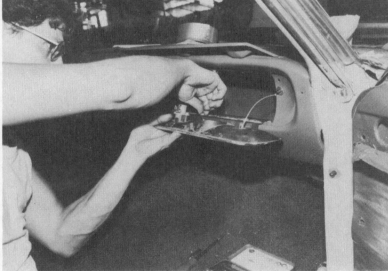

13: Loosely attach the door on the hinge and line it up before tightening the bolts. Small holes on the sides are for rubber stops that keep the door from scratching the metal.

14: Install the dash pad before installing the radio speaker. Push the pad into place and attach screws on top of dash to start. You'll probably need an awl to find many of the other screw holes since the holes in reproduction dash pads often are a little bit off.

Installing Carpets

1: Install the rear carpet section first. Spray or brush glue on the floor where padding will be placed.

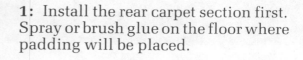

2: Cut the padding to fit and glue the underside of the padding as well, then press it firmly into place. Lay the rear carpet down, tucking it under the edges of the rear quarter panel. Screw the forward end of the rear carpet down on each side so it won't slide.

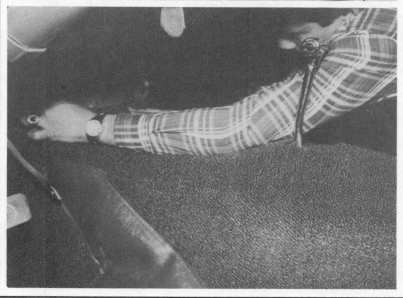

3: Lay the front carpet, cutting a slit where the shift lever will come through. Before you start cutting, smooth the carpet into place so you don't cut in the wrong spot.

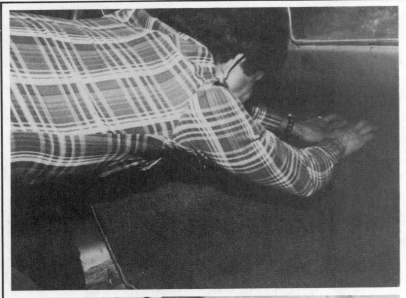

4: Tuck the forward edges under the dash. Also cut a hole for the headlight dimmer switch. Locate bolt holes and mark them with chalk so you'll know where to cut later.

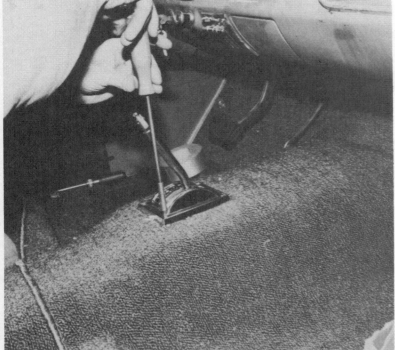

5: Once you've positioned the carpet, screw down the shift quadrant, trimming excess carpet to make it fit. You may have to trim small amounts on the edges as well, though reproduction carpets usually are good fits. The kick panels and door sill scuff plates will help secure the carpet.

Installing Interior Trim and Door Panels

1: If you removed the rear panels for painting, you'll need a rivet gun. The piece across the back under the rear window is riveted on the bottom and screwed on the top.

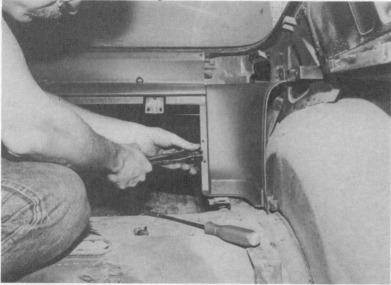

2: The lower corner piece slips in behind the back panel and is riveted also.

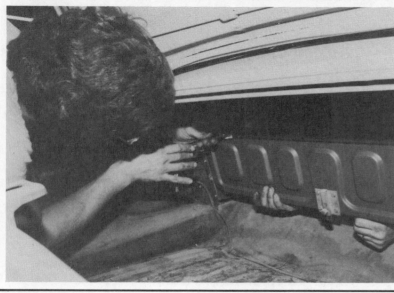

3: The trap door is bolted to hinges. You'll need a helper to hold it in place while you tighten the bolts.

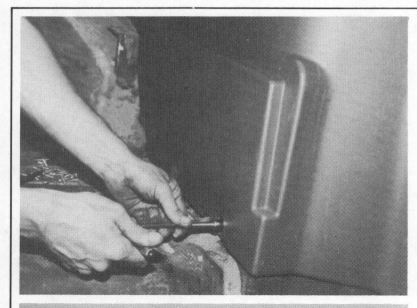

4: The lower rear quarter panel is bolted along the bottom and screwed up the side. Reconnect the courtesy light first.

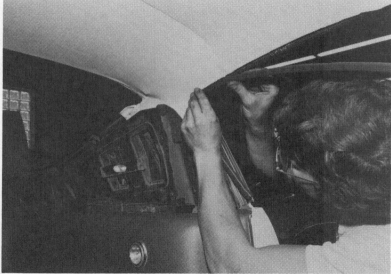

5: The windlace is merely pushed back into place or its groove, though you have to line up the ends before starting to put it on.

6: The vent panel is held by screws. Panels on our Mustang were held by a variety of screw sizes and it was trial-and-error to find where they went. A good idea is to tape the screws to the back of the panel next to the hole they were removed from.

7: Screw the trim moldings into place after all the panels are on.

8: On fastbacks, rear of headliner is trimmed by molded panels that are held by one screw each and a center clip.

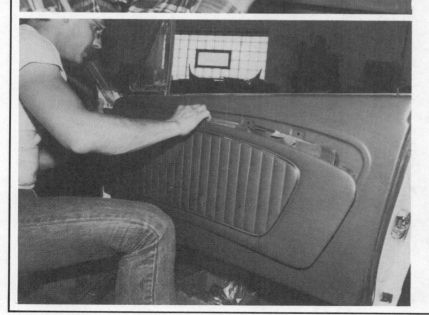

9: Door panels are held by retaining clips that mount in slots on the reverse side and are pushed into holes on the door. Handle with care; the cardboard backing on the door panels is pretty flimsy and it's easy to tear if you have to take it off the door.

10: Armrest base and pad screw together. It's a good idea to mark the door panel with chalk before mounting it so you know where to find screw holes for the armrest. Use the old door panel as a guide.

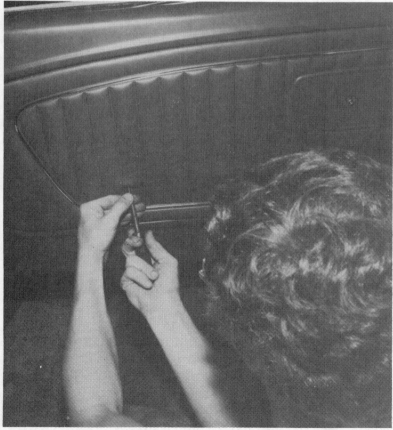

11: With the door panel mounted, use an awl to find the screw holes and the way they are angled.

12: Screw the armrests into place.

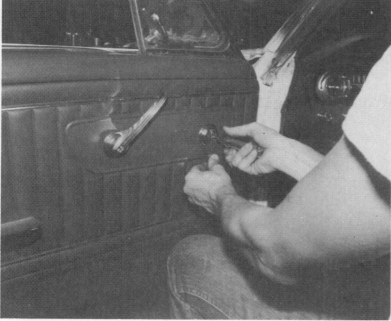

13: Attach door handle and window crank. Ours were attached with hex screws, though other models have clips or Phillips screws. The door handle has to be angled up towards the front so the window crank will clear it.

Installing Seats

1: In fastbacks, the first step is to mount the carpeted bottom panel. Place spacers on the hinges so the trap door will line up properly with the panel. Tighten bolts on each side and two screws through the carpet.

2: Attach the folding seatback to the hinges at the front of the bottom panel.

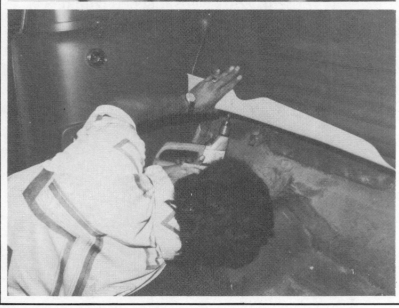

3: Hang the upholstered seatback on the upper hooks and push into place at the bottom. Attach the retaining screws to the molding along the bottom.

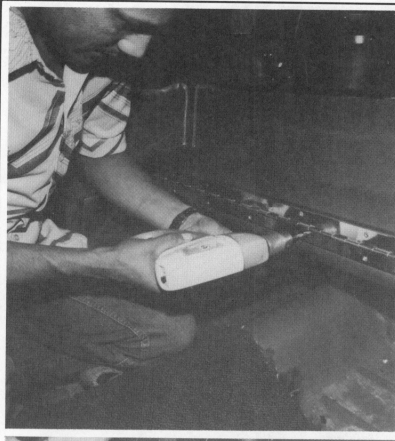

4: This folding piece is attached by a row of screws. Fold the seatback down and tighten the screws.

5: Raise the seatback and mount the cushion onto brackets at the base of the seatback, pushing it into place.

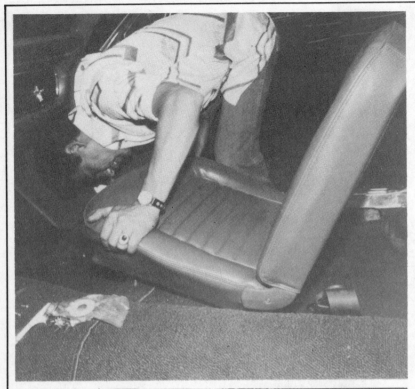

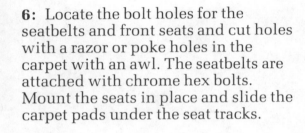

6: Locate the bolt holes for the seatbelts and front seats and cut holes with a razor or poke holes in the carpet with an awl. The seatbelts are attached with chrome hex bolts. Mount the seats in place and slide the carpet pads under the seat tracks.

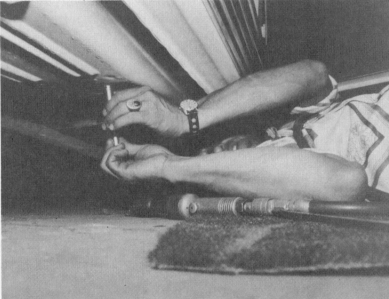

7: It's back under the car to tighten the seat bolts. Replace the rubber plugs in the bolt holes, otherwise you'll get water in the interior.

Installing a Windshield

If you are planning to install a windshield or rear window yourself, we would recommend you have professionals do it instead. Improper sealing will result in a waterfall over your dashboard. A slip of the hands when installing can result in a chipped or broken windshield. We'll show you the procedure used on our Mustang and add another warning: many body shops hire glass and trim experts like ours to do their work.

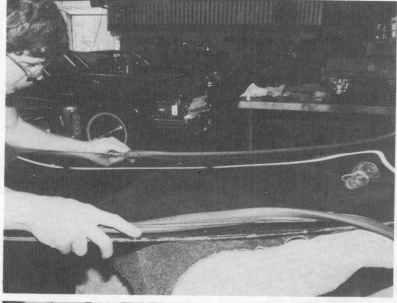

1: Slip the rubber windshield gasket securely onto the windshield, making sure it's seated properly.

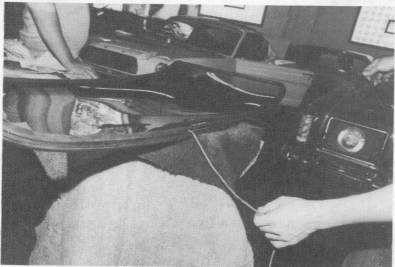

2: The rubber gasket has a groove that will fit around a lip on the inside of the window frame. Slip a 3/16-inch nylon rope into that groove all around the windshield. The rope has to be long enough so you'll have at least 10 inches of rope left hanging after you've gone all around the windshield. Leave the ends hanging from the center of the bottom part of the windshield.

3: With a helper, carefully mount the windshield on the frame. Check the alignment on both sides to make sure it is in place.

Installing a Windshield

4: With a helper firmly pushing the windshield in place from the outside, gently pull the rope out of the gasket. As you pull the rope, the gasket will slip into place over the lip of the frame. If you don't use rope, you'll have to pull the gasket over the lip by hand or with the help of a screwdriver, which can be an awfully long job. Be careful with a screwdriver; you could scratch the glass.

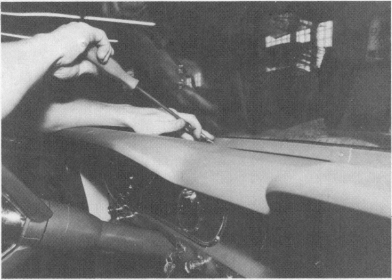

5: Screw in the inside windshield moldings along the top of the dash. You'll need an awl to find the holes through the rubber gasket.

6: Brush sealer primer around the windshield before applying sealer. It dries quickly, like paint primer. Without the primer, the sealer won't stick well.

Installing a Windshield

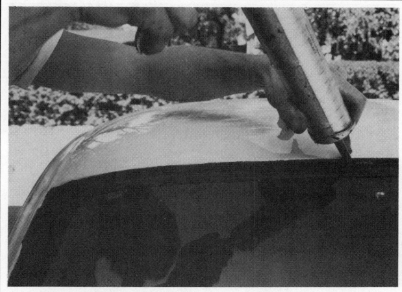

7: Apply window sealer carefully with a caulking gun in the seam between the frame and the rubber gasket.

8: While the sealer is still moist, press the windshield moldings into place. If you mount them before the sealer is dry you'll get a better bond. Push the moldings in until they are secured to the retaining clips.

9: Wipe off excess sealer with a cleaning solvent before it hardens.

Cleaning the Engine

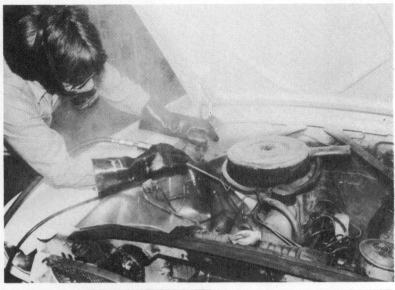

Give the engine compartment a thorough cleaning before you do mechanical work and painting. With a clean engine, you'll be able to tell more about what shape it's in and it will also be easier to spot fluid leaks. The engine in our Mustang badly needed cleaning.

Let the engine run for several minutes before applying a degreasing fluid; it works better on a warm engine. Cover the distributor and carburetor with plastic bags. If you're going to take the distributor apart soon after washing, you don't have to worry about getting it wet. You can dry it while it's apart.

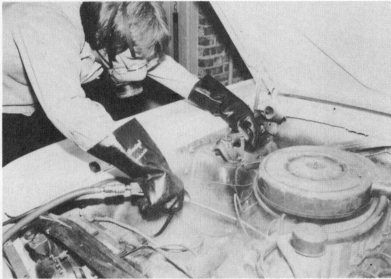

1: Apply liberal amounts of degreaser to remove crud that has built up over the years. Spray cans are adequate, but using a spray gun attached to an air hose will help loosen grease and dirt.

2: Do the top part of the engine compartment first, then steadily work your way to the bottom.

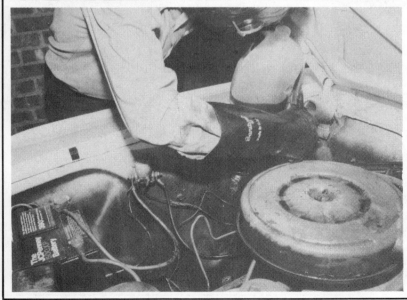

3: You'll probably have to use a scraper and brush to clean the worst spots. Pour additional degreaser directly on stubborn areas and give it lots of elbow grease.

4: When you rinse, start at the top again so you're washing the degreaser and dirt downward.

5: The more force you have in your hose, the easier it will be to rinse away grease.

6: Wipe off leftover grease marks with a rag. Anyone who works on engines prefers to work on a clean one.

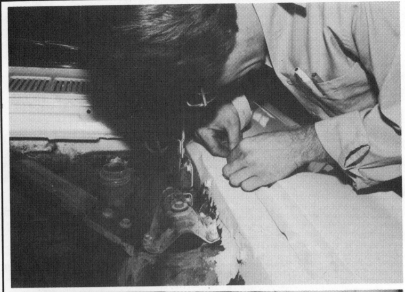

Painting the Engine

Engine colors on 1965 Mustangs depend which engine is in the car. The block and heads were always black, but the valve covers and air cleaner were red-orange on 6-cylinders, medium blue on the 260-cid V-8, and gold on the 289 (the snout on the air cleaner was painted black on the 289). Starting with 1966, all engines were blue. Paint the valve covers and air cleaner off the car, first cleaning them thoroughly with a degreaser.

Save yourself some masking time and eliminate potential problems by removing the hood before you paint the engine compartment. You'll have more working room with the hood off the car and won't have to worry about stray paint.

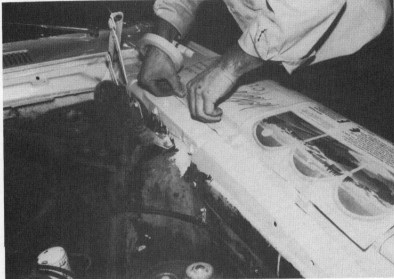

1: Mask the edges of the fenders first with tape; lining it up carefully and sealing it tightly. A crooked edge of loose tape will let paint run onto the fender.

2: Tape newspaper or heavier paper over the tape strips. Tape it securely, making sure all edges and gaps are covered. If you use newspaper, cover with 2–3 sheets at a time.

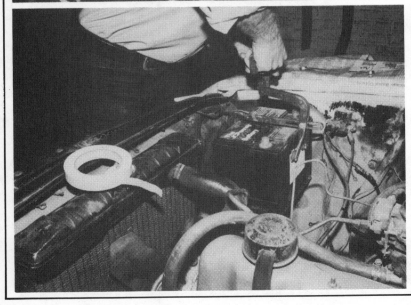

3: Remove the battery; disconnect electrical wires and either remove them or tuck them out of the way. Tape exposed terminals. Also remove oil dipstick and put tape over the tube.

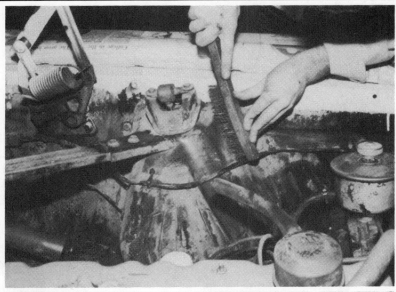

4: A wire brush will remove rust and loose paint from the inner fenders and firewall. Use an air hose to blow off the dust or wipe it with a rag.

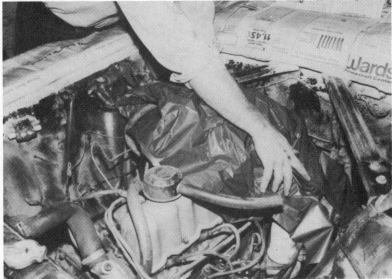

5: Cover the engine with a large plastic or paper. Also cover or remove other pieces that you don't want painted. For example, take off the radiator cap and cover the hoses with plastic or paper.

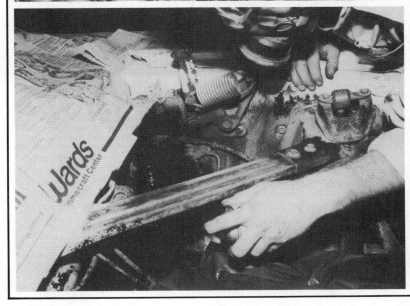

6: Paint the firewall and inner fenders from the bottom up. By starting at the bottom, you won't be leaning on areas that you've already painted. The inner fenders and firewall are painted black.

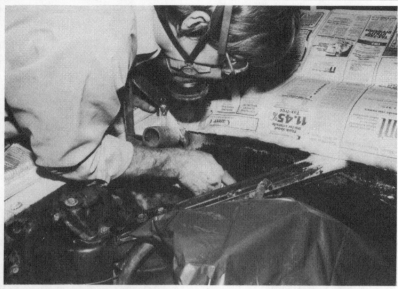

7: Some hard-to-reach spots will require that you aim the spray can with an educated guess because you won't be able to see where you're painting. Move wires out of the way and paint around them.

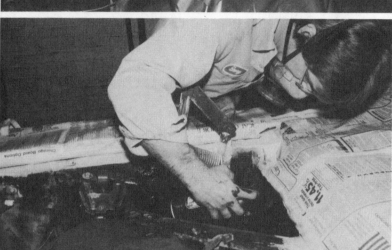

8: Look at the engine from every angle you can to find bare patches that you missed.

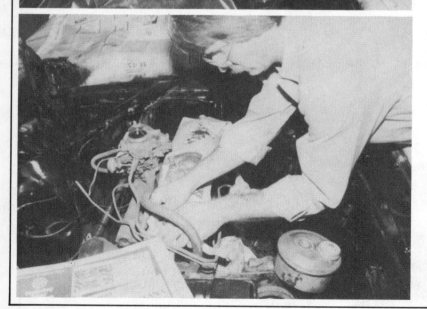

9: Once the paint is dry on the inner fenders and firewall, remove the valve covers (if you haven't already) and cover the valves with paper. You also should cover the alternator, exhaust pipes, oil filter, distributor (remove the wires) and other parts that don't get painted.

Painting the Engine

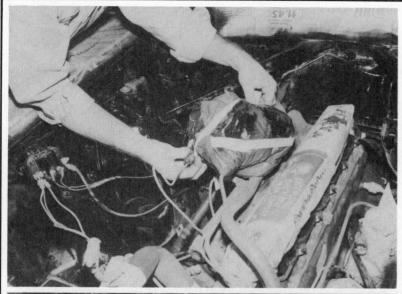

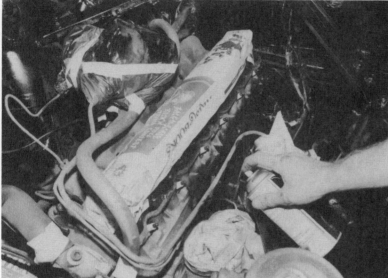

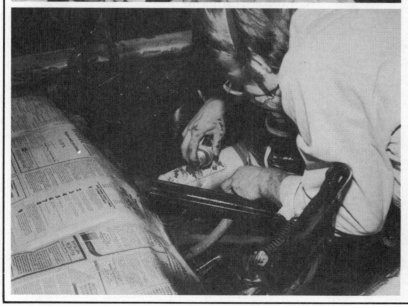

10: Cover the carburetor with a large piece of plastic, taping it securely in place. Tape hose fittings and clamps. A good rule of thumb is to paint over parts that will be replaced later, like spark plugs and hoses. That way all the holes are plugged and you don't have to mask them.

11: A single coat of black engine enamel should do the job on the block and heads. On '65 Mustangs you could get an engine block in any color you wanted, as long as it was black. Ford switched to blue blocks in 1966.

12: Even with the roomy compartment around a 6-cylinder you'll have to be agile to get at some of the lower areas. Try going under the car to get the most difficult areas.

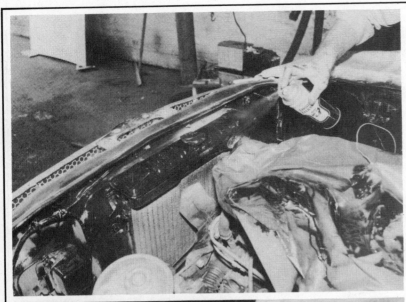

13: The radiator, fan (and fan shroud), battery tray, starter, and oil filler cap also are painted black.

14: Remove masking tape while the paint is still damp. If you wait until it's dry, you might be pulling off paint that overlaps the tape.

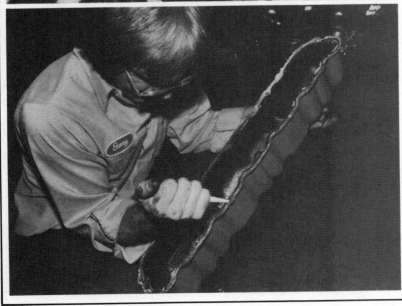

15: If you tore the valve cover gasket when you took it off, you'll have to replace it. If not, make sure the old one is in good shape before putting it on again. Apply a silicone sealer to the gasket for a tighter seal.

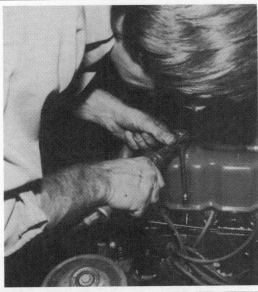

16: Bolt down the valve cover. Replace the battery and other parts you removed.

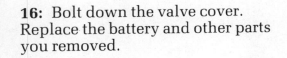

17: With the air cleaner back in place on top of a freshly painted engine compartment, the bright underhood area will make your Mustang even more appealing.

18: Paying close attention to detail will result in a spotless engine compartment like this beauty.

233

The Completed Restoration: Our Mustang is Transformed from a Beater to a Beauty

Those of us who saw the Mustang as it arrived from California still find it hard to believe that the photographs on these pages are of the same car. The tattered and faded fastback we first saw is now a horse of a different color, spiffed up inside and out, and as photogenic as the day it was built.

MUSTANG PARTS, ACCESSORIES, AND PRICE GUIDE

The Original Ponycar was as much a product of canny marketing strategy as it was Lee Iacocca's brilliant thinking. As discussed in the history section, the key to the Mustang's marketing was Ford's decision to offer a long list of extra-cost accessories for an attractive, well-equipped basic package. This wide choice of options allowed the buyer to customize his or her car to a degree rarely, if ever, possible before. Check off the appropriate blanks on the order form, wait a little while, and out of Ford's factory would come a lithe economy Mustang, a posh luxury Mustang, a brutal high-performance Mustang, or whatever combination of these you had selected. This kind of adaptability did much to make Mustang so popular with a range of buyers as wide as the options available.

Mustangs, especially the early ones, have now become collector's items. But not all Mustangs are worth the same, even disregarding varying states of condition. The reason: options. Because of the way Ford sold the car, the way any particular Mustang is equipped has much more to do with what it's worth now as a collectible than is the case with most other cars (with the possible exceptions of other ponycars like Chevy's Camaro and the large-displacement muscle machines of the '60s). Certain accessories may be rare but don't have much bearing on collector values because they're not desirable items.

What options and accessories *should* you look for on an old Mustang? That's the subject of this section. In the pages that follow you'll find detailed price listings by model year for the many factory and dealer-installed accessories available for 1965–73. Each list is followed by a Collector Comments section discussing new options for the year, with plus and minus points for various items, and some indication of their relative worth today. Similar listings are provided for the 1974–78 Mustang II and the 1979–82 Mustang but only with a shorter single Collector Comments section for each of these generations, not each model year.

In all cases, we have tried to make the lists as complete as possible, even to the point of detailing the content of the many option packages or groups offered through the years. Prices shown are in contemporary dollars, and are factory suggested retail prices in effect at the start of each model year. Vehicle list prices and a rundown of standard equipment are provided at the top of each model year list.

By looking through the listings and noting the Collector Comments, you can quickly become as much an expert on desirable Mustang accessories as on desirable Mustang models. But even if you're not in the market for a collectible Mustang, you'll find browsing through this section both fun and informative. No car can be all things to all people, but Mustang probably came closer to this ideal than any other car ever built in America. Ford may have said it best back in 1972: "Designed to be designed by you."

1965 hardtop with vinyl roof, spinner wheel covers

1965 PRICES

	List Price
2-door hardtop, 6-cyl.	$2368
2-door hardtop, 8-cyl.	2480
2-door convertible, 6-cyl.	2614
2-door convertible, 8-cyl.	2722
2+2 2-door fastback, 6-cyl.	2589
2+2 2-door fastback, 8-cyl.	2697

STANDARD EQUIPMENT

170-cid 101-bhp 6-cylinder engine (200-cid 120-bhp from autumn 1964 on) or 260-cid 164-bhp V-8 (289-cid 200-bhp from autumn 1964 on), 3-speed manual transmission w/ floorshift, front bucket seats, padded instrument panel, full wheel covers, cloth-and-vinyl (hardtop) or all-vinyl upholstery, color-keyed carpeting, sports steering wheel, cigarette lighter, door courtesy lights, glovebox light, front and rear bumper guards, heater/defroster.

OPTIONAL EQUIPMENT

Engines
289-cid 2bbl. 200-bhp V-8 (incl. in above prices)	$106
289-cid 4bbl. 225-bhp V-8	158
289-cid 4bbl. 271-bhp HP V-8 (incl. Special Handling Package and 6.95×14 Dual Red Band nylon tires)	
w/o GT Equipment Group	328
w/GT Equipment Group	276

Transmissions
Cruise-O-Matic 3-speed automatic	
6-cyl.	176
200- and 225-bhp V-8s	185
Four-speed manual	
6-cyl.	113
V-8s	184

Power assists
Power brakes	42
Power steering	84
Power top, convertible	53

Performance equipment
Front disc brakes, V-8s only (N/A with power brakes)	57

Limited-slip differential	42
Rally-Pac (clock & tachometer)	69
Special Handling Package (200- and 225-bhp V-8s only) (incl. increased-rate front and rear springs, larger front and rear shock absorbers, 22.1:1 steering ratio, larger-diameter front stabilizer bar)	31
GT Equpment Group, 225- and 271-bhp V-8s only (incl. dual exhaust system w/bright extensions, Special Handling Package, front disc brakes, fog lamps, GT stripes, five-dial instrument cluster, GT ornamentation)	165
Wheels, styled steel, 14" (V-8s only)	120

Optional tires
All 6-cyl. models have (5) 6.50×13 4-ply BSW rayon tires standard.	
(5) 6.50×13 WSW	33
(5) 6.95×14 BSW	7
(5) 6.95×14 WSW	41
All 8-cyl. models (except w/271 HP V-8) have (5) 6.95×14 4-ply BSW tires standard.	
(5) 6.95×14 WSW	33
(5) 6.95×14 BSW, nylon	16
(5) 6.95×14 WSW, nylon	49
(5) 6.95×14 dual red band nylon	49
All models with 271-bhp Hi-Performance V-8 have (5) 6.95×14 4-ply Dual Red Band nyon tires standard.	
(5) 6.95×14 BSW, nylon	N/C
(5) 6.95×14 WSW, nylon	N/C

Saftey equipment
Emergency flashers	19
Padded sunvisors (except 2+2)	6
Rear seatbelts	15
Deluxe front seatbelts, retractable	7
Deluxe front and rear seatbelts (front retractable)	25
Visibility Group (incl. remote-control mirror, day/night mirror, two-speed electric wipers, windshield washer	36

Comfort/convenience and appearance equipment
Accent Group (incl. bodyside paint stripes and rocker panel moldings; deletes rear quarter ornament)	
Hardtop, convertible	27
2+2 fastback	14
Air conditioner	277
Backup lamps	10
Heavy-duty battery	7
Closed emission system (California type)	5
Console, full-length	50
Console (for air conditioner)	32
Interior Decor Group (incl. unique luxury trim, padded sunvisors, woodgrain instrument panel appliqué, deluxe woodgrain steering wheel, five-dial insrument cluster, door courtesy lights)	107
Full-width front-seat w/center armrest, hardtop, convertible	24
Tinted glass with banded windshield	30

Pushbutton AM radio (w/antenna)	58
Rocker panel moldings (except 2+2)	16
Deluxe steering wheel	32
Vinyl roof, hardtop	74
Wheel covers with knock-off centers	18
Wire wheel covers, 14″......................	45
MagicAire heater delete (credit)	(32)
Seatbelts delete (credit)	(11)

The following options are not available with the 271-bhp Hi-Performance V-8: air conditioner, three-speed manual transmission, Cruise-O-Matic, limited-slip differential, power steering, rayon tires.

The following options are not available with the GT Equipment Group: backup lamps, rocker panel moldings, power brakes, Accent Group, and all options not available with the HP V-8.

Rear bumper guards are not included with GT Equipment group, nor are rocker panel moldings on 2+2. Full-width seat with center armrest not available with Interior Decor Group, GT Equipment, or console.

Dealer-installed accessories

Door edge guards	3
Rocker panel moldings, set	20
Deluxe spinner wheel covers, 13″ or 14″	29
Simulated wire wheel covers, 13″ or 14″	58
Luggage rack	35
Tonneau cover, white or black	53
Spotlight, left	30
Vanity mirror	2
License plate frame	5
Fire extinguisher	34
Compass	8
AM radio	54
Rear seat speaker	12
Studio-Sonic Sound System (reverb unit)	23
Round left door mirror	4

Universal left door mirror	2
Left remote-control door mirror	13
Matching right door mirror	7
Inside day/night mirror	5
Backup lights	10
Power brakes	47
Glovebox lock	2
Remote-control trunk release	7
Windshield washer	15
Rally-Pac	16

Note: Accessory tables may not include every option available in each year. Only Mustang-only dealer accessories are shown; universal options, such as tissue dispensers, are omitted.

Collector Comments—1965

Technically, Mustangs made in calendar year 1964 are considered 1965 models. Ford said so in early sales literature, though not in factory service manuals. It should be noted that the early models differ in some ways from the later cars. Besides a change in the engine lineup between "1964½" and 1965 (referred to in the history section), the early direct-current generator was later replaced by a more efficient and powerful alternator. This is an easy way to distinguish between the two groups, but it is not absolutely foolproof.

In general, the "1964½" cars bring slightly more than the "true" 1965 models, all things being equal. As you might expect, the V-8 cars, especially those with 271-bhp Hi-Performance 289 V-8 command the highest prices. As a rule, other V-8s are worth from 10–15 percent more than comparable six-cylinder models. The HP cars command as much as a 50 percent price premium because they are both more rare and more highly sought-after. If you are buying one, make sure that it is a true "Hi-Po" in both serial number and engine.

1965 2+2 fastback with GT Equipment Group

The most common 1965 driveline is a non-HP V-8 combined with Cruise-O-Matic, and even today most collectors prefer the automatic to the manual. Approximately 64 percent of 1965 model year production was V-8, and some 54 percent was accounted for by Cruise-O-Matic. Surprisingly, 14 percent of original buyers elected the optional four-speed, and a full 32 percent were happy with the standard three-speeder. The two optional transmissions elevate a Mustang's worth almost equally, with the four-speed having a slight edge. The six coupled to the Dagenham (British-built) four-speed is perhaps the most desirable of the inline-engine cars, and is quite rare to boot.

Among other options, power steering is fairly common, with 25 percent of production so fitted. Power brakes and disc brakes are more rare, with 4 and 7 percent installation figures, respectively. Air conditioning adds measurably to a car's value, especially in warm-weather areas. There are any number of appearance options that add value, if only a little. In order of significance from most to least these include: styled steel wheels, Rally-Pac, deluxe woodgrain steering wheel, Accent Group, console, tonneau cover, and vinyl roof. A consideration of original prices for such items will give some idea as to their relative worth today on the collector market.

One particularly desirable '65 option can add up to 30 percent to a Mustang's value now: the GT Equipment Group. Check for completeness on a car claimed to have this package because many GT components (for example, the five-dial instrument cluster or the fog lamps) were available individually over the counter.

Other than the HP V-8, the most valuable 1965 option is, believe it or not, the factory AM/FM stereo radio, which seems to have been fitted to only a few late-production cars. This can bring up to $1000. An AM radio with 8-track stereo tape player was also offered, but this would not approach half the value of the AM/FM unit.

1966 convertible

1966 PRICES

	List Price
2-door hardtop	$2416
2-door convertible	2653
2+2 2-door fastback	2607

STANDARD EQUIPMENT

200-cid 1bbl. 120-bhp 6-cylinder engine, 3-speed manual transmission w/floorshift, front bucket seats, pleated vinyl upholstery and interior trim, sports steering wheel, padded instrument panel and sunvisors, five-dial instrument cluster, full carpeting, heater/defroster, front and rear seatbelts, left door mirror, windshield washers w/electric wipers, backup lamps, emergency flasher, door courtesy lights, rocker panel moldings, full wheel covers, **2+2 fastback** adds: Silent-Flo interior ventilation system.

OPTIONAL EQUIPMENT

Engines
289-cid 2bbl. 200-bhp V-8	$106
289-cid 4 bbl. 225-bhp V-8	158
289-cid 4 bbl. 271-bhp V-8 (incl. Special Handling Package and 6.94×14 Dual Red Band nylon tires)	
w/o GT Equipment Group	328
w/GT Equipment Group	276

Transmissions
Cruise-O-Matic 3-speed automatic	
6-cyl.	175
200- and 225-bhp V-8s	185
271-bhp V-8	216
Four-speed manual	
6-cyl.	113
V-8s	184

Power assists
Power brakes	42
Power steering	84
Power top, convertible	53

Performance equipment
Heavy-duty battery, 55 amp	7
Front disc brakes, V-8s only (N/A w/power brakes)	57
GT Equipment Group, 225- and 271-bhp V-8s only (incl. dual exhaust system, foglamps, special ornamentation, disc brakes, Special Handling Package, GT stripes less rocker panel moldings)	152
Limited-slip differential	42
Rally-Pac (clock and tachometer)	69
Special Handling Package, 200- and 225-bhp V-8s only (incl. increased-rate front and rear springs, larger front and rear shock absorbers, quicker steering ratio, larger-diameter front stabilizer bar)	94

Safety equipment
Two-speed windshield wipers	13
Glass, tinted and banded windshield	30
Glass, tinted, windshield only	21
Deluxe seatbelts, front and rear, front retractors and warning light	15
Visibility Group (incl. remote-control door mirror, day/night mirror, two-speed electric wipers)	30

Comfort/convenience equipment
Air conditioner (tinted glass recommended)	311
AM radio/"Stereosonic" tape system (radio req.)	128
Full-width front seat w/armrest (NA 2+2)	24

Luggage rack, decklid (NA 2+2) 32
AM radio and antenna 58

Appearance equipment
Accent stripe (deletes rear quarter ornamentation) 14
Console, full-length 50
Console (for air conditioner) 32
Deluxe steering wheel, simulated woodgrain 32
Interior Decor Group (incl. special trim, deluxe
    woodgrain steering wheel, rear courtesy lights,
    pistol-grip door handles) 94
Vinyl roof, hardtop 74
Wire wheel covers 58
Wheel covers with knock-off centers 19

Special equipment
Closed crankcase emission system (avail. only
    w/exhaust ECS; NA w/271-bhp V-8) 5
Exhaust Emission Control System (N/A 271-bhp
    V-8) 45

Delete options
MagicAire heater (credit) . . . . (32)

Optional tires
All models exc. w/271-bhp Hi-Performance V-8
    have (5) 6.95×14 4-ply BSW/rayon tires
    standard.
        (5) 6.95×14 WSW 33
        (5) 6.95×14 BSW, nylon 16
        (5) 6.95×14 WSW, nylon 49
        (5) 6.95-14 Dual Red Band, nylon 49
All models w/271-bhp Hi-Performance V-8 have
    (5) 6.95×14 Dual Red Band nylon tires standard.
        (5) 6.95×14 BSW, nylon . . . . N/C
        (5) 6.95×14 WSW, nylon . . . . N/C

Dealer-installed accessories
Door edge guards 3
Rocker panel moldings, set 19
Deluxe wheel covers with spinners, 13″ or 14″ 29
Simulated wire wheel covers, 13″ or 14″ 58

Luggage rack 35
Tonneau cover, black or white 53
Spotlight, left 30
Vanity mirror 2
License plate frame 5
Fire extinguisher 34
Compass 8
AM radio 54
Rear seat speaker 12
Studio-Sonic Sound System (reverb unit) 23
Round left door mirror 4
Universal left door mirror 13
Matching right door mirror 7
Inside day/night mirror 5
Backup lights 10
Power brakes 47
Glovebox lock 2
Remote-control trunk release 7
Windshield washers 15
Rally-Pac 76

Collector Comments—1966

Mustang powertrains for 1966 remained much the same as for '65. For the first time, the HP 289 V-8 was available with a special version of Cruise-O-Matic which, as before, seemed to interest buyers more than the optional four-speed manual. A mere 7.1 percent of production (all engines) was fitted with four-on-the-floor this year, a whopping 62.8 percent with Cruise-O-Matic, and 30.1 percent with standard three-speed manual.

As with the '65s, the most desirable body style among '66 models is the deluxe-interior convertible, the hardtop the least desirable. One interesting point involves the "full width front seat option," or more simply the bench seat. Only 1 percent of '66s carried it compared to 3 percent of '65s. However, limited demand today has kept the bench-seat cars, rare as they are, only even in value with an otherwise equal bucket-seat counterpart. Another factor here may be that the Interior Decor Group was not offered with the bench seat option.

1966 convertible with styled steel wheels

Installation of eight-cylinder engines fell significantly for 1966, to 58.3 percent, the only time this would occur during the first-generation years. Other options and their installation percentages are: power steering 29%, power brakes 3%, front disc brakes 7%, tinted glass 7%, vinyl top 10%, and air conditioner 10%.

Values for 1966 options parallel 1965 in all cases, with the proviso that the 1966 car as a whole is worth somewhat less. As before, the top-dollar model is a convertible with the HP 289 V-8, four-speed, GT Equipment and Interior Decor Groups, accessories like air conditioner and power steering.

1967 hardtop

1967 PRICES

	List Price
2-door hardtop	$2461
2-door convertible	2698
2+2 2-door fastback	2592

STANDARD EQUIPMENT

200-cid 1bbl. 120-bhp 6-cylinder engine, 3-speed manual transmission w/floorshift, front bucket seats, full carpeting, all-vinyl upholstery and door trim, sports steering wheel, padded instrument panel and sunvisors, heater/ defroster, front and rear seatbelts, laminated safety windshield glass, outside rearview mirror, electric wipers w/washer, backup lamps, emergency flasher, door courtesy lights.

OPTIONAL EQUIPMENT

Engines
289-cid 2bbl. 200-bhp V-8	$106
289-cid 4bbl. 225-bhp V-8	158
289-cid 4bbl. 271-bhp V-8 (incl. w/GT Equipment Group)	434
390-cid 4 bbl. 320-bhp V-8	264

Transmissions
Cruise-O-Matic 3-speed automatic	
6-cyl.	188
200- and 225-bhp V-8s	198
271- and 320-bhp V-8s	233
Four-speed manual	
6-cyl. or 225-bhp V-8	184
Other V-8s	233
Heavy-duty three-speed manual (req. w/390 V-8)	79

Power assists
Power front disc brakes	65
Power steering	84
Power top (convertible)	53

Performance equipment
GT Equipment Group, V-8s only	205
Limited-slip differential	42
Competition Handling Package (w/GT Group only)	389
Wide-Oval tires (V-8 required)	62

Comfort/convenience and appearance equipment
Styled-steel wheels	
2+2	94
Others	115
Tinted windows and windshield	30
Convenience control panel	40
Fingertip speed control (V-8 and Cruise-O-Matic req.)	71
Remote-control left door mirror (std. 2+2)	10
Safety-glass rear window, convertible	32
SelectAire conditioning	356
Pushbutton AM radio	58
Pushbutton AM/FM radio	134
Stereo-Sonic tape system (AM radio req.)	128
Folding rear seat and access door, 2+2 (sport deck option)	65
Full-width front seat (NA 2+2)	24
Tilt-Away steering wheel	60
Decklid luggage rack (NA 2+2)	32
Comfort-weave vinyl trim (NA convertible)	25
Center console (radio req.)	50
Deluxe steering wheel	32
Exterior Decor Group	39
Lower back panel grille	19
Interior Decor Group	
Convertible	95
Others	108
Two-tone paint, lower back grille	13
Accent paint stripe	14
Vinyl roof, hardtop	74
Wheel covers (std. 2+2)	21
Wire wheel covers	
2+2	58
Others	80
Typical whitewall tire option	33
Rocker panel moldings (std. 2+2)	16
MagicAire heater (delete)	(32)

Collector Comments—1967

Mustang received its first major restyling for 1967 as well as several new options. First and foremost of these was availability of the 390-cid "Thunderbird Special" 4-barrel V-8 with 320 horsepower, the first of Ford's big-blocks that would see duty in the 'Stang. Other powertrains were the same as for 1965–66. Approximate value adjustments would be +10 percent for the 200-bhp 289, +15 percent for the 225-bhp unit, and +30 percent for the 271 HP small-block. The 390 slots in between the latter two at +20 percent.

Also newly available for 1967 was a Competition Handling Package that included limited-slip differential and a 3.25:1 minimum final drive ratio. This option is quite rare, and adds about the same value as a four-speed, which is to say a good deal. It was available only in combination with the GT Equipment Group, which by itself adds about 25–30 percent.

Options adding 5 percent or more to a '67 car's value today are SelectAire conditioner, power convertible top, styled steel wheels, AM/FM radio (not nearly as rare this year as in 1965–66), Exterior Decor Group with the ribbed rear "grille," and add-on under-dash air conditioner (1967 was the first year for built-in A/C). Adding less than 5 percent are power steering and brakes (with the former being about twice as desirable as the latter), tachometer, limited-slip differential, deluxe seatbelts, tinted windows and windshield, luggage rack, Tilt-Away steering wheel (borrowed from the Thunderbird and new for '67), deluxe steering wheel, console, Protection Group, and the Convenience Control Panel, a set of four warning lights for door ajar, low fuel, etc.

Though the restyle was successful, the original Mustang was a hard act to follow. Sales dropped markedly, and values on the collector market now reflect this. Today, a '67 is worth approximately 10–20 percent less than a similarly equipped '66, with the smallest margin being between convertibles. It's also possible that the '67s are currently undervalued. Though their new styling is considered debatable by some, they did benefit from the experience Ford had garnered with the 1965–66 models. And the '67s offered the widest choice of performance and luxury accessories of any Mustang to date. It was a forecast of the direction the original ponycar would take in later years.

One final aspect of the '67s may not be appreciated fully for a few more years yet, but may add luster to their appeal: these would be the last Mustangs untainted by federal regulations. And among car collectors today, there's a lot to be said for that.

1968 convertible with two-tone hood paint

1968 PRICES

	List Price
2-door hardtop	$2602
2-door convertible	2814
2+2 2-door fastback	2712

STANDARD EQUIPMENT

200-cid 1bbl. 115-bhp 6-cylinder engine, 3-speed manual transmission w/floorshift, front bucket seats, full carpeting, all-vinyl upholstery and door trim, sports steering wheel, heater/defroster, front and rear seatbelts, padded instrument panel and sunvisors, laminated safety windshield glass, outside rearview mirror, electric wipers w/ washer, backup lamps, emergency flasher, door courtesy lights, impact-absorbing steering column, other required safety and production equipment.

OPTIONAL EQUIPMENT

Engines

250-cid 1bbl. 155-bhp I-6	NA
289-cid 2bbl. 195-bhp V-8	$106
302-cid 2bbl. 220-bhp V-8	NA
302-cid 4bbl. 230-bhp V-8	172
390-cid 4bbl. 325-bhp V-8	264
427-cid 4bbl. 390-bhp V-8	NA
428-cid 4bbl. 335-bhp V-8	NA

Transmissions

SelectShift Cruise-O-Matic 3-speed automatic	
6-cyl.	191
289 V-8s	201
390 V-8	233

1967 interior with console, Convenience Control Panel

Four-speed manual (NA w/6-cyl.)	
289 V-8s	184
390 V-8	233

Power assists

Power front disc brakes, V-8s only (req. w/390 V-8 or GT Equipment Group)	65
Power steering	84
Power top, convertible	53

Performance equipment

GT Equipment Group, 230- or 325-bhp V-8s w/power brakes (NA w/Sports Trim Group or optional wheel covers)	147
Tachometer (V-8s only)	54
Limited-slip differential, V-8s only	42
Wide-Oval tires, V-8s only	79

Comfort/convenience and appearance equipment

Glass backlight, convertible	39
Tinted glass	30
Convenience Group (console req. with SelectAire)	32
Fingertip speed control (V-8 and SelectShift req.) .	74
Remote-control left door mirror	10
SelectAire conditioner	360
Pushbutton AM radio	61
AM/FM stereo radio	181
Stereo-Sonic Tape System (AM radio req.)	133
Sport deck rear seat, 2+2 only	65
Full-width front seat, hardtop, 2+2 only (NA w/console)	32
Tilt-Away steering wheel	66
Center console (radio req.)	54
Interior Decor Group	
Convertible and models with full-width front seat	110
Others w/o full-width front seat	124
Two-tone hood paint	19
Accent paint stripe	14
Vinyl roof, hardtop	74
Wheel covers (NA w/GT or V-8 Sports Trim Group)	34
Whitewall tires	33

Collector Comments—1968

The Mustang options roster became more complex for '68. The 230-bhp and 271-bhp 289 V-8s were replaced by a new 302 V-8 with 230 bhp. The 2-barrel 289 lasted until mid-year, then was superceded by 220-bhp 2-barrel 302. The 115-bhp 200-cid six was augmented by a 250-cid six with 155 bhp lifted from the Ford truck line. To counter Chevrolet's growing escalation of the horsepower war, Ford introduced two new high-performance engines, an extremely rare Hi-Performance 302 and the big-block 427 4-barrel, also rare, with 390 bhp. Later in the year, Ford added the 428 Cobra Jet, grossly underrated at 335 bhp. This car is also extremely rare, and is now worth half again as much as a base-engined pony. The 427 would command about a 40 percent premium, the 390 a 20 percent gain, and the small-block V-8s up to 10 percent. The big six is worth only about 5 percent extra over the base engine. The HP 302 is so rare that it's impossible to estimate its present value.

Transmission choices remained as before, with a few exceptions. Six-cylinder engines were no longer available with four-speed, and a heavy-duty three-speed was still standard with the 390. Curiously, the 427 was available only with beefed-up Cruise-O-Matic.

Installation percentages for 1968 options confirm Mustang's shift toward luxury. Performance was still important, but it was becoming secondary to comfort and

1968 2+2 fastback with GT Equipment Group

convenience features. V-8 installations climbed to 71 percent of production, automatic transmission appeared on 72 percent (four-speeds were but a mere 6 percent), air conditioning was on 18 percent, power steering (necessary with the big-blocks and/or a full option load) on 52 percent, vinyl top 19 percent, Tilt-Away steering wheel 3 percent. Power front disc brakes accounted for only 13 percent of production, though this would increase dramatically to 31 percent of the 1969 models.

Fully five different wheel treatments were available for 1968. In order of desirability, these are the styled steel wheels, wire wheel covers, deluxe wheel covers (with red plastic centers), standard full wheel covers, and hubcaps (which appeared with both Ford and Mustang insignia). Few Mustangs were delivered with the lowly hubcap; most came with the full wheel cover, a single stamping with radial spokes and a large brushed-finish central hub.

Ford heavily promoted a special Mustang model in the spring and summer of 1968. This was the Sprint package, which added GT stripes, a pop-open gas cap, and full wheel covers to six-cylinder models plus Wide-Oval tires, styled steel wheels, and foglamps to V-8 cars. The Sprint option adds approximately 10 percent to a car's value today. The GT Equipment Group, more functional and less cosmetic, would add up to 25 percent.

Desirable minor options for '68s don't change much from earlier years. Each is a plus in itself, and a number of them together can add substantially to a car's value. General pricing for '68 models on the collector market matches 1967 values.

The new Sports Trim Group for '68 consisted of woodgrain dash appliqué, two-tone hood paint, Comfort-Weave vinyl front seat inserts (except convertibles), and wheel lip moldings on sixes plus argent-finished styled steel wheels and E70-14 WSW tires with V-8. This group adds an extra 5 percent to the price of a typical '68. The fingertip speed control is fairly rare (0.2 percent of production) and is equally desirable. Other useful options to look for are rear window defogger (offered for the first time this year but not on the drop-top), AM/FM stereo radio, Traction-Lock differential, front disc brakes, and tempered glass backlight for the convertible.

1969 Mach 1 fastback with 428 Cobra Jet V-8

1969 PRICES

	List Price
2-door hardtop, 6-cyl.	$2635
SportsRoof 2-door fastback, 6-cyl.	2635
2-door convertible, 6-cyl.	2849
Grandé 2-door hardtop, 6-cyl.	2866
2-door hardtop, V-8	2740
SportsRoof 2-door fastback, V-8	2740
2-door convertible, V-8	2954
Grandé 2-door hardtop, V-8	2971
Mach 1 2-door fastback, V-8	3199
Boss 302 2-door fastback, V-8	3588

STANDARD EQUIPMENT

200-cid 1bbl. 120-bhp 6-cylinder engine or 302-cid 2bbl. 220-bhp V-8 as above, 3-speed manual transmission w/floorshift, front bucket seats, full carpeting, all-vinyl upholstery and door trim, courtesy lights, applicable required safety and protection equipment. **Mach 1 adds:** 351-cid 2bbl. 250-bhp V-8, ''shaker'' hood with scoop, pin-type hood locks, special exterior striping, chrome styled steel wheels, fiberglass-belted tires, high-back bucket seats, dual color-keyed racing mirrors, electric clock, wood-rim 3-spoke steering wheel, simulated teak appliqué on doors and instrument panel. **Grandé has** (in addition to base equipment): luxury hopsack cloth and vinyl upholstery, simulated teak appliqué on doors and instrument panel, special sound insulation package, dual color-keyed racing mirrors, bodyside striping, wire wheel covers, additional chrome exterior moldings, electric clock.

OPTIONAL EQUIPMENT

Engines

250-cid, 1bbl. 155-bhp I-6 (NA Mach 1)	26
302-cid, 2bbl. 220-bhp V-8 (NA Mach 1)	105
351-cid, 2bbl. 250-bhp V-8 (std. Mach 1)	163
351-cid, 4bbl. 290-bhp V-8	
Mach 1	26
Others	189
390-cid, 4bbl. 320-bhp V-8	
Mach 1	100
Others	158
428-cid, 4bbl. 335-bhp V-8	
Mach 1	224
Others	288
428-cid, 4bbl. 335-bhp Cobra Jet V-8	
Mach 1 (incl. Ram Air)	357
Others	421

Transmissions

SelectShift Cruise-O-Matic	
6-cyl. engines	191
302 and 351 V-8s	201
390 and 428 V-8s	222
Four-speed manual	
302 and 351 V-8s	205
390 and 428 V-8s	254

Power assists

Power disc brakes (NA w/200-cid I-6)	65
Power steering	95
Power top, convertible	53

Performance equipment

GT Equipment Group (NA on Grandé or w/6-cyl. or 302-cid V-8)	147
Tachometer, V-8s only	54
Handling suspension (NA Grandé or w/6-cyl. and 428 V-8 engines)	31
Competition suspension (std. Mach 1 and GT; 428 V-8 required)	31

Comfort/convenience and appearance equipment

Glass backlight, convertible	39
Limited-slip differential, 250 I-6 and 302 V-8	42
Traction-Lok differential (NA sixes and 302 V-8)	64
Intermittent windshield wipers	17
High-back front bucket seats (NA Grandé)	85
Color-keyed dual racing mirrors (std. Mach 1, Grandé)	19
Power ventilation (NA w/SelectAire)	40
Electric clock (std. Mach 1, Grandé)	16
Tinted windows and windshield	32
Speed control (V-8 and auto. trans. req.)	74
Remote-control left door mirror	13
SelectAire conditioner (NA 200 I-6 or 428 V-8 w/four-speed)	380
Pushbutton AM radio	61
AM/FM stereo radio	181
Stereo-Sonic Tape System (AM radio req.)	134
Rear seat speaker, hardtop and Grandé	13
Rear seat deck, SportsRoof and Mach 1	97
Full-width front seat, hardtop (NA w/console)	32
Tilt-Away steering wheel	66
Rim-Blow deluxe steering wheel	36
Console	54
Interior Decor Group (NA Mach 1, Grandé)	101
w/dual racing mirrors	88
Deluxe Interior Decor Group, SportsRoof and convertible	133
w/dual racing mirrors	120
Deluxe seatbelts with reminder light	16
Vinyl roof, hardtop	84
Wheel covers (NA Mach 1, GT, Grandé; incl. w/Exterior Decor Group)	21
Wire wheel covers (NA Mach 1, GT; std. Grandé)	
w/Exterior Decor Group	58
w/o Exterior Decor Group	80
Exterior Decor Group (NA Mach 1, Grandé)	32
Chrome styled steel wheels (std. Mach 1; NA Grandé or w/200 I-6)	117
w/GT Equipment Group	78
w/Exterior Decor Group	95
Adjustable head restraints (NA Mach 1)	17

1969 Grandé hardtop

Collector Comments—1969

Ford took a somewhat different approach to Mustang options for 1969 with the new Mach 1 and Grandé models as well as the awe-inspiring Boss 302 and Boss 429. With these, a buyer could now get a specific set of options as a package. The Grandé was a luxury version of the standard hardtop. The Mach 1 was essentially a performance edition of the slick-looking fastback, which this year picked up the name SportsRoof in Ford advertising.

The 1969 bodyshell was all-new and sleeker, though dimensions and general styling themes remained unmistakably Mustang. Many collectors today feel the '69s are the handsomest of the breed—aggressive yet lean. These cars seemed to reflect what the market wanted: hotter-than-ever peformance, the likes of which shall not be seen again. The zoomier offerings were undoubtedly showroom draws, even for those buyers who ended up with one of the tamer Mustangs. And while performance remained a strong sales factor this year, Mustang entered the upper end of the ponycar field for the first time not just because of the Grandé but because of the widest array of comfort and convenience equipment yet offered.

This was the final year for the GT Equipment Group as a separate option not tied to a particular model. The Mach 1 had all the GT pieces and more, but the GT group by itself is something of a rarity, and worth an extra 25 percent.

Engine offerings this year were led by the mighty 428 Cobra Jet, available with or without Ram-Air induction, and rated in either case at 335 bhp. Either option would increase a vehicle's current value by 35 to 40 percent. The 390 V-8 is worth about 15 percent additional. The 4-barrel 351 small-block is good for 20 percent, and you can add 10 percent for the 2-barrel version of same or the 302. The larger of the two available sixes is worth a mere 5 percent.

Both of the specialty Boss models are rare, and command prices two and three times higher, respectively, than a "cooking" '69. Significant options for the Boss 302 included Traction-Lok and Detroit Locker rear axles, Autolite "in-line" 4-barrel carbs on "Cross-Boss" intake manifolds, and 15×7 chrome Magnum 500 wheels (argent versions were standard). On the Boss 429, value is affected more by engine type, either "S" or "T" specifications, than anything else. The 820S engine is the heavy-duty version and very scarce, worth perhaps 5 to 10 percent more now than the milder 820T mill. The only other significant option for this car is the Detroit Locker No-Spin axle, giving a 5 percent value return today.

Returning to standard production models, the Sports-Roof and Mach 1 fastbacks are desirable as the raciest-looking of the three body styles, and could be worth some

40 to 60 percent more than a '69 hardtop. Hardtops come in slightly below their 1968 counterparts, say 5 to 10 percent, except for the Grandé, which would run about the same but had no direct '68 equivalent. Convertibles are worth approximately twice the base hardtop figure on today's market.

Desirable options for '69 parallel those listed for '68. Interior appointments can be confusing because there were two similar-sounding packages, the Interior Decor Group and the Deluxe Interior Decor Group. Neither was available on Mach 1 or Grandé, as both models already had most of the items standard. The Deluxe Group was not available on the standard hardtop, and high-back bucket seats could be ordered with either package.

Equipment installation rates for '69 models are especially interesting compared to those in previous years. The V-8 rate soared to a new high, 82 percent, and fully 12 percent of production carried four-speed manual shift. The latter gained at the expense of the three-speed manual. Automatic was installed in 71 percent of the cars, about the same as the year before. Power steering orders climbed to 66 percent, and power brakes jumped to 31 percent, more than double the '68 rate. SelectAire conditioning jumped five points to 23 percent.

The 1969 model year, and to some extent 1970 as well, represented the zenith of the enthusiast's influence on Dearborn's products. The performance fan was certainly well served by the Mach 1, which outsold every other model in the '69 lineup, and by the limited-production Boss Mustangs. But this was only a short-lived diversion in Mustang's course toward more luxury and road-hugging weight, more comfort and convenience. This trend would culminate in the all-new 1971 design, the biggest Mustang in history.

1970 PRICES

1970 Mach 1 fastback

	List Price
2-door hardtop, 6-cyl.	$2721
SportsRoof 2-door fastback, 6-cyl.	2771
2-door convertible, 6-cyl.	3025
Grandé 2-door hardtop, 6-cyl.	2926
2-door hardtop, V-8	2822
SportsRoof 2-door fastback, V-8	2872
2-door convertible, V-8	3126
Grandé 2-door hardtop, V-8	3028
Mach 1 2-door fastback	3271
Boss 302 2-door fastback	3588

STANDARD EQUIPMENT

200-cid 1bbl. 115-bhp 6-cylinder engine or 302-cid 2bbl. 220-bhp V-8 as above, 3-speed manual transmission w/floorshift, high-back front bucket seats, full carpeting, all-vinyl upholstery and door trim, courtesy lights, applicable required safety and protection equipment. **Mach 1 adds:** 351-cid 2bbl. 250-bhp V-8, unique grille and parking lamps, dual twist-type hood lock pins, black or white hood paint, hood scoop, E70-14 fiberglass-belted tires, white-wall tires, cast wheel covers, competition suspension package, dual color-keyed racing mirrors, deluxe 3-spoke Rim-Blow steering wheel, knitted-vinyl seat trim, center console, electric clock. **Grandé has** (in addition to base equipment): black or white landau vinyl roof, deluxe 2-spoke steering wheel, woodtone appliqué on instrument panel and doors, houndstooth-check upholstery, electric clock, dual accent paint stripes, dual color-keyed racing mirrors, wheel covers. **Boss 302 has** (in addition to base equipment): special 302-cid 4bbl. 290-bhp V-8, color-keyed dual racing mirrors, hubcaps w/trim rings, front spoiler, space-saver spare tire, fiberglass-belted Wide-Oval tires, quick-ratio steering, competition suspension package.

OPTIONAL EQUIPMENT

Engines
250-cid, 1bbl. 155-bhp I-6 (NA Mach 1)	$ 39
302-cid, 2bbl. 220-bhp V-8 (NA Mach 1)	101
351-cid, 2bbl. 250-bhp V-8 (std. Mach 1)	145
351-cid, 4bbl. 300-bhp V-8	
Mach 1	48
Others	194
428-cid, 4bbl. 335-bhp Cobra Jet V-8	
Mach 1	311
Others	457
w/Ram Air, Mach 1	376
w/Ram Air, others	522

Transmissions
SelectShift Cruise-O-Matic	
6-cyl. or 302 and 351 V-8s (NA Boss 302)	201
428 V-8s	222
Four-speed manual (std. Boss 302; NA 6-cyl.)	205

Power assists
Power front disc brakes (std. Boss 302; NA w/200 I-6)	65
Power steering	95

Comfort/convenience equipment
SelectAire conditioning (NA w/200-cid, Boss 302, or 428-cid w/four-speed)	380
Electric clock, rectangular (NA Grandé, Mach 1 or w/Decor Group)	16
Console (std. Mach 1)	54
Convenience Group	
Grandé, Mach 1, Boss 302, or w/Decor Group	32

Others	45
Rear window defogger, hardtops only	26
Tinted glass, complete	32
Color-keyed dual racing mirrors (std. Grandé, Mach 1, Boss 302, and w/Decor Group)	26
Deluxe seatbelts with reminder light	15
Sport Deck rear seat, SportsRoof, Mach 1, Boss 302 only	97
Deluxe 3-spoke Rim-Blow steering wheel (std. Mach 1)	39
Tilt-Away steering wheel	45
Intermittent windshield wipers	26
Space-Saver spare (std. Boss 302; NA w/200 I-6)	
with E70 or F70×14 WSW or F70×14 RWL tires	7
with E78×14 WSW tires	13
with E78×14 BSW tires	20

Audio equipment

AM radio	61
AM/FM radio	214
Stereo-Sonic Tape System (AM radio req.)	134

Appearance options

Bumper guards, front	13
Decor Group (NA Mach 1, Grandé)	
Boss 302, others exc. convertible	78
Convertible	97
Rocker panel moldings (incl. w/Decor Group; NA Grandé, Mach 1, Boss 302)	16
Dual accent paint stripes, Mach 1 only (std. Grandé)	13
Vinyl roof	
Grandé (landau vinyl roof std.)	26
Hardtop	84
Sport slats, SportsRoof only (dual racing mirrors req.)	65
Trim rings w/hubcaps (std. Boss 302; N/C Grandé, Mach 1)	26
Wheel covers (std. Grandé, NA Boss 302, Mach 1)	26
Sports wheel covers (std. Mach 1; NA w/200 I-6)	
Grandé, Boss 302	32

Others	58
Wire wheel covers (NA Boss 302, Mach 1)	
Grandé	53
Others	79
Magnum 500 chrome wheels, Boss 302 only	129
Argent styled steel wheels (N/C Mach 1; NA Boss 302 or w/200 I-6)	
Grandé	32
Others	58

Performance equipment

Drag Pack axle, 428 V-8s w/3.91 or 4.30 axle ratio	155
Optional rear axle ratios	13
Traction-Lock differential	43
Heavy-duty 55-amp. battery (std. 200 I-6 & 351 2bbl. V-8 w/SelectShift), 250 I-6, 302 V-8 w/manual trans.	13
Heavy-duty 70-amp. battery (std. 351 4bbl. V-8), 200 I-6 & 351 2bbl. V-8 w/SelectShift	13
Extra cooling package (incl. w/SelectAire and 428 V-8; NA Boss 302)	13
Shaker hood scoop, Boss 302, 351 V-8s (incl. w/428 Cobra Jet V-8)	65
Rear spoiler, SportsRoof, Mach 1, Boss 302	20
Quick-ratio steering (std. Boss 302)	16
Competition suspension (std. Mach 1, Boss 302; incl. w/428 V-8s; NA w/sixes)	31
Tachometer and trip odometer, V-8s only	54

Collector Comments—1970

The 1970 Mustang was basically a continuation of '69 themes. There were few styling alterations of note, the most obvious being a return to two headlamps instead of four. The sport slats that had first appeared on the '69 Boss 302 were now available for any SportsRoof fastback, including the Mach 1, and required dual racing mirrors. The slats add an extra 5 to 10 percent in value today. Several interesting vinyl top styles were offered this year, includ-

1970 Grandé hardtop

ing a blue and green houndstooth and a Saddle Kiwi design featuring western trim with a leather look. Either of these rarities is worth a 5 percent premium if in good condition.

Engine options for 1970 were unaltered except for the elimination of the big-block 390 V-8, so collector values duplicate those of '69. The same applies to overall vehicle prices, with not enough design differences between the two model years for collectors to express much of a preference for the '69 over the '70 or vice-versa. Similarly equipped 1969s and '70s in similar condition should therefore be priced virtually the same in all cases.

The GT Equipment Group was deleted from the 1970 options slate, so enthusiastic drivers had to be content with the competition suspension package, which came in two versions. There was one for the 4-barrel 351 and 428 V-8s teamed with automatic transmission. The other one was intended for the manual-shift 428 cars, and had staggered rear shocks. The latter is now worth twice as much, 10 percent versus 5 percent. A new 1970 extra was the Drag Pack, which consisted of stronger con rods, heavy-duty oil cooler, and a modified rotating assembly. This was offered mainly for drag strip use as the name indicated, and was available only with the 428. It's worth approximately 10 percent extra now, more if the rear axle also has the Detroit Locker No-Spin differential and ultra-short 4.30:1 gearing. Clearly, the buyer who wanted to go like blazes could still do so in a 1970 Mustang.

The Boss Mustang was on the wane in 1970. Most comments about the '69 models apply to their 1970 successors. The 820T engine in the Boss 429 was now joined by a new 820A. The subtle differences between these mills illustrate that things other than performance were beginning to tie up Dearborn engineers: minor tweaks to the ''Thermo-actor'' emissions control system are the only contrasting features. It was a sign of the times. But in view of what was to come—or rather, what wouldn't—1970 was hardly a bad year for Mustang performance.

1971 SportsRoof fastback (prototype)

1971 PRICES

	List Price
2-door hardtop, 6-cyl.	$2911
SportsRoof 2-door fastback, 6-cyl.	2973
2-door convertible, 6-cyl.	3227
Grandé 2-door hardtop, 6-cyl.	3117
2-door hardtop, V-8	3006
SportsRoof 2-door fastback, V-8	3068
2-door convertible, V-8	3320
Grandé 2-door hardtop, V-8	3212
Mach 1 2-door fastback, V-8	3268
Boss 351 2-door fastback, V-8	4124

STANDARD EQUIPMENT

250-cid 1bbl. 145-bhp 6-cylinder engine or 302 2bbl. 210-bhp V-8 as above, 3-speed manual transmission w/floorshift, mini front console w/ashtray, armrests, color-keyed loop-pile carpeting, courtesy lights, cigarette lighter, all-vinyl upholstery and door trim, high-back front bucket seats, E78-14 belted BSW tires. **SportsRoof adds:** tinted back window, back panel tape stripe. **Convertible adds:** under-dash courtesy lights, color-keyed top boot, power-operated vinyl convertible top. **Mach 1 has** (in addition to base equipment): 302-cid 2bbl. 210-bhp V-8 engine, choice of hood w/ or w/o NACA-type scoops, E70-14 Wide-Oval whitewall tires, color-keyed spoiler, honeycomb grille and back panel, competition suspension package, dual color-keyed racing mirrors w/left remote control, dual exhausts, pop-open gas cap, wheel trim rings w/hubcaps, ''Mach 1'' fender decals, black or argent lower body and front and rear valence panels. **Boss 351 has** (in addition to base equipment): 351-cid 4bbl. 330-bhp HO V-8 engine, Dual Ram Induction w/functional NACA-type hood scoops, black or argent hood paint and lower body color, twist-type hood locks, 4-speed manual transmission w/Hurst shifter, color-keyed dual racing mirrors, F60-15 RWL belted tires, hubcaps w/wheel trim rings, space-saver spare tire, special exterior striping, dual exhaust system, competition suspension package including staggered rear shocks, special cooling package, 3.91:1 Traction-Lok differential, engine rpm limiter, full instrumentation including tachometer and trip odometer, 80 amp/hour battery, power front disc brakes, black front spoiler. **Grandé has** (in addition to base equipment): luxury cloth-and-vinyl seat trim, molded door trim panels w/integral armrests and courtesy lights, deluxe 2-spoke steering wheel, electric clock, dual color-keyed racing mirrors w/left remote control, bright pedal pads, dual bodyside paint stripes, vinyl roof, wheel covers, rocker panel and wheel lip moldings.

OPTIONAL EQUIPMENT

Engines

302-cid, 2bbl. 210-bhp V-8 (std. Mach 1)	$ 95
351-cid, 2bbl. 240-bhp V-8	140
351-cid, 4bbl. 285-bhp V-8	188
429-cid, 4bbl. 370-bhp Cobra Jet V-8 (power disc brakes, Cruise-O-Matic or close-ratio four-speed, special tires req.)	467
429-cid, 4bbl. 370-bhp Cobra-Jet V-8 w/Ram Air (same options as above req.)	531

Transmissions

SelectShift Cruise-O-Matic (NA Boss 351)
| 250 I-6 or 302 and 351 V-8s | 217 |

Collector Comments—1971

Mustang grew in every dimension except height for 1971, putting on extra pounds that would turn the once-lithe polo pony into a more sedate trotter. Bodyshell and styling were completely new, though traditional Mustang appearance cues were retained. The model lineup was much the

1971 Mach 1 fastback

same as the year before: hardtop, SportsRoof fastback, and convertible among standard cars; Mach 1 and Grandé as the specialty offerings; and the new Boss 351, replacing the previous Boss 302 and 429 as the racers' choice. Production had been dropping for the past several years, and dipped to a new low of around 150,000 units at the close of the '71 model year. Obviously, Mustang was beginning to lose favor with many buyers.

Powerteams for the year proliferated. Base engine for all models except Mach 1 and Boss 351 was the reliable 250-cid six with 145 bhp. Mach 1's base power now came from a 210-bhp 2-barrel 302, optional in other models. There were four 351s: a 2-barrel, 240-bhp unit; a 4-barrel packing a rated 285 bhp; the new H.O. version, standard for the Boss 351, delivering 330 bhp; and a lower-compression Cobra Jet with 4-barrel carb and 280 advertised horses. The big-block 428 was dropped, replaced by the race-bred 429 rated at 370 bhp with or without optional Ram-Air induction. There was also a Super Cobra Jet boasting 375 bhp, which made the '71 Mustang a true screamer.

Reflecting their lower popularity when new, the '71s are now worth only 75 to 80 percent as much as corresponding 1969–70 models. Adjustments for engines would be as follows: add 10 percent for either 2-barrel V-8 (302 or 351); 15 percent for the normal 4-barrel 351; 20 percent for the 351 Cobra Jet; 35 percent for the 429 CJ, 35–40 percent for the Ram-Air CJ, and 50 percent for the Super CJ with Ram Air. What made a CJ into a Super Cobra Jet? Mainly the Drag Pack option, which included a long-duration, high-lift cam with solid lifters; stronger connecting rods; modified rotating assembly; and either Traction-Lok differential with 3.91:1 ratio or Detroit Locker axle with 4.11:1 gearing.

Significant 1971 options important to look for now include the competition suspension (worth an extra 10–15 percent), the Mach 1 Sports Interior (+10 percent), and the Decor Group (also 10–15 percent). A first for Mustang this year was power windows. Only 2 percent of production was so fitted, making this option worth an extra 10 percent today.

Option installation rates for '71 reveal that performance was becoming less and less a factor in Mustang sales. Fully 90 percent were fitted with V-8s versus only 10 percent with sixes. However, automatic found its way into 84 percent of production, with the four-speed manual accounting for just 5 percent, the lowest ever for this option. Power steering was specified on 86 percent of the cars, power brakes and air conditioning on 41 percent each.

The most collectible '71 Mustang would have to be the slick Boss 351. Few were produced, and few good-condition examples survive today. Given equal states of condition, a Boss 351 should be worth two to two-and-a-half times as much as a base hardtop. As the last Boss Ford would build, it also has collector appeal now as a one-year-only model.

1972 convertible with Decor Group

1972 PRICES

	List Price
2-door hardtop, 6-cyl.	$2729
SportsRoof 2-door fastback, 6-cyl.	2786

2-door convertible, 6-cyl.	3015
Grandé 2-door hardtop, 6-cyl.	2915
2-door hardtop, V-8	2816
SportsRoof 2-door fastback, V-8	2873
2-door convertible, V-8	3101
Grandé 2-door hardtop, V-8	3002
Mach 1 2-door fastback, V-8	3053

STANDARD EQUIPMENT

250-cid 1bbl. 95-bhp 6-cylinder engine or 302-cid 2bbl. 136-bhp V-8 as above, 3-speed manual transmission w/floorshift, E78-14 belted BSW tires, rocker panel and wheel lip moldings, lower back panel appliqué with bright moldings, color-keyed dual racing mirrors, wheel covers, all-vinyl upholstery and door trim, high-back front bucket seats, mini-console, color-keyed loop carpeting, deluxe 2-spoke steering wheel w/woodtone insert, cigarette lighter. **SportsRoof adds:** tinted rear window, fixed rear quarter windows. **Convertible adds:** power-operated vinyl convertible top, color-keyed top boot, knitted-vinyl seat trim, molded door panels w/integral armrests, tinted windshield, glass backlight. **Mach 1 has** SportsRoof equipment plus: 302-cid 2 bbl. 136-bhp V-8, E70-14 bias-belted wide-oval WSW tires, competition suspension package, choice of hood w/ or w/o NACA-type scoops, color-keyed front spoiler, honeycomb grille and back panel appliqué, black or argent lower body and front and rear valence panels, rear back panel tape stripe, "Mach 1" front fender decals, wheel trim rings w/hubcaps. **Grandé has** (in addition to base equipment): vinyl roof, bodyside tape striping, E78-14 BSW tires, special wheel covers, trunk mat, Lambeth cloth and vinyl seat trim, molded door panels w/integral armrests, bright pedal pads, deluxe instrument panel trim, electric clock.

OPTIONAL EQUIPMENT

Engines

302-cid, 2bbl. 136-bhp V-8 (std. Mach 1)	$ 90
351-cid, 2bbl. 168-bhp V-8	132
351-cid, 4bbl. V-8 (req. Cruise-O-Matic w/3.25 axle ratio or four-speed manual w/3.50 axle ratio plus competition suspension)	209
Emissions system (req. in Calif.)	14

Transmissions

SelectShift Cruise-O-Matic	210
Four-speed manual w/Hurst shifter	199

Power assists

Power front disc brakes	64
Power windows	NA
Power steering (req. w/Tilt-Away steering wheel)	NA

Comfort and convenience equipment

SelectAire conditioning (incl. 55-amp. alternator and extra cooling package; NA w/6-cyl. engine in combination w/3-speed manual transmission)	379

Console	
w/Mach 1 Sports Interior, Grandé	55
Others	70
Convenience Group (incl. trunk light, glove compartment light, map light, underhood light, "lights on" warning buzzer, automatic seatback releases, under-dash courtesy lights (std. convertible), parking brake warning light, glove compartment lock)	47
Electric rear window defroster (incl. 61-amp. alternator on Mach 1 and models w/air conditioning; 55-amp. alternator others)	44
Tinted glass, complete	
Convertible	14
Others	37
Instrumentation Group (incl. tachometer, trip odometer, and oil pressure, ammeter, temperature gauges; incl. w/Mach 1 Sports Interior)	
w/Mach 1 Sports Interior and console	50
w/Mach 1 Sports Interior w/o console	35
Grandé w/o console	57
Others	73
Color-keyed dual racing mirrors (incl. left remote control; std. Mach 1, Grandé)	24
AM radio	61
AM/FM radio (incl. two front door speakers)	197
Sport deck rear seat (incl. F78×14 Space-Saver spare tire)	89
Mach 1 Sports Interior (incl. knitted-vinyl trim, high-back bucket seats with accent stripes, electric clock, engine gauges, door trim panels w/integral pull handles and armrests, color-accented deep-embossed carpet runners, deluxe black instrument panel appliqué with woodtone center section, rear seat ashtray)	119
Deluxe 3-spoke Rim-Blow steering wheel	36
Tilt-Away steering wheel (power steering req.) . . .	42
Stereo-Sonic Tape System (AM radio req.; incl. two front door speakers; NA AM/FM)	124

Handling and performance equipment

Optional axle ratios (NA California for 302 V-8 w/Cruise-O-Matic)	12
Traction-Lok rear axle	44
Heavy-duty 70 amp battery (std. Mach 1 w/351 2bbl V-8 w/air conditioning and electric rear window defroster)	14
Extra cooling package (incl. w/air conditioning) . .	13
Dual Ram-Air Induction System, 351 V-8s only (incl. functional NACA-type hood scoops, black or argent two-tone hood paint, hood lock pins, "Ram-Air" engine decals)	60
Rear spoiler, SportsRoof only	30
Competition suspension (incl. extra heavy-duty front and rear springs, extra heavy-duty front and rear shock absorbers, rear stabilizer bar, std. Mach 1; NA 6-cyl. models)	29

Appearance and protection equipment

Deluxe seatbelts w/warning light (std. convertible exc. for shoulder belts)	16

Front and rear bumper guards (incl. w/Protection Group) 29

Decor Group, hardtop and convertible (incl. lower bodyside black or argent paint w/bright upper edge moldings, unique grille w/sport lamps, color-keyed spoiler/bumper and hood and fender moldings, trim rings w/hubcaps; deletes std. rocker panel moldings, wheel lip moldings, and wheel covers; NA w/Protection Group) 72

Door edge guards 6

NACA-type hood, Mach 1 302 only (std. Mach 1 w/351 V-8) .... N/C

Color-Glow metallic paint 36

Protection Group (incl. bodyside protection moldings w/color-keyed vinyl inserts, front and rear bumper guards; deletes bodyside tape stripe on Grandé; NA w/Decor Group, Mach 1) 42

Vinyl roof (incl. "C" pillar tri-color ornament; std. Grandé) 82

Bodyside tape stripes, black or argent, Mach 1 or w/Decor Group only 24

Trim rings w/hubcaps (std. Mach 1; incl. w/Decor Group)
    Grandé 8
    Others 32

Wheel covers 24

Sports wheel covers
    Grandé 30
    Mach 1 or w/Decor Group 22
    Others 54

Magnum 500 chrome wheels (incl. F78×14 Space-Saver spare tire)
    Grandé 119
    Mach 1 or w/Decor Group 111
    Others 143

Tire options

For models w/(5) B78×14 BSW tires standard.
  Incl. F78×14 Space-Saver spare tire. Opt. tires NA w/6-cyl. or standard wheel covers.
    (5) E70×14 WSW 36
    (5) F70×14 WSW 63
    (5) F70x14 B/WL 75
    (5) F60×15 B/WL .... NA

For models w/(5) E70×14 WSW tires standard.
  Incl. F78×14 Space-Saver spare tire. Opt. tires NA w/6-cyl. or standard wheel covers.
    (5) F70×14 WSW 27
    (5) F70×14 B/WL 39
    (5) F60×15 B/WL 55

Collector Comments—1972

Mustang production declined again for the 1972 campaign, sinking to just under 125,000 cars, the lowest yearly total ever. In virtually all respects the '72s were identical with the '71s and—except the convertible—are worth the same. The 1972 ragtop brings more primarily because of its higher-grade standard interior.

The main 1972 changes concerned powerteam availability. Ironically, a big reason why Mustang became so big for 1971, the 429 big-block, was eliminated. Engine choices were slashed to five as Dearborn's engineers concentrated on meeting federal emission standards. Base engine for all but Mach 1 was the time-tested 250-cid six, now rated at 95 bhp (by the newly adopted SAE net rating method). Next was the 302 2-barrel V-8 with 136 bhp, standard in Mach 1, and good for a 10 percent value plus in other models today. Add the same for the 2-barrel 351 (168 bhp). The 4-barrel 351 Cobra Jet adds 20 percent. Late in the year a detuned Boss 351 4-barrel unit called the 351 H.O. became available; it is rare, and adds 35 percent to current values. As always, figure 10 percent or so for four-speed manual or three-speed automatic over the base three-speed manual.

Ford offered two special models with red, white, and blue trim called Sprint, following previous packages of the same name. The better Sprint included Magnum 500 wheels and F60×15 RWL tires, and commands a 15 percent premium now. Allow 10 percent for the lesser package. The Mach 1 Sports Interior and the Decor Group

1972 Mach 1 Fastback

each increase a 1972 car's value by 10 percent.

Initially, dual racing mirrors color-keyed to the exterior were fitted to all 1972s, but Ford later reverted to a single mirror on standard models and the duals became optional again. Any association with racing must have been seen as a liability by Ford product planners, because several performance-oriented options fell by the wayside—the Detroit Locker No-Spin differential, for example. Even the competition suspension, though still available (and worth 10–20 percent today) was greatly toned down.

Desirable options this year are SelectAire conditioning, Dual Ram-Air Induction, Instrumentation Group, Traction-Lok differential, the 15×7 Magnum 500 chrome wheels, AM/FM stereo radio, power windows (fitted to only 2 percent of production), and sport deck rear seat (SportsRoof fastbacks only).

Equipment installations moved even further away from go and more toward show. V-8 engines amounted to 94 percent of production, automatic transmission 90 percent. Only 3 percent of '72s came off the line with the four-speed. Air conditioning and tinted windows were carried by 49 and 56 percent, respectively. Power steering accounted for 90 percent, power front disc brakes 55 percent. Cruise control, which previously never ran above 0.3 percent, was not available, the first time since 1968. The Tilt-Away steering wheel installation figure climbed a point to 4 percent, the first gain in five years.

1973 Grandé hardtop

1973 PRICES

	List Price
2-door hardtop, 6-cyl.	$2760
SportsRoof 2-door fastback, 6-cyl.	2820
2-door convertible, 6-cyl.	3102
Grandé 2-door hardtop, 6-cyl.	2946
2-door hardtop, V-8	2897
SportsRoof 2-door fastback, V-8	2907
2-door convertible, V-8	3189
Grandé 2-door hardtop, V-8	3088
Mach 1 2-door fastback, V-8	3088

STANDARD EQUIPMENT

250-cid 1bbl. 95-bhp 6-cylinder engine or 302-cid 2bbl. 136-bhp V-8 as above, 3-speed manual transmission w/ floorshift, E78-14 bias-belted BSW tires, rocker panel and wheel lip moldings, lower back panel appliqué w/bright molding, chrome rectangular left door mirror, all-vinyl upholstery and door trim, mini front console, color-keyed loop-pile carpeting, deluxe 2-spoke steering wheel w/woodtone insert, cigarette lighter, seatbelt reminder system, door courtesy lights. **SportsRoof adds:** tinted back window, fixed rear quarter windows. **Convertible adds:** under-dash courtesy lights, power-operated vinyl convertible top, color-keyed vinyl top boot, glass backlight, knitted-vinyl seat trim, power front disc brakes. **Grandé has** (in addition to base equipment): color-keyed dual racing mirrors, vinyl roof, bodyside tape striping, special wheel covers, trunk mat, Lambeth cloth and vinyl seat trim, molded door panels with integral armrests, bright pedal pads, deluxe instrument panel, electric clock. **Mach 1 has** (in addition to base equipment): 302-cid 2bbl. 136-bhp V-8 engine, competition suspension package, choice of hood w/ or w/o NACA-type hood scoops, E70-14 bias-belted WSW Wide-Oval tires, color-keyed dual racing mirrors, black grille and back panel tape stripe, wheel trim rings w/hubcaps, tinted back window, all-vinyl upholstery and door trim, high-back front bucket seats.

OPTIONAL EQUIPMENT

Engines

302-cid 2bbl. V-8 (std. Mach 1)	$ 87
351-cid 2bbl. V-8	128
351-cid 4bbl. V-8 (incl. 55 amp. alternator, heavy-duty 55 amp. battery, special intake manifold, special valve springs and dampers, large-capacity 4300-D carburetor, 2.5-inch-diameter dual exhaust outlets, modified camshaft, four-bolt main bearing caps. Requires Cruise-O-Matic (3.25 axle ratio) or 4-speed manual (3.50 axle ratio) transmission, power front disc brakes, competition suspension)	194
California emission testing	14

Transmissions

SelectShift Cruise-O-Matic	204
Four-speed manual w/Hurst shifter (NA w/6-cyl.)	193

Power assists

Power front disc brakes (std. convertible; req. w/ 351 V-8s)	62
Power windows	113
Power steering (req. w/Tilt-Away steering wheel)	103

Comfort/convenience equipment

SelectAire conditioning (incl. extra cooling package; NA 6-cyl. w/3-speed manual transmission)	368
Console	
Grandé	53
Others (incl. electric clock)	68
Convenience Group (incl. trunk light, glove compartment light, map light, underhood light, "lights on" warning buzzer, automatic seatback releases, under-dash courtesy lights (std.	

convertible), parking brake warning light, glove compartment lock) 46

Electric rear window defroster (NA convertible or w/6-cyl.) 57

Tinted glass, complete
Convertible 14
Others 36

Instrumentation Group (incl. tachometer, trip odometer, and oil pressure, ammeter, and temperature gauges; incl. w/Mach 1 Sports Interior; NA 6-cyl.)
Grandé w/o console 55
Others 71

Color-keyed dual racing mirrors (std. Grandé, Mach 1) 23

AM radio 59
AM/FM stereo radio 191
Sport deck rear seat, SportsRoof, Mach 1 only 86
Deluxe 3-spoke Rim-Blow steering wheel 35
Tilt-Away steering wheel (power steering req.) . . . 41
Deluxe leather-wrapped 2-spoke steering wheel . . 23
Stereo-Sonic Tape System (AM radio req.) 120
Intermittent windshield wipers 23

Handling and performance equipment
Optional axle ratios 12
Traction-Lok differential 43
Heavy-duty 70 amp/hr. battery (std. hardtop and convertible w/351 2bbl. in combination w/Instrument Group or SelectAire) 14
Extra-cooling package (std. w/SelectAire; NA 6-cyl.) 13
Dual Ram Induction, 351 2bbl. V-8 (incl. functional NACA-type hood with black or argent two-tone paint, hood lock pins, "Ram-Air" engine decals) 58
Rear deck spoiler, SportsRoof, Mach 1 only 29
Competition suspension (incl. extra heavy-duty front and rear springs, extra heavy-duty front and rear shock absorbers; std. Mach 1; NA 6-cyl.) 28

Appearance equipment
Deluxe seat and shoulder belts (std. convertible exc. shoulder belts) 15
Deluxe Bumper Group (incl. rear rubber bumper inserts and full-width horizontal rub strip) 25
Rear bumper guards 14
Decor Group (incl. black or argent lower bodyside paint w/bright upper edge moldings, unique grille w/sport lamps, trim rings w/hubcaps; deletes rocker panel and wheel lip moldings w/ Decor Group) 51
Door edge guards (incl. w/Protection Group) 6
Color-keyed front floor mats 13
Metallic Glow paint 35
Two-tone hood paint
Mach 1 18
Others 34
Protection Group (incl. vinyl-insert bodyside moldings, spare tire lock, door edge guards;

deletes bodyside tape stripe on Grandé; NA Mach 1 or w/Decor Group)
Grandé 23
Others 36

Vinyl roof, hardtops (incl. C-pillar tri-color ornament; std. Grandé) 80
Three-quarter vinyl roof, SportsRoof only 52
Mach 1 Sports Interior, V-8 SportsRoof, Mach 1 only (incl. knitted vinyl trim, high-back bucket seats w/accent stripes, Instrumentation Group, door trim panels w/integral pull handles and armrests, color-accented deep embossed carpet runners, deluxe black instrument panel appliqué w/woodtone center section, bright pedal pads, rear seat ashtray) 115
Black or Argent bodyside stripes, w/Decor Group only 23
Trim rings w/hubcaps (std. Mach 1 and w/Decor Group)
Grandé 8
Others 31
Sports wheel covers
Grandé 56
Mach 1, Decor Group 48
Others 79
Forged aluminum wheels
Grandé 119
Mach 1, Decor Group 111
Others 142

Collector Comments—1973

As befits the last of the "true" Mustang ponycars, the 1973 models are worth a slight bit more—say 2–3 percent—than comparable '72s. Convertibles are especially desirable, though more were sold than the previous year because Ford had announced plans in advance to discontinue the ragtop for the downsized 1974 Mustang II, which most everyone knew was on the way. At one time, convertibles commanded much higher prices than other '73 models as the "last" factory-built Ford soft-tops. Now that the body style has been revived for 1983, it remains to be seen what effect this will have on '73 convertible values.

Only minor styling changes marked the last of the "fat" Mustangs, a revised grille with vertical parking lamps being the most obvious. Interiors were basically unaltered, as were engine choices. Either of the optional 2-barrel V-8s is worth an extra 10 percent over a six-cylinder car, and the 4-barrel 351 adds 20 percent. Other option values are the same as for '72. One new item for 1973 was forged aluminum dish-type slotted wheels, which replaced the Magnum 500s available for so many years. These are worth 5–10 percent extra on today's market.

Ford tried another type of option packaging this year with the Basic Equipment Groups A and B. The former comprised Cruise-O-Matic, power steering and front disc brakes, AM radio, and whitewall tires. To these, the B group added air conditioning, tinted glass, and full-length center console. Respective value gains are 10–15 percent

1973 convertible with Decor Group, two-tone hood

and 20–25 percent compared with a car not so equipped.

Even though it had grown to outlandish proportions for a "sporty compact," Mustang remained an eminently "optionable" car. Of course, the choice performance extras were mostly gone by 1973, but there was still at least a modicum of scoot available, plus enough luxury and convenience features to warm the heart of the most ardent LTD fancier. Nevertheless, Ford knew it needed a different sort of a pony to meet the exigencies of the fuel-short, emissions-throttled '70s. And it had one all ready to go for 1974: the smaller, lighter, tighter Mustang II.

1974 Ghia hardtop

1974 PRICES

	List Price
2-door hardtop	$2895
2+2 3-door fastback	3088
Ghia 2-door hardtop	3325
Mach 1 3-door fastback	3518

STANDARD EQUIPMENT

2.3-liter (140-cid) 85-bhp 4-cylinder engine, 4-speed manual transmission w/floorshift, solid-state ignition, front disc brakes, tachometer, steel-belted WSW radial tires, low-back front bucket seats, vinyl upholstery and door trim, color-keyed carpeting, woodtone instrument panel appliqué, European-type armrests, full wheel covers. **2+2 adds:** fold-down rear seat, styled steel wheels. **Ghia has** (in addition to base equipment): color-keyed deluxe seatbelts, dual color-keyed remote-control door mirrors, Super Sound Package, shag carpeting, woodtone door panel accents, digital clock, super-soft vinyl or Westminister cloth interior trim, color-keyed vinyl roof, spoke-style wheel covers, **Mach 1 has** 2+2 equipment plus: 2.8-liter (171-cid) 105-bhp V-6 engine, dual color-keyed remote-control door mirrors, Wide-Oval steel-belted BSW radial tires, black lower bodyside paint, decklid striping, styled steel wheels w/trim rings.

OPTIONAL EQUIPMENT

Engine
2.8-liter (171-cid) 105-bhp V-6 (std. Mach 1) $229

Transmission
SelectShift Cruise-O-Matic 212

Option packages
Convenience Group (incl. dual color-keyed remote-control door mirrors, right visor vanity mirror, inside day/night mirror, parking brake boot, rear ashtray)

w/Luxury Interior Group	41
Mach 1 or w/Rallye Package	21
Others	57

Light Group (incl. underhood, glovebox, map, ashtray, and instrument panel courtesy lights plus trunk or cargo area courtesy light and warning lamps for parking brake, door ajar, and headlamps-on) 44

Luxury Interior Group (incl. super-soft vinyl upholstery, deluxe door panels with large armrests and woodtone accents, deluxe rear quarter trim, 25 oz. cut-pile carpeting, sound package, parking brake boot, door courtesy lamps, rear ashtray; std. Ghia) 100

Maintenance Group (incl. manual, spare bulbs, fire extinguisher, flares, warning flag, fuses, tire gauge, bungee cord, lube kit, trouble light, pliers, screwdriver, crescent wrench) 44

Rallye Package (2.8 V-8 req.; NA Ghia; incl. Traction-Lok differential, steel-belted RWL tires, extra-cooling package, competition suspension, dual color-keyed remote-control door mirrors, styled steel wheels, sport exhaust system, digital clock, leather-wrapped steering wheel)

Mach 1	150
2+2	284
Others	328

Other
SelectAire conditioning 383
Anti-theft alarm system 75
Traction-Lok differential 45

Heavy-duty battery	14
Color-keyed deluxe seatbelts (std. Ghia)	17
Front and rear bumper guards	37
Digital clock (std. Ghia)	36
Console	43
Electric rear window defroster	59
California emission equipment	19
Full tinted glass	37
Dual color-keyed door mirrors (std. Ghia; Mach 1)	36
Rocker panel moldings	14
Vinyl-insert bodyside moldings	50
Glamour paint	36
Pinstripes	14
Power brakes	45
Power steering	106

Radios

AM	61
AM/FM monaural	124
AM/FM stereo	222
AM/FM stereo w/tape players	346

Competition suspension (incl. heavy-duty springs, adjustable shocks, rear anti-roll bar, 195/70 B/WL tires)	37
Flip-out rear quarter windows, 2+2, Mach 1	29
Vinyl roof, hardtop only (std. Ghia)	83
Fold-down rear seat	61
Super Sound Package (std. Ghia)	22
Leather-wrapped steering wheel	30
Sunroof	149
Luggage compartment trim	28
Picardy velour cloth trim, Ghia	62
Wheel trim rings (std. Ghia)	32

1975 2+2 hatchback

1975 PRICES

	List Price
2-door hardtop	$3529
2+2 3-door fastback	3723
Ghia 2-door hardtop	3897
Mach 1 3-door fastback	4093

STANDARD EQUIPMENT

2.3-liter (140-cid) 83-bhp 4-cylinder engine, 4-speed manual transmission w/floorshift, solid-state ignition, front disc brakes, tachometer, steel-belted BSW radial tires, low-back front bucket seats, vinyl upholstery and door trim, color-keyed carpeting, woodtone instrument panel appliqué, European-type armrests, full wheel covers. **2+2 adds:** fold-down rear seat, styled steel wheels. **Ghia has** (in addition to base equipment): color-keyed deluxe seatbelts, dual color-keyed remote-control door mirrors, steel-belted WSW radial tires, Super Sound Package, shag carpeting, woodtone door panel accents, digital clock, choice of Westminster cloth or super-soft vinyl interior trim, color-keyed vinyl roof, spoke-style wheel covers. **Mach 1 has** 2+2 equipment plus: 2.8-liter (171-cid) 97-bhp V-6 engine, dual color-keyed remote-control door mirrors, Wide-Oval steel-belted BSW radial tires, black lower bodyside paint, decklid striping, styled steel wheels w/trim rings.

OPTIONAL EQUIPMENT

Engines

2.8-liter (171-cid) 105-bhp V-6 (std. Mach 1)	$253
5.0 liter (302-cid) 122-bhp V-8	
Mach 1	172
Others	199

Transmission

SelectShift Cruise-O-Matic	227

Option packages

Convenience Group (incl. dual color-keyed remote-control door mirrors, right visor vanity mirror, inside day/night mirror, parking brake boot, rear ashtray)	
w/Luxury Interior Group	48
Mach 1, models w/Rallye Package or Exterior Accent Group	29
Others	65
Light Group (incl. underhood, glovebox, ashtray, dashboard courtesy lights plus map light and door ajar and headlamps-on warning lamps)	33
Security Lock Group (incl. locking gas cap, inside hood release lock, spare tire lock)	14
Luxury Interior Group (incl. super-soft vinyl seat/door trim w/large armrests, deluxe rear quarter trim, door courtesy lights, color-keyed seatbelts, shag carpeting, parking brake boot, rear ashtray, super sound package)	100
Ghia Silver Luxury Group, Ghia only (incl. Silver metallic paint, silver Normande-grain half-vinyl roof, stand-up hood ornament, cranberry striping, silver bodyside moldings, all-cranberry interior in Media velour cloth, color-keyed sunvisors/headliner, center console)	151
Maintenance Group (incl. manual, bulbs, fire extinguisher, flares, warning flag, fuses, tire gauge, bungee cord, lube kit, trouble light, pliers, screwdriver, crescent wrench)	45

Rallye Package (incl. Traction-Lok differential, 195/70 RWL tires, extra-cooling package, bright exhaust tips, competition suspension package, dual color-keyed remote-control door mirrors, leather-wrapped steering wheel, styled steel

wheels w/trim rings)

Mach 1	168
2+2	218
Others	262
Protection Group (incl. door edge guards, front floormats, license plate frames)	
Mach 1	19
Others	27

Others

Exterior Accent Group	151
SelectAire conditioning	401
Anti-theft alarm system	71
Traction-Lok differential	46
Heavy-duty battery	14
Deluxe color-keyed seatbelts (std. Ghia)	17
Power brakes	51
Front and rear bumper guards	31
Digital quartz clock	37
Console	63
Electric rear window defroster	59
California emission equipment	41
Extended range fuel tank	18
Full tinted glass	41
Fuel monitor warning light	14
Decklid luggage rack	43
Dual color-keyed door mirrors (std. Ghia, Mach 1)	36
Rocker panel moldings	14
Color-keyed vinyl-insert bodyside moldings	51
Glass moonroof	422
Radios	
AM	63
AM/FM monaural	124
AM/FM stereo	213
AM/FM stereo w/8-track or cassette tape player	333
Glamour paint	43
Vinyl roof, hardtop only (std. Ghia)	83
Fold-down rear seat (std. 2+2, Mach 1)	61
Leather-wrapped steering wheel	30
Power steering	111
Pinstripes	18
Sunroof	195
Competition suspension (incl. heavy-duty springs, adjustable shocks, rear anti-roll bar, 195/70 B/WL tires)	
Ghia or w/Exterior Accent Group	43
Mach 1	25
Others	55
Velour cloth trim	63
Flip-out rear quarter windows, 2+2, Mach 1	31

1976 PRICES

	List Price
MPG 2-door hardtop, 4-cyl.	$3525
MPG 2+2 3-door fastback, 4-cyl.	3781
MPG Ghia 2-door hardtop, 4-cyl.	3859
2-door hardtop, V-6	3791
2+2 3-door fastback, V-6	4047

1976 2+2 hatchback with Stallion Package

Ghia 2-door hardtop, V-6	4125
Mach 1 3-door fastback, V-6	4209
2-door hardtop, V-8	3737
2+2 3-door fastback, V-8	3992
Ghia 2-door hardtop, V-8	4071
Mach 1 3-door fastback, V-8	4154

STANDARD EQUIPMENT

2.3-liter (140-cid) 92-bhp 4-cylinder engine (optional 2.8-liter (171-cid) 103-bhp V-6 and 5.0-liter (302-cid) 139-bhp V-8 shown in above prices), 4-speed manual transmission w/floorshift, front disc brakes, tachometer, BSW bias-ply tires, low-back front bucket seats, vinyl upholstery, cut-pile carpeting, woodtone interior accents, wheel covers, door panels with integral armrests. **2+2 adds:** fold-down rear seat, styled steel wheels. **Ghia has** (in addition to base equipment): color-keyed deluxe seatbelts, dual color-keyed remote-control door mirrors, steel-belted WSW radial tires, Super Sound Package, shag carpeting, digital clock, choice of Westminster cloth or super-soft vinyl interior trim, color-keyed vinyl roof, deluxe wheel covers. **Mach 1 has** (in addition to 2+2 equipment): 2.8-liter (171-cid) 103-bhp V-6 engine, dual color-keyed remote-control door mirrors, Wide-Oval steel-belted RWL radial tires, black lower bodyside paint, decklid striping, styled steel wheels w/trim rings.

OPTIONAL EQUIPMENT

Transmission

SelectShift Cruise-O-Matic	$239

Option packages

Exterior Accent Group (incl. pinstriping, color-keyed bodyside moldings, dual color-keyed remote-control door mirrors, wheel trim rings on 2+2, styled steel wheels on hardtop, WSW tires)	169
Luxury Interior Group (incl. super-soft vinyl or cloth-and-vinyl trim, large armrests, deluxe door and rear-quarter trim, door courtesy lights, color-keyed deluxe seatbelts, trunk carpeting on hardtops, 18 oz. cut-pile carpeting, parking brake boot, rear ashtray, Super Sound Package)	117
Security Lock Group (incl. locking gas cap, locking inside hood release, spare tire lock)	16

Protection Group (incl. door edge guards exc. Mach 1, front floormats, locking gas cap, spare tire lock, license plate frames)

    Mach 1 36
    Others 43

Convenience Group (incl. intermittent wipers, passenger visor vanity mirror, day/night rearview mirror) 35

Light Group (incl. underhood, glovebox, ashtray and trunk lights plus instrument panel courtesy lights, cargo area light on 2+2, map light, door ajar and headlamps-on warning lights

    w/sunroof or moonroof 28
    w/o sunroof or moonroof 41

Rallye Package (incl. Traction-Lok differential, competition suspension, special exhaust system w/bright extensions, extra-cooling package, RWL tires, styled steel wheels w/trim rings, dual color-keyed remote-control door mirrors exc. Mach 1, leather-wrapped steering wheel, quartz digital clock)

    Mach 1 163
    Others w/V-6, w/o air conditioner 399
    Others w/V-8 or V-6 & w/air conditioner 267

Ghia Luxury Group (incl. Normande-grain half-vinyl roof, full-length bodyside tape striping, hood ornament, Media velour cloth upholstery, console), Ghia only 177

Cobra II Package, 2+2, Mach 1 only (incl. racing stripes, front and rear spoilers, non-functional hood scoop, Cobra emblems, louvered flip-out rear quarter windows, dual remote-control door mirrors, 2.8-liter (171-cid) V-6 engine, brushed-metal door and instrument panel appliqués) ... 312

Cobra II Modification Package 287

Stallion Package (incl. special black hood-and-roof paint, Stallion front fender decals) .... NA

Others

SelectAire conditioning	420
Anti-theft alarm system	83
Optional axle ratio	13
Traction-Lok differential	48
Heavy-duty battery	14
Color-keyed deluxe seatbelts (std. Ghia)	17
Power brakes	54
Front & rear bumper guards	34
Digital quartz clock (std. Ghia)	40
Electric clock	17
Console	59
Electric rear window defroster	67
California emission equipment	49
Extended range fuel tank	24
Full tinted glass	43
Engine block heater	17
Dual-note horn	6
Fuel monitor warning light	18
Decklid luggage rack, hardtop, Ghia	51
Dual color-keyed door mirrors (std. Ghia, Mach 1)	42
Color-keyed vinyl-insert bodyside moldings	60

Rocker panel moldings	19
Glass moonroof	470
Glamour paint	54
Tu-Tone paint/tape treatment	84
Radios	
AM	71
AM w/8-track or cassette tape player	192
AM/FM monaural	128
AM/FM stereo	173
AM/FM stereo w/tape player	299
Vinyl roof, hardtop (std. Ghia)	83
Power steering	117
Leather-wrapped steering wheel	33
Pinstripes	27
Sunroof	230
Velour cloth trim	99
Wheel trim rings (std. Mach 1)	35
Flip-out rear quarter windows, 2+2, Mach 1	33
Luggage compartment light (incl. w/Light Group)	4
LH color-keyed door mirror	14
Tinted windshield	24

1977 2+2 hatchback with Cobra II Package

1977 PRICES

	List Price
2-door hardtop	$3745
2+2 3-door fastback	4016
Ghia 2-door hardtop	4099
Mach 1 3-door fastback	4485

STANDARD EQUIPMENT

2.3-liter (140-cid) 89-bhp 4-cylinder engine, 4-speed manual transmission w/floorshift, front disc brakes, tachometer, BSW bias-ply tires, low-back front bucket seats, vinyl upholstery and door trim, integral armrests, cut-pile carpeting, pecan woodtone accents, full wheel covers. **2+2 adds:** fold-down rear seat, styled steel wheels. **Ghia has** (in addition to base equipment): luxury all-vinyl or cloth-and-vinyl upholstery, luxury decor trim panels, deluxe parking brake boot w/rear ashtray, half-vinyl color-keyed roof, opera windows, bodyside pinstriping, color-keyed vinyl-insert bodyside moldings, deluxe wheel covers. **Mach 1 has** (in addition to base equipment): 2.8-liter (171-cid) 93-bhp V-6, black lower bodyside and back panel paint treatment, color-keyed dual remote-control door mirrors, special Mach 1 striping and insignia, styled steel wheels w/trim rings, RWL radial tires, bright lower bodyside moldings.

OPTIONAL EQUIPMENT

Engines
2.8-liter (171-cid) 93-bhp V-6 (std. Mach 1) $289

5.0-liter (302-cid) 139-bhp V-8
    Mach 1 59
    Others 230
2.3-liter (140-cid) 89-bhp 4-cyl., Mach 1 (credit) . . (289)

Transmission
SelectShift Cruise-O-Matic 253

Option groups
Exterior Accent Group (incl. dual sport mirrors,
    pinstriping, color-keyed vinyl-insert wide
    bodyside moldings, styled steel wheels w/trim
    rings, whitewall tires), 2+2, hardtop 216
Appearance Decor Group (incl. two-tone paint,
    accent tape stripes, wheel trim rings, all-vinyl or
    cloth upholstery, brushed-aluminum instrument
    panel appliqué)
        Hardtops 152
        2+2, Mach 1 96
Convenience Group (incl. interval wipers,
    passenger visor vanity mirror, day/night
    rearview mirror, plus pivoting rear quarter
    windows on 3-door models)
        3-doors w/o Cobra II package 71
        Others 37
Luxury Interior Group (incl. choice of cloth or
    vinyl upholstery, oversize armrests, deluxe door
    trim, color-keyed seatbelts, 14 oz. cut-pile
    carpeting, large parking brake boot w/rear
    ashtray) 124
Protection Group (incl. door edge guards exc.
    Mach 1, front floormats, license plate frames; NA
    w/Cobra II package)
        2+2, Mach 1 39
        Others 46
Light Group (incl. underhood, glovebox, ashtray,
    trunk or cargo area, and under-dash courtesy
    lights plus door ajar and headlamps-on warning
    lamps)
        w/manual or flip-up sunroof 29
        Others 43
Ghia Sports Group, Ghia only (incl. black or tan
    paint w/black Odense grain or Chamois Lugano
    grain vinyl roof, chamois or black vinyl-insert
    bodyside moldings, blackout grille, luggage
    rack with color-keyed leather hold-down straps
    and bright buckles, cast aluminum wheels with
    chamois-painted spokes, chamois seat trim w/
    black upper straps, black instrument panel/
    console/door trim appliqués, center console,
    leather-wrapped sport steering wheel, black
    parking brake handle) 422
Rallye Package (incl. extra-cooling package,
    heavy-duty springs, adjustable shocks, rear
    stabilizer bar, dual color-keyed door mirrors)
    Mach 1 or w/Cobra II or Exterior Accent
      Group 43
        Others 88
Cobra II Package (incl. choice of four colors with
    color-keyed red/blue/green racing stripes or
    black w/gold stripes, front and rear spoilers,

louvered flip-out rear quarter windows, Cobra II
emblems, blackout grille, color-keyed dual sport
mirrors, styled steel wheels w/trim rings, RWL
radial tires, brushed-aluminum instrment panel
and door trim appliqués 535

Other
SelectAire conditioning 446
Heavy-duty battery 16
Deluxe color-keyed seatbelts (std. Ghia) 18
Power brakes 58
Front and rear bumper guards 36
Digital quartz clock (std. Ghia) 42
Console 76
Electric rear window defroster 73
California emission equipment 52
Full tinted glass 48
High-altitude emission equipment 39
Decklid luggage rack, hardtop, Ghia 54
Dual sport mirrors 45
Color-keyed vinyl-insert bodyside moldings 64
Rocker panel moldings 20
Metallic glow paint 58
Radios
    AM 76
    AM/FM monaural 135
    AM/FM stereo 184
    AM w/stereo 8-track tape player 204
    AM/FM stereo w/8-track tape player 317
Sunroof 147
Full vinyl roof, hardtop 90
Fold-down rear seat (std. 2+2, Mach 1) 77
Four-way manual driver seat 33
Power steering 124
Leather-wrapped sport steering wheel
    2+2, Mach 1 35
    Others 49
Pinstripes 28
Engine block heater 18
Luggage compartment light 4
Inside day/night mirror 6
Left door sport mirror 16
Tinted windshield 25

1978 2+2 hatchback with Rallye Appearance Package, T-roof

1978 PRICES

	List Price
2-door hardtop	$3555
2+2 3-door fastback	3798
Ghia 2-door hardtop	3972
Mach 1 3-door fastback	4253

STANDARD EQUIPMENT

2.3-liter (140-cid) 88-bhp 4-cylinder engine, 4-speed manual transmission w/floorshift and woodtone shift knob, front disc brakes, BSW bias-ply tires, left chrome door mirror, stainless steel full wheel covers, low-back front bucket seats, vinyl upholstery and door trim, color-keyed carpeting, integral European-style armrests, pecan woodtone interior accents, glovebox lock, inside hood release. **2+2 adds:** styled steel wheels, bias-belted RWL or WSW tires, fold-down rear seat, cargo area carpeting, sports steering wheel, blackout grille, front spoiler. **Ghia has** (in addition to base equipment): deluxe color-keyed seatbelts, choice of cloth or deluxe all-vinyl upholstery, luxury decor door trim with large armrests, deluxe parking brake boot w/rear ashtray, color-keyed half-vinyl roof, bodyside pinstriping, color-keyed vinyl-insert bodyside moldings, deluxe wheel covers. **Mach 1 has** 2+2 equipment, plus: 2.8-liter (171-cid) 90-bhp V-6 engine (exc. Calif.), RWL steel-belted radial tires, dual color-keyed remote-control door mirrors, black lower bodyside/back panel/valence panel paint, back panel accent tape, styled steel wheels w/trim rings, bright lower bodyside moldings, Mach 1 insignia.

OPTIONAL EQUIPMENT

Engines
2.8-liter (171-cid) 90-bhp V-6 (std. Mach 1)	$324
5.0-liter (302-cid) 139-bhp V-8 (incl. w/King Cobra Option)	
Mach 1	13
Others	312
2.3-liter (140-cid) 88-bhp 4-cyl., Mach 1 (credit) . .	(324)

Transmission
SelectShift Cruise-O-Matic	
w/V-8 or King Cobra Option	225
Others	263

Option groups
Appearance Decor Group (incl. two-tone lower body paint, dual accent paint stripes, white-painted styled steel wheels w/trim rings. Corinthian all-vinyl or Stirling cloth upholstery, brushed aluminum instrument panel appliqué)

Hardtops	160
2+2	112

Exterior Accent Group (incl. dual sport mirrors, full-length bodyside pinstriping, wide color-keyed vinyl-insert bodyside moldings, styled steel wheels w/trim rings, WSW tires) 224

Convenience Group (incl. interval wipers, passenger visor vanity mirror, day/night rear view mirror; 3-door also has pivoting rear quarter windows)

3-doors w/o Cobra II pkg. or T-roof	69
Others	35

Fashion Accessory Package (incl. bodyside pinstriping, Fresno cloth-and-vinyl upholstery, illuminated visor vanity mirror, door trim convenience pockets, large parking brake boot w/coin tray, 4-way manual driver's seat, Appearance Protection Group, illuminated entry system, rear ashtray) 228

Ghia Sports Group, Ghia only (incl. half-vinyl roof in Black Odense or Chamois Lugano grain, color-keyed vinyl-insert bodyside moldings, full-length accent stripes, black grille, cast aluminum wheels with chamois-painted spokes, black engine-turned instrument panel and door trim appliqués, leather-wrapped sport steering wheel, black manual-shift knob or bright auto. trans. selector handle, center console w/tray, black parking brake handle) 355

Luxury Interior Group (incl. cloth or vinyl upholstery, large armrests, deluxe door trim, color-keyed seatbelts, 18 oz. cut-pile carpeting, large parking brake boot, rear ashtray) 155

Appearance Protection Group (incl. chrome door edge guards exc. Mach 1 and Cobra II, front floormats, license plate frames)

Mach 1, Cobra II (incl. front license bracket) . .	28
Others w/front license bracket	36
Mach 1, Cobra II w/o front license bracket	24
Others w/o front license bracket	33

Rallye Appearance Package, 2+2 only (incl. gold bodyside and hood stripes, black moldings and door handles, black wiper arms, black front spoiler, gold grille and taillight surrounds, black dual sport door mirrors, white styled steel wheels w/trim rings, black or white vinyl upholstery w/gold-ribbed Touraine cloth inserts, sport steering sheel, gold welting and door panel moldings, color-keyed carpeting) . . . 166

Rallye Package (incl. extra-cooling package, heavy-duty springs, adjustable shock absorbers, dual sport door mirrors)

Mach 1, models w/Exterior Accent Group or Rallye Appearance Pkg	37
Others	87

Light Group (incl. underhood, glovebox, ashtray, trunk or cargo area and under-dash courtesy lights plus door ajar and headlamps-on warning lights)

w/flip-up roof or T-roof	40
Others	45

Cobra II Package, 2+2, Mach 1 only (incl. front & rear spoilers, black louvers on backlight and rear quarter windows, flipper rear quarter windows, tri-color racing stripes, Cobra II insignia, black grille, styled steel wheels w/trim rings, black sport mirrors, RWL tires, hood scoop, Rallye Package, and black wiper arms, rocker panel and upper door moldings) 730

King Cobra Option, 2+2 only (incl. V-8 engine, power brakes, power steering, RWL tires, Rallye Package, unique tape treatment, King Cobra insignia on bodysides and rear deck spoiler, distinctive hood scoop w/emblem, front air dam, color-keyed dual sport door mirrors) 1277

Other

Collector Comments— Mustang II

Compared to the 1965–73 Mustangs, options and accessories have much less bearing on desirability of Mustang IIs. The reason, quite simply, is that the Mustang II is not now a collectible, and may never be. Even the most exciting offerings of these years, the 1976–78 Cobra II and 1978 King Cobra, were more imitations of their Shelby predecessors than true high-performance machines, though the V-8 King Cobra was quick by 1978 standards. So, singling out the more desirable Mustang II options is, at the moment, an academic exercise.

Among the highly optioned specialty or package models, the Mach 1 has far and away the greatest collector potential—even more than the Cobra variations. It came with the top performance equipment in each of the Mustang II's five model years, including the 2.8-liter V-6 and steel-belted radial tires. The competition suspension package for 1974 was theoretically available on any model, but most Mustang IIs leaving the factory with it were Mach 1s. You can tell if a car has it by checking underneath for the rear stabilizer bar, one of its key components.

The Ghia hardtop was the must luxurious Mustang II, but most of those suffered from being too "loaded" with frills. Also, most had the optional automatic transmission, which really ate into Mustang II performance, and the

1978 2+2 hatchback with King Cobra Option

model's standard vinyl top and opera window roof treatment were passé even in 1974. Nonetheless, a surprising degree of quality was built into the Ghia (it was supposed to be the most brilliant of what Lee Iacocca called his "little jewels"), and you can still find good ones today for remarkably little money.

An interesting option applied first to the Ghia for 1975 was the glass moonroof. It's a practical feature that also adds to comfort and driving fun. The special Silver Ghia that year was a desirable package model, tastefully furnished in plush materials and comprehensively equipped. Other new '75 extras included an extended-range (17-gallon) fuel tank and forged aluminum wheels. Bolted onto more roadable machinery, those wheels might be worth more (in appearance if not hard cash) than a whole 1975 Mustang II.

Because Ford didn't change the Mustang II much over its five-year production run, options didn't change much either. For 1976, the moonroof was extended to other models, and could be ordered with either a silver or brown tint. It was hardly a substitute for a true convertible or even a T-top, though Ford would get around to the latter for 1978.

The most interesting news (if that's the word for it) for '76 was the return of the Cobra name on an option group for the 2+2 fastback. This package could also be ordered on the Mach 1, which created the amusing official designation Mustang II Mach 1 Cobra II. You may smile, but Carroll Shelby didn't, nor did fans of the genuine article. As the Cobra II had the same mechanicals as the Mach 1, the only thing that set it apart was cosmetics—and those were of dubious distinction. Somehow, the package managed to evoke the look of the 1965–66 Shelby-Mustangs with their white paint and broad blue racing stripes, but the Cobra II had a hood scoop that didn't work above an engine with far less guts than the original Shelby-modified 289 V-8.

Ford had reinstated the 302-cid derivative of its legendary small-block as an option for the 1975 Mustang II. This means that a Cobra II so equipped can be made into quite a little terror what with all the bolt-on speed parts available

for this engine on the aftermarket. Even so, this "cosmetic performance" car will never have the investment potential of an early Mustang, even one of the low-line 1965–66 models. But it can be fun, and makes an interesting daily driver (with the bonus of hatchback practicality) for collectors on a budget.

Wheel choices had expanded to at least five different types by the time the 1977 Mustang IIs were announced. These included the "lacy spoke" aluminum jobs, the same thing with white-painted spokes and red trim rings, and dapper-looking wire wheel covers. All these are good finds today, and chances are you can sell them for more than you paid at the local junkyard.

If handling is your thing and you're thinking about a Mustang II, be sure to look for the Rallye Package. It comprised heavy-duty springs, adjustable shocks, and a matching rear stabilizer bar to go with the standard front one, plus an increased-capacity cooling system and dual racing-type door mirrors. Just be sure you like to go around corners quickly, because the tradeoff with this option is a very harsh ride, the inevitable result of stiffening an already crude cart-sprung live rear axle.

Carmakers tend to pull out all the stops for a model's last year, and so it was with Ford for the 1978 Mustang II, offered with the widest choice of options this model would see. Among the most desirable is the T-top, which gave you twin lift-off glass panels that could be stored in the trunk in special vinyl pouches. Not many cars had this option, so it's worth looking for today. The year also brought a simple but effective dress-up treatment in the Rallye Appearance Package, detailed in the listings. It was very much patterned along the lines of the John Player/Lotus Grand Prix cars, with gold accents against black body paint. Another nice 1978 option group was the Fashion Accessory Package, aimed mainly at women buyers according to Ford, and most usually ordered on the notchback hardtops. It consisted of bright-pattern upholstery fabrics, illuminated visor vanity mirror, door map pockets, and the like.

The King Cobra option, also new for '78, was the ultimate in paint-on performance. Though it looked more macho than the Cobra II, it was basically a toothless tiger in stock tune. Again, if you're handy with a wrench you can give one of these the extra muscle it needs to live up to its looks—that is, if you like the looks enough in the first place to go to that kind of trouble. The Cobra II package for '78 got a different look, with wider (and louder) side striping and "go-faster" black louvers for the back window that made it look less like a shrunken GT-350. Shelby lovers must have been horrified.

As for collectibility, you can dismiss all the low-line Mustang IIs as well as the fancy Ghia. Though it sold well when new, Mustang II just doesn't have the technical innovation or design significance to merit more than a passing nod among car collectors today. The same holds true for the Cobra II and King Cobra, with the qualification that they may be long-shot collectibles in the future. Whether they achieve genuine collector status and begin to appreciate in value will depend on many factors as yet unknown: the state of the general economy over the next decade, availability of pre-1974 Mustangs, and whether or not cars of the '70s generate the same widespread nostalgia/enthu-

1978 hardtop with Fashion Accessory Package

siasm that currently surrounds cars of the '50s and '60s.

In the meantime, a Mustang II can provide reliable, economical daily transportation, and even offers a little flair in the bargain despite design compromises dictated by federal mandates and the state of the automotive engineering art in the early '70s. Asking prices are in the cellar now, and parts are equally cheap and in good supply (most as close as your nearest Ford dealer). All this may not be enough to send you running out to buy a Mustang II now, but it doesn't hurt.

1979 hardtop with Sport Option, two-tone paint, TRX suspension

1979 PRICES

	List Price
2-door coupe	$4071
3-door coupe	4436
Ghia 2-door coupe	4642
Ghia 3-door coupe	4824

STANDARD EQUIPMENT

2.3-liter (140-cid) 88-bhp 4-cylinder engine, 4-speed manual transmission w/floorshift, front disc brakes, B78-13 BSW bias-ply tires, full instrumentation including tachometer and oil pressure gauge and ammeter, day/night rearview mirror, cigarette lighter, high-back front bucket seats, color-keyed carpeting, carpeted lower door panels, deluxe steering wheel (2-door), sport steering wheel (3-door), fold-down back seat (3-door), full wheel covers (2-door), sport wheels (3-door), wide black bodyside moldings (3-door), woodtone instrument panel appliqué, black left door mirror, inside hood release, glovebox lock, parking brake warning light. **Ghia adds:** low-back bucket seats, Ghia door trim w/map pockets, sports steering wheel, Light Group, roof-mounted passenger assist handle, right visor vanity mirror, Ghia sound package, carpeted trunk (2-door), bright belt and rocker panel moldings, turbine wheel covers, 14-inch BSW steel-belted radial tires, Ghia badges on door panels and decklid.

OPTIONAL EQUIPMENT

Engines
2.8-liter (171-cid) 109-bhp V-6	$273
2.3-liter (140-cid) 131-bhp turbocharged 4-cyl.	542
5.0-liter (302-cid) 140-bhp V-8 (N/C w/Cobra Pkg.)	514

Transmission
SelectShift automatic (NA w/Turbo-4 high-altitude areas)	307

Option groups

Exterior Accent Group (incl. bright belt moldings, pinstriping, black bumper rubstrip extensions w/dual accent stripes, black rocker panel moldings)	72
Interior Accent Group (incl. low-back bucket seats w/crinkle-grain vinyl upholstery, passenger vanity mirror, inertia seatback releases, color-keyed deluxe seatbelts, deluxe sound package, carpeted cargo area; NA Ghia)	
2-doors	120
3-doors	108
Cobra Package (incl. 2.3-liter turbocharged 4-cyl. engine, turbo warning light w/audible overboost indicator and oil temperature warning system, 8000-rpm tachometer, black engine-turned instrument panel appliqué, Cobra insignia on door panels and dash, hood scoop w/bright TURBO nameplate, Cobra door decals, black exterior moldings, wide black bodyside moldings, bright dual tailpipe extensions, Michelin 195/65R-390 TRX tires, metric forged aluminum wheels, special suspension w/heavy-duty front and rear stabilizer bars and special shock valving, aluminum rear brake drums and semi-metallic front disc brake pads, 3.45:1 axle ratio, sport steering wheel)	1173
Cobra Hood Graphics	78
Light Group (incl. pivoting map light, ashtray and glovebox lamps, engine and luggage compartment lamps; std. Ghia)	
w/o Open-Air Roof	37
w/Open-Air Roof	25
Power Lock Group (incl. power door locks and electric trunklid/hatchback release)	99
Appearance Protection Group (incl. carpeted front floormats, door edge guards)	
w/front license bracket	36
w/o front license bracket	33
Sport Option (incl. black exterior moldings, black bodyside moldings w/rubstrip extensions, 13-inch sport wheels, sport steering wheel)	175
Handling Suspension (incl. rear stabilizer bar, adjusted bushing and spring rates and shock valving; requires optional radial tires)	33

Other

Air conditioner	484
Heavy-duty battery	18
Deluxe seatbelts (std. Ghia)	20
Lower bodyside protection	30
Front license bracket	NC
Power brakes	70
Console (incl. graphic warning light display and electronic digital clock)	140
Mud/stone deflectors	23
Electric rear window defroster	84
California emission system	76
High-altitude emission system	33
Sport-tuned exhaust	34
Tinted glass	59

Left remote-control door mirror	18
Dual remote-control door mirrors	52
Bodyside moldings	39
Rocker panel moldings	24
Wide bodyside moldings	66
Metallic glow paint	41
Tu-Tone paint	78
Radio equipment	
AM	72
AM w/digital clock	119
AM/FM	120
AM/FM stereo	176
AM/FM stereo w/cassette or 8-track tape	243
Premium sound system	67
Dual rear speakers	42
Radio flexibility option	90
Open-air roof	199
Vinyl roof	102
4-way manual driver's seat	35
Speed control	
2-doors w/o Sport Option	116
Others	108
Power steering	141
Leather-wrapped sport steering wheel	
2-drs. w/o Sport Option	53
Others	41
Tilt steering wheel	
2-drs. w/o Sport Option	81
Others	69
Trim	
Cloth	20
Cloth (Accent)	29
Cloth (Ghia)	42
Leather	282
Turbine wheel covers	
3-door or w/Sport Option	10
Others	39
Forged aluminum metric wheels (incl. w/Cobra Pkg.)	
3-door or w/Sport Option	269
Ghias	259
Others	298
Intermittent wipers	35
TRX 190/65R-390 Blackwall Michelin tires (incl. w/Cobra Pkg.; req. metric wheels)	
Mustang	241
Ghia	117

1980 PRICES

	List Price
2-door coupe	$4884
3-door coupe	5994
Ghia 2-door coupe	5369
Ghia 3-door coupe	5512

STANDARD EQUIPMENT

2.3-liter (140-cid) 88-bhp 4-cylinder engine, 4-speed manual transmission w/floorshift, front disc brakes, P184/80R-13 BSW steel-belted radial tires, full instrumentation including tachometer and ammeter and oil pressure gauge,

1980 hatchback with Cobra Package

day/night rearview mirror, high-back front bucket seats, deluxe carpeting, carpeted lower door panels, deluxe steering wheel (2-door), sports steering wheel (3-door), full wheel covers (2-door), sport wheels (3-door), woodtone instrument panel appliqué, black left door mirror, inside hood release, glovebox lock, parking brake warning light, wide black bodyside moldings (3-door), cigarette lighter, fold-down back seat (3-door), mini-spare tire, maintenance-free battery, electronic voltage regulator. **Ghia adds:** low-back bucket seats, color-keyed cut-pile carpeting, Ghia door trim w/map pockets, luxury rear seat trim panels, luxury 4-spoke steering wheel, Light Group, roof-mounted passenger assist handle, right visor vanity mirror, color-keyed deluxe seatbelts, Ghia sound insulation package, carpeted trunk (2-door), pinstriping, Ghia badges on door panels and decklid, P-metric 14-inch BSW steel-belted radial tires, turbine wheel covers, belt and rocker panel moldings.

OPTIONAL EQUIPMENT

Engines

3.3-liter (200-cid) 85-bhp 6-cyl.	$219
2.3-liter (140-cid) 131-bhp turbocharged 4-cyl.	481
4.2-liter (255-cid) 117-bhp V-8	
w/Cobra Pkg. (credit)	(144)
Others	338

Transmission

SelectShift automatic	340

Option packages

Exterior Accent Group (incl. pinstriping, black rocker panel moldings and rubstrip extensions, bumper rubstrip accent stripes), 2-doors only	63
Interior Accent Group (incl. low-back bucket seats w/crinkle-grain vinyl upholstery, inertia seatback releases, deluxe color-keyed seatbelts, passenger visor vanity mirror, deluxe sound package, carpeted trunk on 2-door)	
2-doors	134
3-doors	120
Cobra Package, 3-door only (incl. 2.3-liter turbocharged 4-cyl. engine, sport-tuned exhaust w/bright tailpipe extension, special suspension system w/heavy-duty front and rear stabilizer	

bars and special shock valving, semi-metallic front disc brake pads, Michelin 190/65R-390 TRX radial tires, metric forged aluminum wheels, 3.45 axle ratio, Turbo warning light w/audible overboost indicator and oil pressure warning system, black engine-turned instrument panel appliqué, unique front-end styling w/integral air dam and dual fog lamps, non-functional hood scoop, dual black remote-control door mirrors, black lower bodyside paint, black exterior moldings and door handles, rear spoiler) 1482

Cobra hood graphics	88
Light Group (incl. dual-beam map/dome light, ashtray and glovebox lamps, engine and cargo area lamps; std. Ghia)	41
Power Lock Group (incl. power door locks plus remote trunklid/hatchback release)	113
Appearance Protection Group (incl. carpeted front floormats, door edge guards)	
w/front license bracket	41
w/or front license bracket	38
Sport Option (incl. black exterior moldings, black bodyside moldings w/rubstrip extensions, 13-inch sport wheels, sport steering wheel)	
w/Carriage Roof	168
w/o Carriage Roof	186
Handling Suspension (incl. rear stabilizer bar, adjusted bushing and spring rates and shock valving; requires optional radial tires)	35

Others

Air conditioner	583
Heavy-duty battery	20
Deluxe seatbelts (std. Ghia)	23
Lower bodyside protection	34
Front license bracket	NC
Power brakes	78
Cargo area cover, 3-doors	44
Console (incl. graphic warning light display and electronic digital clock)	166
Mud/stone deflectors	25
Electric rear window defroster	96
California emission system	253
High-altitude emission system	36
Sport-tuned exhaust	38
Tinted glass	65
Hood scoop	31
Liftgate louvers, 3-doors	141
Luggage rack, roof	86
Left remote-control door mirror	19
Dual remote-control door mirrors	58
Bodyside moldings	43
Rocker panel moldings	30
Wide bodyside moldings	74
Metallic glow paint	46
Tu-Tone paint	88
Radio equipment	
AM	93
AM/FM	145

AM/FM stereo	183
AM/FM stereo w/cassette or 8-track tape	271
Premium sound system	94
Dual rear speakers	38
Radio flexibility option	63
Carriage roof, 2-doors only	625
Open-air roof	
Ghia or w/Light Group	204
Others	219
Vinyl roof, 2-doors only	118
4-way manual driver's seat	38
Recaro bucket seats	531
Speed control	
2-doors w/o Sport Option	129
Others	116
Power steering	160
Leather-wrapped sport steering wheel	
2-doors w/o Sport Option	56
Others	44
Tilt steering wheel	
2-doors w/o Sport Option	90
Others	78
Trim	
Cloth	21
Cloth (accent)	30
Cloth (Ghia)	46
Leather	349
Turbine wheel covers	
3-door or w/Sport Option	10
Others	43
Forged aluminum metric wheels (for TRX tires; incl. w/Cobra Pkg.)	
3-door or w/Sport Option	323
Ghias	313
Others	355
Intermittent wipers	39
Rear window wiper/washer	79
TRX 190/65R 390 blackwall Michelin tires (incl. w/Cobra Pkg; req. metric wheels)	
Mustang	150
Ghia	125

1981 hatchback with Cobra Package, T-roof

1981 PRICES

	List Price
2-door coupe	$5980
3-door coupe	6216
Ghia 2-door coupe	6424
Ghia 3-door coupe	6538

STANDARD EQUIPMENT

2.3-liter (140-cid) 88-bhp 4-cylinder engine, 4-speed manual transmission w/floorshift, front disc brakes, P185/80R-13 BSW steel-belted radial tires, full instrumentation including tachometer and ammeter and oil pressure gauge, day/night rearview mirror, AM radio, high-back front bucket seats w/recliners, deluxe carpeting, carpeted lower door panels, deluxe steering wheel (2-door), sport steering wheel (3-door), fold-down rear seat (3-door), full wheel covers (2-door), sport wheels (3-door), cigarette lighter, black left door mirror, inside hood release, glovebox lock, carpeted cargo area (3-door), woodtone instrument panel appliqué. **Ghia adds:** low-back bucket seats w/inertia seatback releases, luxury color-keyed cut-pile carpeting, luxury door trim panels w/map pockets, luxury 4-spoke steering wheel, Light Group (map/dome light plus lamps for ashtray, glovebox, engine and luggage compartments) passenger visor vanity mirror, color-keyed deluxe seatbelts, Ghia sound insulation package, dual black remote-control door mirrors, bright rocker panel moldings, pinstriping, Ghia badges on door panels and decklid, 14-inch P-metric BSW steel-belted radial tires, turbine wheel covers.

OPTIONAL EQUIPMENT

Engines

3.3-liter (200-cid) 88-bhp 6-cyl. (incl. 4-speed overdrive man. trans.)	$213
2.3-liter (140-cid) 131-bhp turbocharged 4-cyl. (incl. w/Cobra Pkg.; NA w/auto. trans.)	610
4.2-liter (255-cid) 120-bhp V-8 w/Cobra Pkg. (credit)	(321)
Others	289

Transmissions

SelectShift automatic (req. w/V-8)	332
5-speed manual, 4-cyl. engines only	152

Option packages

Interior Accent Group (incl. deluxe sound package, low-back bucket seats w/higher-level vinyl upholstery, inertia seatback releases, luxury door trim panels, deluxe seatbelts, passenger visor vanity mirror, carpeted trunk on 2-door)

2-doors	139
3-doors	126

Cobra Package (incl. 2.3-liter turbocharged 4-cylinder engine, sport-tuned exhaust w/bright tailpipe extensions, handling suspension w/heavy-duty front and rear stabilizer bars and special shock valving, Michelin 190/65R-390 TRX BSW radial tires on forged aluminum metric wheels, 3.45:1 performance axle ratio, 8000-rpm tachometer, turbo monitoring system, black engine-turned instrument panel appliqué, integral front air dam and dual fog lamps, rear spoiler, non-functional hood scoop, dual black remote-control door mirrors, black lower bodyside paint, black exterior moldings and door handles, black bodyside moldings), 3-door only ... 1586

Cobra hood graphics	85

Light Group (incl. pivoting map light, lamps for ashtray, glovebox, engine compartment, cargo area) ... 40

Power Lock Group (incl. power door locks plus electric remote trunklid/hatchback release)

2-doors	110
3-doors	87

Appearance Protection Group (incl. deluxe carpeted front floormats, door edge guards, rear license plate frame if needed) ... 40

Handling suspension (incl. larger front stabilizer bar, rear stabilizer bar, adjusted spring and bushing rates and special shock valving; requires optional radial tires) ... 34

Sport Option, 2-doors only (incl. sport wheel treatment, black window frames and rocker panel moldings, sport steering wheel)

w/Carriage Roof	91
w/o Carriage Roof	110

Others

Air conditioning	524
Optional axle ratio	18
Traction-Lok differential	63
Heavy-duty battery	20
Deluxe seatbelts (std. Ghia)	22
Lower bodyside protection	33
Front license bracket	NC
Power brakes	76
Cargo area cover, 3-doors	43
Console (incl. graphic warning light display and electronic digital clock)	162
Mud/stone deflectors	24
Electric rear window defroster	99
California emission system	246
High-altitude emission system	35
Sport-tuned exhaust, V-8s only	37
Tinted glass	73
Hood scoop (incl. w/Cobra Pkg.)	30
Liftgate louvers, 3-doors	138
Luggage rack, roof	84
Left remote-control door mirror	18
Dual remote-control door mirrors	56
Rocker panel moldings	29
Metallic glow paint	45
Tu-Tone paint, lower	85

Radio equipment

AM delete (credit)	(61)
AM/FM	51
AM/FM stereo	88
AM/FM stereo w/cassette tape	174
AM/FM stereo w/8-track tape	162
Premium sound system	91
Dual rear speakers	37
Radio flexibility option	61

Carriage Roof, 2-doors only	610

Open-air roof

Ghia or w/Light Group	199
Others	213

"T"-bar roof, 3-doors only 823
Vinyl roof, 2-doors only 115
Recaro bucket seats 732
Speed control
    2-doors w/o Sport Option 126
    Others 113
Power steering 156
Leather-wrapped sport steering wheel
    2-doors w/o Sport Option 88
    Others 76
Trim
    Cloth and vinyl 29
    Cloth (Ghia) 45
    Leather 340
Turbine wheel covers (std. Ghia)
    3-door or w/Sport Option 10
    Others 41
Forged aluminum metric wheels (for TRX tires;
    incl. w/Cobra Pkg.)
    3-door or w/Sport Option 315
    Ghias 305
    Others 346
Power windows 133
Intermittent wipers 38
Rear window wiper/washer 77
Michelin TRX 190/65R 390 BSW tires (incl.
    w/Cobra Pkg.; metric wheels req.)
    Mustang 146
    Ghia 122

1982 GT hatchback with H.O. V-8, Recaro seats, TR Package

1982 PRICES

	List Price
L 2-door coupe	$6345
GL 2-door coupe	6844
GL 3-door coupe	6979
GLX 2-door coupe	6980
GLX 3-door coupe	7101
GT 3-door coupe	8308

STANDARD EQUIPMENT

2.3-liter (140-cid) 88-bhp 4-cylinder engine, 4-speed manual transmission w/floorshift, remote-control left door mirror, AM radio, deluxe wheel covers, high-back reclining front bucket seats, carpeting, full instrumentation. **GL adds:** deluxe sound insulation, black treatment on exterior moldings, dual bodyside pinstripes, turbine wheel covers, sport steering wheel, low-back reclining bucket seats, upgraded vinyl trim. **GLX adds:** dual bright remote-control door mirrors, luxury-level carpeting, luxury steering wheel, Light Group, upgraded trim. **GT has** over L equipment: wider tires, handling suspension, fog lamps, black dual remote-control door mirrors, cast aluminum wheels, black treatment on exterior moldings, front spoiler, rear spoiler, hood scoop, console w/digital clock, blackout sports interior treatment, GLX seat trim, GL door trim panels.

OPTIONAL EQUIPMENT

Engines
3.3-liter (200-cid) 88-bhp 6-cyl. $213
4.2-liter (255-cid) 111-bhp V-8
    GT (credit) .... (57)
    Others 283
5.0-liter 157-bhp H.O. V-8 (incl. 4-speed manual
    trans.)
    w/TR Performance Pkg. 402
    Others 452

Transmissions
3-speed SelectShift automatic (req. w/6 and 4.2
    V-8) 411
5-speed manual, 4-cyl. only 196

Option packages
Light Group (incl. dual-beam map/dome light plus
    lamps for ashtray, glovebox, engine
    compartment, and cargo area; std. GLX) 49
Power Lock Group (incl. power door locks plus
    electric remote trunklid/hatchback release) 139
Appearance Protection Group (incl. deluxe
    carpeted front floormats, door edge guards, front
    license plate frame if needed) 48
TR Performance Package (incl. larger front
    stabilizer bar, rear stabilizer bar, adjusted shock
    absorber valving and bushing and spring rates,
    Michelin 190/65R-390 TRX radial tires match-
    mounted on metric forged aluminum wheels w/
    anti-theft lug nuts)
    L 583
    GL 533
    GLX, GT 105

Others
Air conditioner 676
Optional axle ratios 76
Traction-Lok differential 24
Lower bodyside protection 41
Front license bracket .... NC
Power brakes 93
Cargo area cover, 3-doors 51
Console (incl. graphic warning light display and
    electronic digital clock) 191
Electric rear-window defroster 124
California emission system 46
High-altitude emission system .... NC

Tinted glass	88
Hood scoop (std. GT)	38
Liftgate louvers	165
Right remote-control door mirror	41
Rocker panel moldings	33
Metallic glow paint	54
Two-Tone paint, lower	104
Radio equipment	
AM delete (credit)	(61)
AM/FM	76
AM/FM stereo	106
AM/FM stereo w/cassette tape	184
AM/FM stereo w/8-track tape	184
Premium sound system	105
Dual rear speakers	39
Carriage Roof, 2-doors only	734
Open-air roof	276
T-bar roof, 3-doors only	1021
Vinyl roof, 2-doors only	137
Recaro front bucket seats	834
Speed control	155
Power steering	190
Leather-wrapped sport steering wheel	55
Tilt steering wheel	95
Handling suspension (std. GT)	50
Power windows	165
Intermittent wipers	48
Rear window wiper/washer, 3-doors only	101

Collector Comments—
Today's Mustangs

Mustang was reborn for 1979. In one stroke, everything wrong with the pudgy-looking Mustang II was put right. It was a great piece of work—in our view a much more integrated design than either the Mustang II or the now highly rated 1965 original. Coming from a company whose styling director was usually seen in a gussied-up Lincoln Versailles, this latest Mustang was something of a miracle. Its crisp, taut lines flowed smoothly from nose to tail, more like something from Europe than Dearborn. (In fact, the rear-end appearance of the Mustang notchback was often compared to that of the prestigious Mercedes-Benz 450SLC.) There wasn't a single wrong angle or tortured bit of sheetmetal on it, a happy benefit of Ford's concern for giving the new car better aerodynamics.

If for no other reason than styling, the current Mustang generation will no doubt become popular with collectors and nostalgia buffs at some time in the future. But there are many other reasons why this should happen, and to find them you need look no further than the options list. Like its predecessors, today's Mustang is offered with a wide array of performance, comfort and convenience, and appearance accessories that allows a customer to transform his or her car into something very special and very personal. So, even though the 1979 generation has yet to become a "classic," it's pertinent to discuss the options that will likely figure into the status of these cars as future collectibles.

Let's start with the interior, initially available in no fewer than eight trim varieties. Two of these are standouts: the leather option and the Ghia treatment. With the former, genuine hide covered the main part of the seats, with vinyl taking over on side bolsters and door panels. Colors were Vaquero (saddle), white, black, chamois, red, and Wedgewood blue. The leather option was available on Ghia models and with the Cobra package, and it really was marvelous: the smell alone was enough to justify its price.

The Ghia interior could also be decked out in a velour cloth reminiscent of that on the Citroën DS-21 Pallas, one of the most elegantly furnished cars ever made. It was a tightly woven, wear-resistant material available in red, chamois, black, Vaquero, or Wedgewood blue. Unlike base models, Ghias came with low-back front buckets with what Ford termed "European-style" headrests. Standard uphol-

1979 hardtop with Sport Option

1983 GLX convertible with H.O. V-8 and 1965 convertible

1983 GT hatchback with H.O. V-8, sunroof, TR package

1982 GT hatchback with H.O. V-8

stery was a good grade of crinkle-grain vinyl, but the cloth trim was dramatically more luxurious and satisfying.

A number of minor interior extras could be ordered on the newer Mustangs to enhance convenience. For example, there was a four-way manual driver's seat that provided all the adjustability of an electric mechanism (up/down and fore/aft) without the complication. Standard on Ghias and a low-cost extra for other models was the Light Group. This had the usual assortment of interior courtesy lights, including a pivoting pencil-beam map light mounted overhead, plus engine compartment and cargo area lamps. A less commonly ordered item was the Power Lock Group, which included a button mounted in the glovebox for electrically releasing the trunklid or hatchback. With the optional center console you automatically got a Honda-like graphic warning light display and electronic digital clock. The former featured a series of LEDs strategically placed on an outline of the car as seen from above. These "lights" monitored such minor mishaps as low windshield washer fluid or a malfunctioning taillamp bulb. The clock not only told you the time but also the day and date at the touch of a button. It also had an elapsed time feature for clocking the length of your journey—or your waiting time in urban traffic jams.

Exterior options fall into two categories: frivolous and functional. An example of the former was surely the Cobra package with its wild tape striping and standard non-functional hood scoop (which also obscured forward vision). Adding insult to aesthetic injury was the extra-cost Cobra Hood Graphics, Ford's fancy way of describing the gaudy snake decal you could get to adorn the hood. It's significant that Ford made the Cobra's "ape-tape" a delete option for '81 to give what the brochure called a "unique" appearance. The factory must have been running low on the stuff anyway, because the Cobra's 1982 successor, the GT, had none of it, and ended up looking much more tasteful. Black liftgate louvers, once called "sports slats," were available for the hatchback's rear window through '81, though we could live without them. In a more subtle vein, pinstriping was standard on Ghias, and could be ordered on base Mustangs to delineate the clean lines of the bodysides and decklid.

As for functional features, there was the neat Flip-Up/Open-Air Roof, a metal or glass panel that enabled you to let the sun shine in without giving up the tight weather protection of a steel top. It could be used as a tilting "vent" to aid interior air flow or could be removed altogether. The T-top with lift-off glass panels was reinstated for hatchbacks beginning with '81. This item had been offered before for 1977–78 Mustang IIs.

One new appearance option for 1980 was the Carriage Roof for notchbacks. This only simulated the top-up appearance of a real convertible, but it was nicely done, available in white only. Ford was working on a real Mustang flip-top, but that would have to wait until 1983.

One good thing about the '79 and newer Mustangs is the instrument panel. It's well laid out, with clearly calibrated dials that cover all basic engine functions including rpm, oil pressure, and battery charge. The most frequently used minor controls—headlamp dimmer, windshield wipers and washer—are catered for by European-style steering column stalks. Ford may have gone a little too far in imitating the imports, though, by putting the horn button at the end of the turn indicator lever, where it can be difficult to find, particularly in a panic situation.

We mention all this because it suggests that the latest Mustangs were designed to appeal to serious drivers. And so they were. Backing that up was a variety of interesting powertrain and chassis options. Starting at the pavement, you could choose the extra-cost 14-inch sport wheels or wire wheel covers. Ghias came with handsome turbine wheel covers that were also available separately for other models. And there were handsome cast aluminum 14-inch-diameter road wheels that made a good match with upgraded radial tires and the optional handling suspension. This gave you a beefier front stabilizer bar, an anti-sway bar at the back (not part of the base chassis), and higher-rate springs, bushings, and shocks.

For the ultimate in roadability, you could get Michelin's low-profile TRX tires, introduced to the U.S. with the '79 Mustang. These featured an odd 390mm diameter (15.35 inches) that required the use of specifically sized metric wheels. These were forged aluminum wheels with a striking three-spoke design and four-lug mounting. The TRX tires and wheels were part of the top handling package that featured special spring and bushing rates and even tighter shock valving to match the stickability of the French tires. In fact, this wheel/tire combination was one of the most European things about the new Mustang, as it had first been used on hot versions of the European Ford Granada. It gives the newer Mustangs terrific handling and roadholding, especially the more powerful models.

Which brings us to engines. The most interesting one for enthusiasts was the turbocharged version of Ford's domestically built overhead cam four. It was offered on 1979–81 models, then was withdrawn because of reliability problems that showed up in customer use. It was standard with the Cobra package, but could also be ordered separately. In either case, you got the special sport-tuned exhaust system with chromed tailpipe extension. Ford added to the turbo's appeal by offering an optional 5-speed manual gearbox (also available with the unblown four) from mid-1980.

Other powerteams were less exotic, at least through '81. The 302 V-8 was withdrawn after 1979 in favor of a debored 4.2-liter (255-cid) derivative that didn't really live up to its promise of better fuel economy. In between this and the fours was Ford's sturdy 3.3-liter (200-cid) straight six, an engine that had been around in one form or another for nearly two decades. Through 1981 you could team it with a 4-speed manual gearbox in which fourth was an overdrive ratio and third the direct (1:1) gear. Three-speed Select-

1983 GLX convertible with H.O. V-8

1983 GLX convertible with wire wheel covers

Shift automatic was available across the board, and for '82 became a "mandatory option" for the six and the 4.2 V-8.

For 1982, Ford adopted European-style model nomenclature for the Mustang line, with L, GL, GLX, and GT in ascending order of price and pizzazz. The GLX was roughly equivalent to the previous Ghia. The GT, as mentioned, replaced the Cobra, but retained its rear spoiler and the low-slung front air dam with integral fog lamps. Black paint or trim was used on the GT for everything from keyholes to wiper arms to dashboard. Genuine Recaro front bucket seats were available as a separate option to enhance the look and feel of sportiness.

To give Mustang genuine high-performance capability, Ford reinstated the 302 V-8 for '82, with so many modifications it was renamed the 302 H.O. (High Output). It packed a healthy 157 horsepower, good for a 0–60 mph time of comfortably under 8 seconds. The V-8 was teamed only with a wide-ratio 4-speed manual gearbox with overdrive top. This combination was available for any Mustang, but we don't doubt most cars so equipped wore GT initials.

The current Mustang herd was five years old when the 1983 models arrived. As if to celebrate the event, Ford instituted a host of refinements. Number one on the list was a glamorous new convertible, the first Mustang ragtop since 1973, in top-line GLX trim. Ford put a lot of engineering thought into this model. For example, most of it was built on Ford's own assembly line and not as a cutting-torch conversion. The top had a glass backlight just like 1967 and later Mustang convertibles did, as well as roll-down rear quarter windows. The convertible was offered with almost every available powerteam, including a revised H.O. V-8 with 4-barrel carb, low-restriction exhaust system, aluminum valve covers, and other changes that knocked a full second off the 0–60 mph time.

This stronger V-8 was the heart of the 1983 GT. Larger tires (up by at least one size on all '83 Mustangs) plus careful chassis tuning were adopted for more neutral handling and less rear axle hop in bumpy corners. Also added as an option with the V-8 was Borg-Warner's T-5 5-speed manual transmission, which made the 1983 5.0-liter GT a real stormer off the line and gave you a gear for just about any situation.

As if all this weren't enough, Mustang came in for its first major appearance changes since 1979. The '83s sported a more rounded nose with a vee'd, sloped-back grille, which Ford claimed reduced air drag by 2.5 percent. At the back, taillights were restyled, and extended to almost full width, interrupted only by the central license plate mount.

There was less news breaking in the small accessories department for '81, where many options were deleted. The reason for this was Ford's urgent need to achieve quality levels comparable to those of Japanese imports. To get that quality, they logically decided to decrease equipment variability in all Ford models. Thus, Mustang lost the rear window washer/wiper option on hatchbacks as well as dual radio speakers, the Carriage Roof (nobody needed that with the return of a real convertible), liftgate louvers, accent tape stripes, righthand remote-control mirror, and the Recaro bucket seats. The Recaros hadn't been very popular.

Also modified was the optional performance suspension. It no longer came exclusively with Michelin TRX tires (though they could be ordered separately), so it was simply called the "Handling" instead of "TR" suspension. Other features of this important option were retained. About the only new options were revised wire wheel covers, a convex righthand rearview mirror (to replace the interior-adjustable type), and cloth "Sport Performance" buckets (to replace the Recaros).

Odds are that the mile-long list of Mustang accessories is a thing of the past, or at least the lists will be a lot shorter in years to come. The need for tighter quality control means that even the most basic Mustang Ls will be more completely equipped than current models, while the upper-class versions like the GT and GLX will have a good many standard features that now cost extra. In view of the public's heightened quality-consciousness, this is all to the good. The Europeans and Japanese have known for years that the less variation in building any car, the better the chances are its workmanship will be high. Like the rest of Detroit, Ford had to learn this the hard way, but there's little doubt the lesson has been learned. The most exciting—and the best-built—Mustangs in history are here now. And enthusiasts can take heart in the knowledge that there are definitely more to come.

MUSTANG SOURCE GUIDE

This section contains a directory of businesses, services, clubs, and publications catering primarily to the Mustang owner. It was compiled by CONSUMER GUIDE® magazine's staff from both general-interest publications for the old-car hobby and periodicals aimed at the Mustang enthusiast. Because of the survey method used, this is not necessarily a complete directory. There may be businesses in your area that can be of assistance even though they do not advertise as being Mustang specialists.

All information presented here has been verified as much as possible by both written questionnaire and direct telephone contact, and is current at time of publication. The reader should note that some information may have changed since this source guide was compiled.

The listings are provided solely as an aid for the reader. They do not constitute endorsement by CONSUMER GUIDE® magazine or PUBLICATIONS INTERNATIONAL, LTD., of any product, service, business, club, or publication mentioned herein.

The purpose of The Mustang Source Guide is to help you get the most enjoyment as possible from your Mustang. It is divided into four parts: parts, services (including restoration assistance), clubs, and publications. You may obtain additional information from any source by writing to the address shown. Where available, either free or for a charge, catalogs of goods and/or services offered are noted. Cross-references are provided for those businesses offering both parts and services. Parts sources with mail order service are so noted. Some parts sources also maintain a retail store as part of their operations. For information on store hours and location, contact the sources in your area.

With this source guide you'll be able to put your Mustang in top condition and keep it running strong. It can also help you identify other Mustang-minded folks in your area. It's been said that Mustang has always been the kind of car that has something for everyone. This source guide will help you discover the many things available for every Mustang, including yours.

Parts

Aftco Restoration Specialty Co. (est. 1959)
P.O. Box 278
Isanti, MN 55040

Shop service and mail order; brochure available.
1965–68 upholstery, door panels, molded carpet sets, convertible tops, boots, well liners, trunk sets.

Airport Motors (est. 1974)
P.O. Box 89
Oak Bluffs, MA 02557

1965–69 Mustangs and used parts. Also, repair service for pre-1970 models.

American Mustang Parts
2216 Cemo Circle
Rancho Cordova, CA 95670

Mail order; free catalog available.
Upholstery, decals, paint, emblems, weatherstripping, accessories. Also, literature.

Anderson's Mustang Corral (est. 1980)
P.O. Box 353
Bonner Springs, KS 66012

Mail order.
New and used parts. Upholstery, carpets, dash, kick panels, weatherstripping. All body parts including chrome trim, bumpers, patch panels, and accessories. Also, body repair service including panel installation, interior painting, seat and trim installation.

Auto Custom Carpet (est. 1947)
316 "J" St.
Anniston, AL 36202

Mail order; catalog available.
1965–73 molded carpet sets (carpet manufacturer).

Auto Krafters (est. 1978)
RR1
Ft. Calhoun, NE 68023

Mail order; free catalog available.
New and used parts for 1965–73, including reproduction
rear spoilers for 1969–73 Mach 1. Also, books and
literature, restoration service.

B&G Classic Car & Parts (est. 1976)
315 S. Hopkins
Titusville, FL 32780

Mail order; free catalog available.
Manufacturer of replacement door panel skin for 1965–73.
NOS, reproduction, and used parts for 1965–73.

Big T Parts Co. (est. 1975)
19337 Greenview
Detroit, MI 48219

Mail order; catalog available.
Carpets, trunk mats, rubber mats. Also, shop manuals,
owner's manuals, parts books, car covers.

Bill's Special Interest Autos
Box 223M
Mill Creek, IN 46365

Mail order; free price list available.
New, used, and rebuilt parts. Also, owner's manuals
through 1973, books.

Bill's Speed Shop (est. 1952)
13951 Millersburg Road SW
Navarre, OH 44662

Mail order; catalog available.
1965–68 and 1974–77 rear quarters, frame rails, floorpans,
torque boxes, shackle rails.

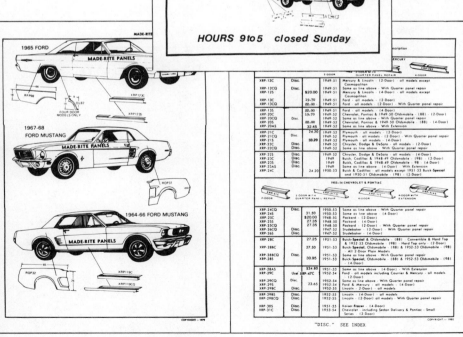

Tony D. Branda Performance (est. 1974)
1434 E. Pleasant Valley Blvd.
Altoona, PA 16602

Mail order; catalog available.
Parts, accessories, and detailing items for Mustang, including Mach 1, Boss 302/351, and Shelby. Also, restoration service.

California Auto Trim (est. 1978)
10949 Tuxford St. #1
Sun Valley, CA 91352

Mail order; catalog available.
Manufacturer of kick panels and headliners. New and used parts, especially for interior; installation available. Also, complete or partial restoration service for 1965–66 (some 1967–68).

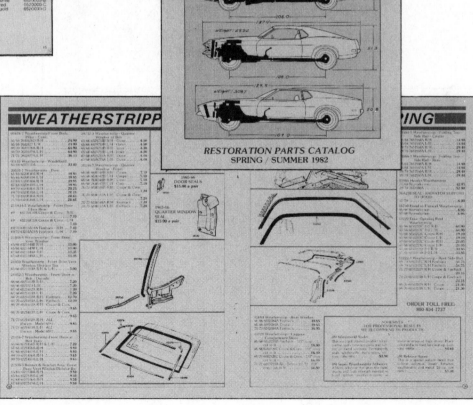

California Mustang Sales and Parts, Inc. (est. 1976)
1249 E. Holt Ave.
Pomona, CA 91767

Mail order; free catalog available.
Original 1965–73 parts. Upholstery, convertible tops, door panels, moldings, weatherstripping, emblems, wheel covers. Also, literature, caps, T-shirts, jackets.

Canadian Mustang (est. 1979)
450 Swift St.
Victoria, B.C., Canada V8W 1S3

Mail order; catalog available.
Parts and restoration supplies.

Central Ohio Mustang (est. 1980)
8600 E. Main St.
Reynoldsburg, OH 43068

Mail order; free parts/price list available.
Restoration parts and supplies.

Champs Mustang Parts (est. 1975)
P.O. Box 545
West Columbia, SC 29172

Mail order only; catalog available.
1965–73 seat covers, carpets, headliners, body parts.

Circle City Mustang
Woolfolk Ave.
Midland City, AL 36350

Mail order; catalog available.
4000 new and reproduction parts. Also decals and literature.

Classic Parts Store (est. 1982)
Box 654
San Fernando, CA 91341

Mail order only; free catalog available.
Reproduction turn signal lever, cigarette lighter assembly, wiper knob, shift handle assembly for automatic transmission, complete T-handle and release knob assembly for automatic transmission.

Cobra Restorers (est. 1977)
3099 Canter Dr.
Kennesaw, GA 30144

Mail order; catalog available.
Engine, body, interior, and trim parts.

Bob Cook Ford Classic Parts (est. 1978)
West State Line
Hazel, KY 42029

Mail order only; catalog available.
New and reproduction parts for 1965–73; over 8000 items.

Corbett's House of Ford Parts (est. 1977)
190 Calhoun St.
Edgewater, MD 21037

Mail order; send needs with Ford part number or body code from data plate and SASE.
NOS parts for 1965–73, including trim moldings, switches, mechanical parts.

Crazy Horse Enterprises
105 S. Ritchie Way
Pasadena, MD 21122

Underbody parts.

Dallas Mustang Parts (est. 1980)
9515 Skillman
Dallas, TX 75243

Mail order; free catalog available.
Complete inventory for all years.

Direct Automotive Products Co. (est. 1980)
7640 Densmore Ave.
Van Nuys, CA 91406

Mail order only.
Custom-tailored car covers, seat covers for 1965–82, bras
for 1978–82.

Eastern Mustang Specialty (est. 1978)
646 South Road
Poughkeepsie, NY 12601

Mail order.
New and used parts for 1965–73. Also, restoration service
(including Shelby) and technical assistance.

Ford Parts Connection of California (est. 1980)
10422 Keokuk Ave.
Chatsworth, CA 91311

Mail order; free catalog available.

Ford Parts Warehouse (est. 1977)
Courthouse Square
Liberty, KY 42539

Mail order; catalog available.

Gelsi's Mustang World (est. 1981)
3576 Northwest Blvd.
Vineland, NJ 08360

Mail order.
New and used parts. Also, cars for sale, repair and
restoration service.

Glazier's Mustang Barn, Inc. (est. 1976)
531 Wambold Rd.
Souderton, PA 18964

Mail order; free catalog available.
New, used, and reproduction parts for 1965–70. Also
literature, appliqués, service signs, car covers.

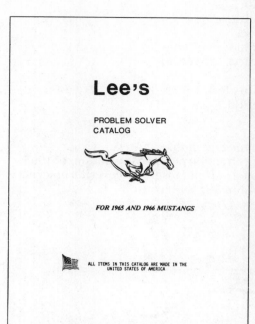

Harris Auto Parts (est. 1976)
8129 Cedarbrook Dr.
Charlotte, NC 28215

Mail order; free catalog available.
Mustang and Shelby parts.

Tom Horne Reproductions (est. 1978)
23032 Hatteras St.
Woodland Hills, CA 91367

Mail order; free catalog available.
Manufacturer, distributor, wholesaler, retailer of
reproduction parts for early Mustangs, including 1965–66
chrome turn signal lever, door-to-window and quarter-
window-pillar rubber seals, inside chrome mirror bracket.
inside day/night mirror, brake pedal trim for automatic
cars, and 1967–68 window-to-door and quarter-window-
pillar rubber seals.

Kanter Auto Parts (est. 1960)
76 Monroe St.
Boonton, NJ 07005

Mail order; free catalog available.
Carpet sets, convertible tops, ball joints, all front
suspension parts, all brake parts.

Kustom Car Care (est. 1976)
111 Old Highway 40
O'Fallon, MO 63366

Restoration shop; parts and complete cars available.

Larry's Mustang Parts (est. 1976)
511 S. Raymond Ave.
Fullerton, CA 92631

Mail order; free price list available.

Lee's Mustang (est. 1978)
351 Buttonwood Lane
Cinnaminson, NJ 08077

Mail order only; catalog available.
1965–67 hardware kits, including trim screw packages,
convertible stud retainers, original radiator hose clamps.
Also, Rally-Pac and fog light wiring harnesses.

Maier Racing Enterprises (est. 1969)
235 Laurel Ave.
Hayward, CA 94541

Mail order; catalog available.
New, used, and reproduction high-performance parts.

Sydney Manchak (est. 1977)
P.O. Box 18025
San Jose, CA 95158

Mail order; free catalog available.

McDonald Ford Parts Co.
RR3, Box 61
Rockport, IN 47635

Mail order only; catalog available.
New parts for 1965–72, including chrome, sheetmetal, weatherstripping, soft trim.

Metro Moulded Parts, Inc. (est. 1918)
9521 Foley Blvd.
Minneapolis, MN 55433

Mail order; catalog available.
New rubber parts, including grommets, pads, weatherstripping.

Mike's Mustang Parts (est. 1980)
3116 Chadwick Dr.
Rockford, IL 61109

Mail order only; send SASE with needs.
1965–73 options, including consoles, tachometers, "Pony" interior items. Also air conditioner and power steering setups and parts.

Mid-America Mustang Parts (est. 1982)
11125 Arcade, Suite E
Little Rock, AR 72212

Mail order; free catalog available.
Interior and trim parts, convertible parts.

Mr. G's Mustang City (est. 1973)
5613 Elliott Reeder Rd.
Ft. Worth, TX 76117

Mail order; free catalog available.
New, used, and reproduction parts. Manufacturer of 1965–66 "Pony" door panel cup and inserts, 1965 grille brackets, and shift seal for automatic with console.

Mr. Mustang, Inc. (est. 1972)
5088 Wolf Creek Pike
Dayton, OH 45426

Mail order; free catalog available.
Large parts inventory. Also, cars for sale, restoration
service.

Muck Motor Sales, Inc. (est. 1921)
10 Campbell Blvd.
Getzville, NY 14068

Mail order.
NOS parts.

Mustang Country (est. 1981)
14625 Lakewood Blvd.
Paramont, CA 90723

New and used parts. Complete line of authentic upholstery
items, with installation available. Also, 1965–73 cars for
sale.

Mustang Country (est. 1980)
3210 Coffey Lane
Santa Rosa, CA 95401

Mail order.
New, used, and reproduction parts including carpet,
upholstery, door panels, headliners, interior paint, body
parts. Also, complete interior restoration facilities and
dismantling service for wrecked cars; owner's manuals,
shop manuals.

Mustang Custom (est. 1977)
2030 Timber Lane
Dayton, OH 45414

Mail order; free catalog available.
Manufacturer, retailer of underbody parts.

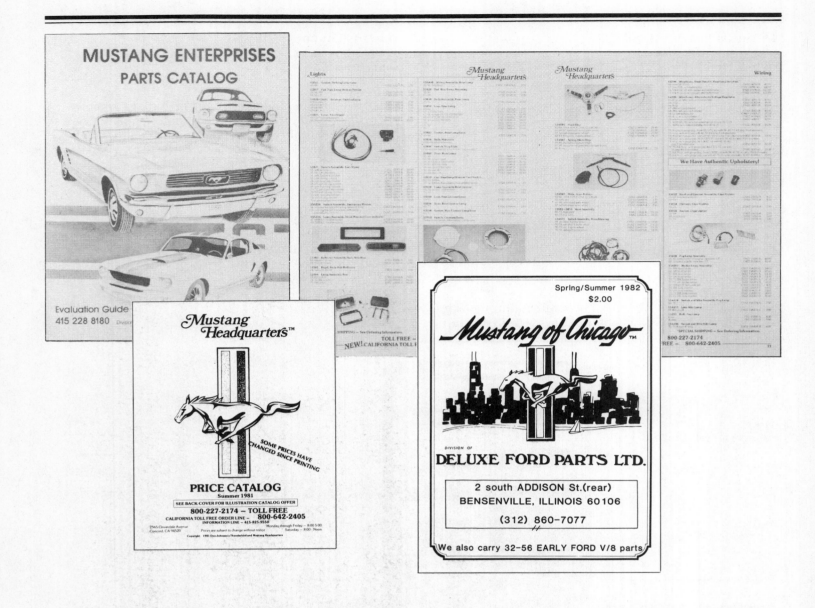

Mustang Enterprises (Div. of Mal's "A" Sales) (est. 1960)
4966 Pacheco Blvd.
Martinez, CA 94553

Mail order; free catalog available.
New parts for 1965–68, including trim and upholstery,
rubber parts, sheetmetal, bumpers.

Mustang Express (est. 1981)
9901 NW 35th St.
Hollywood, FL 33024

Mail order; free catalog available.
1965–67 upholstery and "Pony" upholstery. Also,
1965–68 molded carpets, kick panels, door panels,
convertible tops, trunk mats, headliners, sunvisors, torque
boxes, frame rails, floorpans. Also, stainless steel screw
kits, books.

Mustang Headquarters, Inc. (est. 1978)
2565 Cloverdale Ave.
Concord, CA 94520

Mail order; catalog available.
1965–73 upholstery, sheetmetal, weatherstripping,
suspension parts, accessories. Also, literature.

Mustang Interiors Limited (est. 1981)
P.O. Box 1095
Englewood, CA 90308

Mail order; free price list available.
Interior parts and complete groups.

Mustang Louvers (est. 1977)
2030 Tiger Trail Blvd.
Dania, FL 33004

Mail order.
Rear window sunshade louvers.

Mustang Man (est. 1960)
15514 Mustang Dr.
Fountain Hills, AZ 85269

Mail order only.
Original parts for 1965–66.

Mustang Mart, Inc. (est. 1977)
655 McGlincy Lane
Campbell, CA 95008

Mail order; free catalog available.
1965–70 interior and exterior parts. Also, upholstery shop
specializing in molded door panel repairs for 1965–73
Mustang and Shelby.

Mustang of Chicago (est. 1980)
2 S. Addison St.
Bensenville, IL 60106

Mail order; catalog available.
Complete line of parts for 1965–73 Mustang and Shelby.

Mustang of Ft. Lauderdale (est. 1972)
2205 N. Dixie
Ft. Lauderdale, FL 33305

Mail order; catalog available.
General parts. Also, cars for sale, interior restoration
service, fiberglass repair service.

Mustangs Etc. (est. 1976)
14843 Bessemer St.
Van Nuys, CA 91411

New, used, and reproduction parts. Also repairs,
restoration service, cars for sale.

Mustangs Only World Wide (est. 1968)
1320 Oakland Rd.
San Jose, CA 95112

General parts. Also, mechanical and interior restoration
service.

Mustang Parts (est. 1980)
9 Sallemount Ave.
Warren, NJ 07060

Mail order; catalog available.
1965–73 reproduction and NOS floors, inner rockers,
torque boxes, body patch panels, fenders, quarter panels,
molded carpet sets, upholstery, convertible tops,
headliners, top boots, weatherstripping, trunk mats.

Mustang Parts Store (Div. of T-Bird Parts Store) (est. 1971)
12780 Currie St.
Livonia, MI 48150

Mail order; free brochure available.
Original and reproduction sheetmetal, upholstery, trim,
tires.

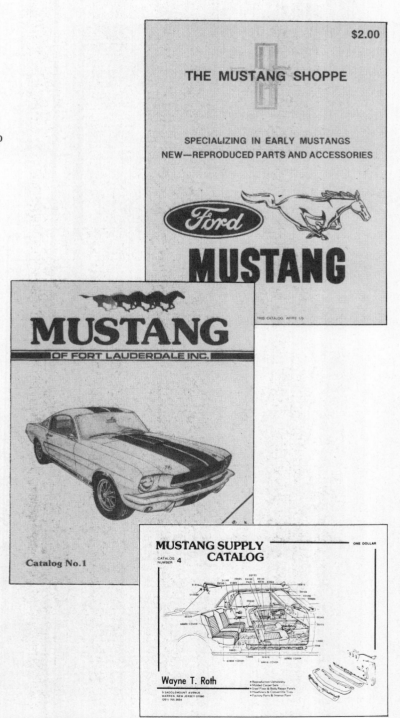

The Mustang Shoppe
8454 S. 34th St.
Scotts, MI 49088

Mail order only; catalog available.
NOS parts, including molded carpets, interior paint, soft trim, upholstery, convertible tops. Reproduction parts, including steel floor and body panels, accessories, weatherstripping. Also, literature.

Mustangs Unlimited, Inc. (est. 1975)
21 Tolland Turnpike
Manchester, CT 06040

Mail order; catalog available.
New and reproduction parts for 1965–73. Also, restoration services, cars bought and sold.

Muscle Parts (est. 1973)
P.O. Box 724
Dearborn, MI 48121

Mail order.
Manufacturer of 1965–70 parts, including full-length floorpans and full steel quarter panels for 1969–70. 1971–73 parts available on special-order basis.

National Parts Depot (est. 1976)
3101 SW 40th Blvd.
Gainesville, FL 32608
and
1495 C Palma Dr.
Ventura, CA 93003

Mail order; free catalog available.
1965–73 sheetmetal, upholstery, soft trim, moldings. Also, literature, decals.

Ohio Mustang Connection (est. 1972)
12981 National Rd. SW
Pataskala, OH 43062

Mail order; free catalog available.
New and used parts and reproduction interior and exterior parts. Also, restoration services, cars bought and sold.

Jim Osborn Reproductions (est. 1976)
3070 Briarcliff Rd. NE
Atlanta, GA 30329

Decals of all kinds; over 7000 stocked.

The Paddock, Inc. (est. 1965)
P.O. Box 30
Knightstown, IN 46148

Mail order; catalog available.
NOS and reproduction steel patch panels ("Paddock Panels") for 1965–70, steel fender apron.

Paddock West—Heritage Pony Car Parts (est. 1982)
446 Tennessee St.
Redlands, CA 92373

Mail order; catalog available.
Mustang factory parts retailer. Also, steel patch panels ("Paddock Panels") and reproduction items.

Pete's Car House (est. 1979)
5831 Rosebud Lane
Sacramento, CA 95841

General repairs; partial to complete restorations.

P.M.I. Parts Locators (est. 1982)
Route 40, Box 5224-F
North Ft. Meyers, FL 33903

Mail order only; free catalog available.
Underbody components, including replacement panels for floor, torque boxes, frame rails. Also, patch panels, parts locating service.

Pony & Corral (est. 1978)
6102 Livingston Rd.
Oxon Hill, MD 20745

Mail order; catalog available.
Door I.D. plates for 1965–69 and general parts.

Pony Enterprises (est. 1981)
P.O. Box 132
Langhorne, PA 19047

Mail order; catalog available.
Hose clamps, screws and bolts, fasteners, clips, detailing items.

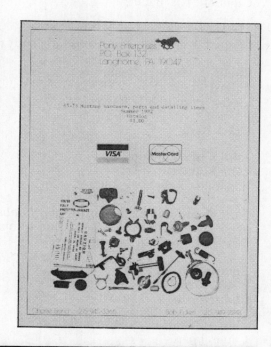

Don Sanderson Ford, Specialty Dept. (est. 1955)
5300 Grand Ave.
Glendale, CA 85301

Mail order.
Large inventory of parts, especially body panels.

Shelby & Mustang Restorers
1 West 5th
Lee's Summitt, MD 64063

Upholstery.

John & Jim Sheldon
2718 Koper Dr.
Sterling Heights, MI 48007

Mail order; send SASE with phone number.
Wheel covers, especially wires and spinners. Original factory radios sold and repaired.

Smartpart (est. 1981)
10422 Keokuk Ave.
Chatsworth, CA 91311

Mail order; free catalog available.
General parts.

Special Interest Cars (est. 1974)
451 Woody Rd.
Oakville, Ontario, Canada L6K 2Y2

Mail order.
New and used parts for 1965–73. Also, "Pony" mats, sales literature, shop manuals, owner's manuals, posters, decals, car covers.

Stillwell's Obsolete Car Parts (est. 1979)
1617 Wedeking Ave.
Evansville, IN 47711

Mail order; catalog available.
Parts for 1965–70, including upholstery, carpet, chrome trim, body panels. Also, shop manuals.

Summitt's Parts & Supplies
RR3, Box 845
King's Mountain, NC 28086

Mail order.
General parts. Also, parts installation service.

Ten Star Auto Panel Distributors, Inc. (est. 1976)
1840 Telegraph Rd.
Dearborn, MI 48128

Mail order; catalog available.
Replacement body panels.

Texas Mustang Parts (est. 1971)
615 Mary
Waco, TX 76701

Mail order; free catalog available.
New parts, including radiators. Also, 1965–67 styled steel wheels, 1965–69 interior items.

TL Auto Interiors (est. 1979)
7869 Trumble Rd.
St. Clair, MI 48079

Mail order.
NOS seat covers for 1965.

Total Radiator Concepts, Inc. (est. 1981)
1200 E. First St.
Los Angeles, CA 90033

Mail order; catalog available.
New radiators and condensers. Also, recoring and repair service for old radiators.

Valley Ford Parts Co. (Valley Obsolete Ford) (est. 1964)
11610 Vanowen St.
North Hollywood, CA 91605

Mail order; catalog available.
Parts for 1965–73 Mustang and Shelby. Parts manufacturer and importer.

Virginia Mustang Supply (est. 1981)
Route 259 West
Broadway, VA 22815

Mail order; catalog available.
Kick panels, general parts.

Douglas Vogel
1100 Shady Oaks
Ann Arbor, MI 48103

Mail order only.
Original keys for 1965–66; original locks for 1965–80.
Also, shop manuals for 1965–80.

Services

Aftco Restoration Specialty Co.
P.O. Box 278
Isanti, MN 55040

Complete restoration facilities.

Anderson's Mustang Corral
P.O. Box 353
Bonner Springs, KS 66012

Interior and exterior repairs.

Auto Krafters
RR1
Ft. Calhoun, NE 68023

Complete restoration facilities.

California Auto Trim
10949 Tuxford St. #1
Sun Valley, CA 91352

Complete or partial restorations for 1965–66 (some 1967–68), especially interiors.

Central Ohio Mustang
8600 E. Main St.
Reynoldsburg, OH 43068

Restoration and repair services.

Crazy Horse Enterprises
105 S. Ritchie Way
Pasadena, MD 21122

Repair service for 1965–70 steering wheels.

Eastern Mustang Specialty
646 South Road
Poughkeepsie, NY 12601

Tune-ups to complete restorations for 1965–73 Mustang and Shelby.

Gelsi's Mustang World
3576 Northwest Blvd.
Vineland, NJ 08360

Repair and restoration service, including rebuilding of floors.

Herforth Motors (est. 1972)
1686 Commonwealth Ave.
Brighton, MA 02135

Repair, renovation, and restoration services, including engines, transmissions, differentials. Electrical repairs. Body work including stripping, welding, painting. Interior repairs: carpets, headliner, upholstery replacements. Vinyl top installation, replacement, reconditioning.

Kustom Kar Kare
111 Old Highway 40
O'Fallon, MO 63366

Complete restoration facilities.

Paul G. McLaughlin, Auto Art (est. 1967)
2829 Cagua Dr. NE
Albuquerque, NM 97110

Mail order only; art creations in various media.

Mr. Mustang Inc.
5088 Wolf Creek Pike
Dayton, OH 45426

Complete restoration facilities.

Muck Motor Sales Inc.
10 Campbell Blvd.
Getzville, NY 14068

Ford dealer with service department.

Mustang Country
14625 Lakewood Blvd.
Paramount, CA 90723

Upholstery installation for 1965–73.

Mustang Country
3210 Coffey Lane
Santa Rosa, CA 95401

Interior restoration facilities. Dismantling service for wrecked Mustangs.

Mustang Custom
2030 Timber Lane
Dayton, OH 45414

Installation of underbody parts.

Mustang Mart, Inc.
655 McGlincy Lane
Campbell, CA 95008

Upholstery shop; repairs to 1965–73 molded door panels
for Mustang and Shelby.

Mustang of Chicago
2 S. Addison St.
Bensenville, IL 60106

General service.

Mustang of Ft. Lauderdale
2205 N. Dixie
Ft. Lauderdale, FL 33305

Interior restoration, fiberglass repairs. Also, cars for sale.

Mustangs Etc.
14843 Bessemer St.
Van Nuys, CA 91411

Service from minor mechanical repairs to full restoration.

Mustangs Only World Wide
1320 Oakland Rd.
San Jose, CA 75112

Mechanical and interior repair service.

Mustangs Unlimited, Inc.
21 Tolland Turnpike
Manchester, CT 06040

Restorations. Also, cars bought and sold.

Ohio Mustang Connection
12981 National Rd. SW
Pataskala, OH 43062

Complete restoration service. Also, cars bought and sold.

Pete's Car House
5831 Rosebud Lane
Sacramento, CA 95841

General repairs to complete restorations.

Pony & Corral
6102 Livingston Rd.
Oxon Hill, MD 20745

General service.

Don Sanderson Ford, Specialty Dept.
5300 Grand Ave.
Glendale, CA 85301

Ford dealer with specialized service department.

Summit's Parts and Supplies
RR3, Box 845
Kings Mountain, NC 28086

Parts installation service.

Total Radiator Concepts, Inc.
1200 E. First St.
Los Angeles, CA 90033

Recoring and repair service for old radiators.

Triple A Enterprises (est. 1980)
P.O. Box 50522
Indianapolis, IN 46250

Reproduction window stickers (factory price labels) for
individual cars. Photocopy sample available.

Literature

American Mustang Parts
2216 Cemo Circle
Rancho Cordova, CA 95670

Sales literature.

Auto Krafters
RR1
Ft. Calhoun, NE 68023

Books and literature.

Big T Parts Co.
19337 Greenview
Detroit, MI 48219

Shop manuals, owner's manuals, parts books, information
books.

California Mustang Sales and Parts, Inc.
1249 E. Holt Ave.
Pomona, CA 91767

Literature.

Circle City Mustang
Woolfolk Ave.
Midland City, AL 36350

Literature.

Glazier's Mustang Barn, Inc.
531 Wambold Rd.
Souderton, PA 18964

Hardcover histories, value guides, fact books, owner's manuals (incl. Shelby), shop manuals, wiring diagrams.

Mustang Country
14625 Lakewood Blvd.
Paramount, CA 90723

Various Mustang publications and books, incl. factory fact books. Also, shop manuals, owner's manuals.

Mustang Country
3210 Coffey Lane
Santa Rosa, CA 95401

Owner's manuals, shop manuals.

Mustang Express, Inc.
9901 NW 35th St.
Hollywood, FL 33024

Various Mustang publications, including factory fact books for 1965–68.

Mustang Headquarters
2565 Cloverdale Ave.
Concord, CA 94520

Literature.

Mustang Monthly Magazine (est. 1977)
410 Brannen Rd.
Lakeland, FL 33803

Mail order; free catalog available.
Publishers of monthly magazine on 1965–73 models, including Shelby. Also publishes books.

The Mustang Shoppe
8454 S. 34th St.
Scotts, MI 49088

Literature.

National Parts Depot
3101 SW 40th Blvd.
Gainesville, FL 32608
    and
1495 C Palma Dr.
Ventura, CA 93003

Literature.

Special Interest Cars
451 Woody Rd.
Oakville, Ontario, Canada L6K 2Y2
1965–73 sales literature, shop manuals, owner's manuals, books, posters.

Stillwell's Obsolete Car Parts
1617 Wedeking Ave.
Evansville, IN 47711

1965–70 shop manuals.

Vintage Auto Literature (est. 1970)
P.O. Box 1281
Highway 33
Moultrie, GA 31768

1965–73 original factory shop manuals, owner's manuals, 1965–72 original factory parts catalogs.

Douglas Vogel
1100 Shady Oaks
Ann Arbor, MI 48103

Original shop manuals for 1965–80.

Clubs

Boss 429 Owners Club
4228 S. Conklin
Spokane, WA 99203

Quarterly newsletter.

Mustang Club of America, Inc. (est. 1976)
P.O. Box 447
Lithonia, GA 30058

Dues: $20 per year ($40 foreign). 4500 members, 62 regional groups. Monthly magazine: *Mustang Times.*

Mustang Owner's Club (est. 1975)
2829 Cagua Dr. NE
Albuquerque, NM 87110

Dues: $10 per year. Over 500 members. Monthly newsletter: *The Pony Express.*

Mustang Owners Club of America
P.O. Box 7321
Van Nuys, CA 91409

Dues: $18 per year. 700 members, 3 regional groups. Quarterly publication: *The Running Horse.*

Shelby American Automobile Club
22 Olmstead Rd.
West Redding, CT 06896

Dues: $22.50 per year ($29.50 for first class mailing; $32.00 foreign). 10 regional groups. Bimonthly magazine: *The Shelby American.*